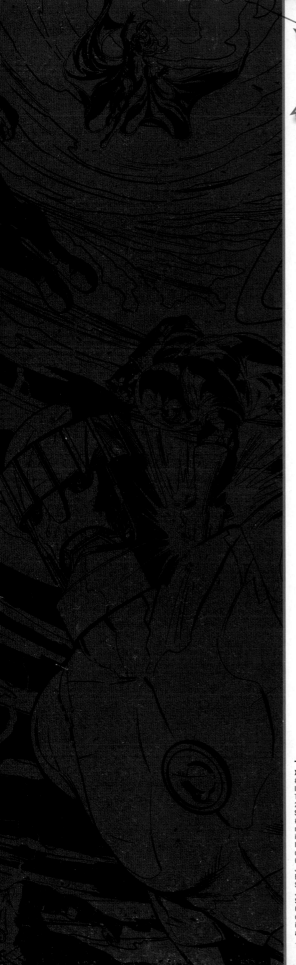

X-MEN

WAR MACHINES

WRITER
VICTOR GISCHLER

ARTIST
WILL CONRAD

WITH
STEVE KURTH & JAY LEISTEN (#22)

COLORISTS
CHRIS SOTOMAYOR

LETTERER
VIRTUAL CALLIGRAPHY'S JOE CARAMAGNA

COVER ART
ADI GRANOV

ASSISTANT EDITOR
JORDAN D. WHITE

ASSOCIATE EDITOR
DANIEL KETCHUM

EDITOR
NICK LOWE

WITHDRAWN

COLLECTION EDITOR: JENNIFER GRÜNWALD
ASSISTANT EDITORS: ALEX STARBUCK & NELSON RIBEIRO
EDITOR, SPECIAL PROJECTS: MARK D. BEAZLEY
SENIOR EDITOR, SPECIAL PROJECTS: JEFF YOUNGQUIST
SENIOR VICE PRESIDENT OF SALES: DAVID GABRIEL
SVP OF BRAND PLANNING & COMMUNICATIONS: MICHAEL PASCIULLO

EDITOR IN CHIEF: AXEL ALONSO
CHIEF CREATIVE OFFICER: JOE QUESADA
PUBLISHER: DAN BUCKLEY
EXECUTIVE PRODUCER: ALAN FINE

X-MEN: WAR MACHINES. Contains material originally published in magazine form as X-MEN (2011) #20-23 and X-MEN (1963) #14. First printing 2012. Hardcover ISBN# 978-0-7851-6187-5. Softcover ISBN# 978-0-7851-6188-2. Published by MARVEL WORLDWIDE, INC., a subsidiary of MARVEL ENTERTAINMENT, LLC. OFFICE OF PUBLICATION: 135 West 50th Street, New York, NY 10020. Copyright © 1965, 2011 and 2012 Marvel Characters, Inc. All rights reserved. Hardcover: $19.99 per copy in the U.S. and $21.99 in Canada (GST #R127032852). Softcover: $14.99 per copy in the U.S. and $16.99 in Canada (GST #R127032852). Canadian Agreement #40668537. All characters featured in this issue and the distinctive names and likenesses thereof, and all related indicia are trademarks of Marvel Characters, Inc. No similarity between any of the names, characters, persons, and/or institutions in this magazine with those of any living or dead person or institution is intended, and any such similarity which may exist is purely coincidental. **Printed in the U.S.A.** ALAN FINE, EVP - Office of the President, Marvel Worldwide, Inc. and EVP & CMO Marvel Characters B.V.; DAN BUCKLEY, Publisher & President - Print, Animation & Digital Divisions; JOE QUESADA, Chief Creative Officer; DAVID BOGART, SVP of Business Affairs & Talent Management; TOM BREVOORT, SVP of Publishing; C.B. CEBULSKI, SVP of Creator & Content Development; DAVID GABRIEL, SVP of Publishing Sales & Circulation; MICHAEL PASCIULLO, SVP of Brand Planning & Communications; JIM O'KEEFE, VP of Operations & Logistics; DAN CARR, Executive Director of Publishing Technology; SUSAN CRESPI, Editorial Operations Manager; ALEX MORALES, Publishing Operations Manager; STAN LEE, Chairman Emeritus. For information regarding advertising in Marvel Comics or on Marvel.com, please contact John Dokes, SVP Integrated Sales and Marketing, at jdokes@marvel.com. For Marvel subscription inquiries, please call 800-217-9158. **Manufactured between 3/12/2012 and 4/9/2012 (hardcover), and 3/12/2012 and 10/8/2012 (softcover), by R.R. DONNELLEY, INC., SALEM, VA, USA.**

10 9 8 7 6 5 4 3 2 1

X-MEN

The world of the X-Men has been shaken up. Since the defeat of the Serpent and his helpers, Colossus has been struggling with taking on the power of the Juggernaut... along with the demonic influence of Cyttorak that comes with it. Meanwhile, a recent re-emergence of old-school, mutant-hunting robot Sentinels lead to much turmoil around the world and within the X-Men, eventually leading to Wolverine leaving the group and taking half the team with him. Now, the mutants who remained with Cyclops on the X-Men's island nation of Utopia find themselves still fighting to represent mutantkind while half the species has abandoned them...

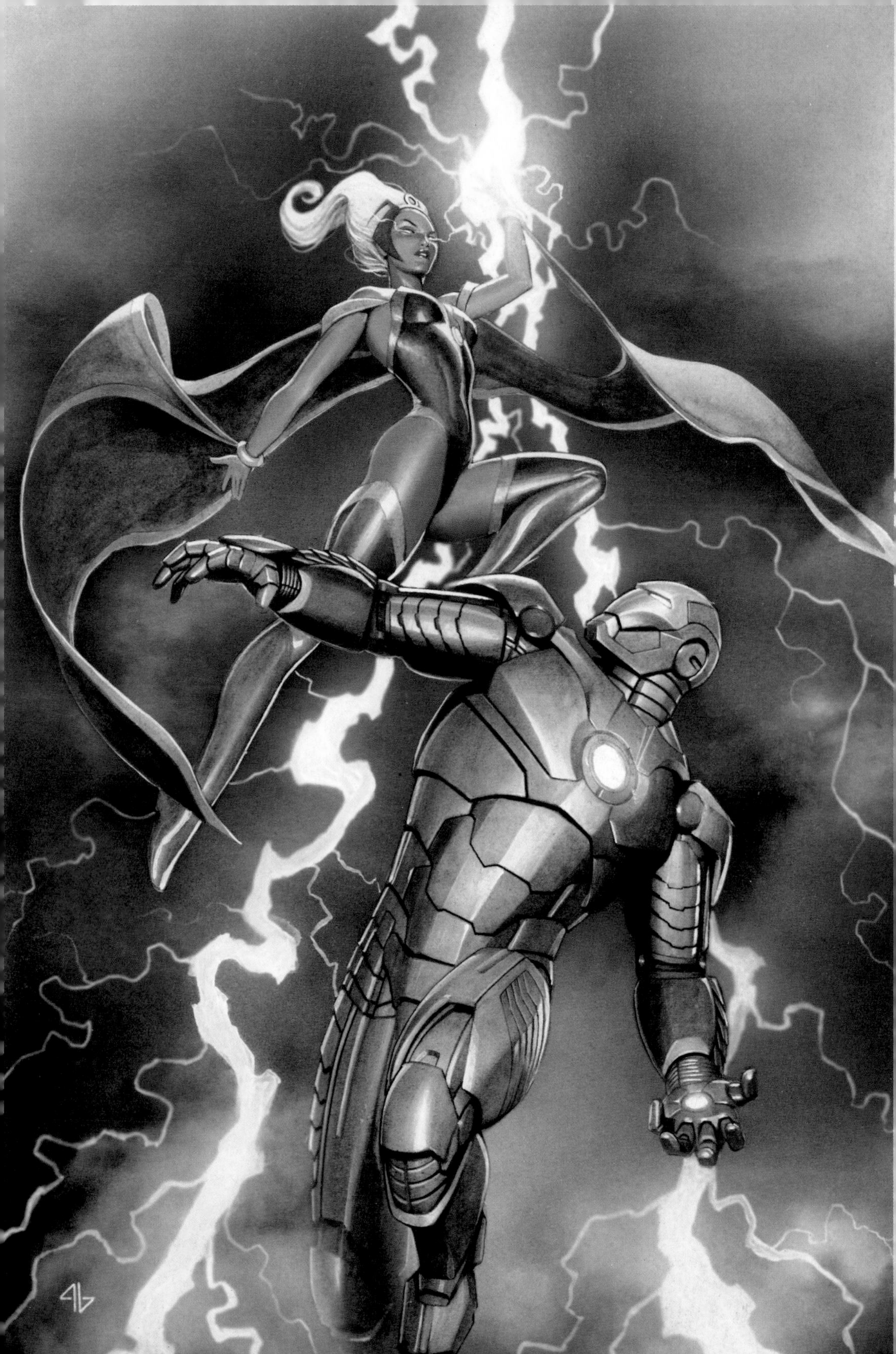

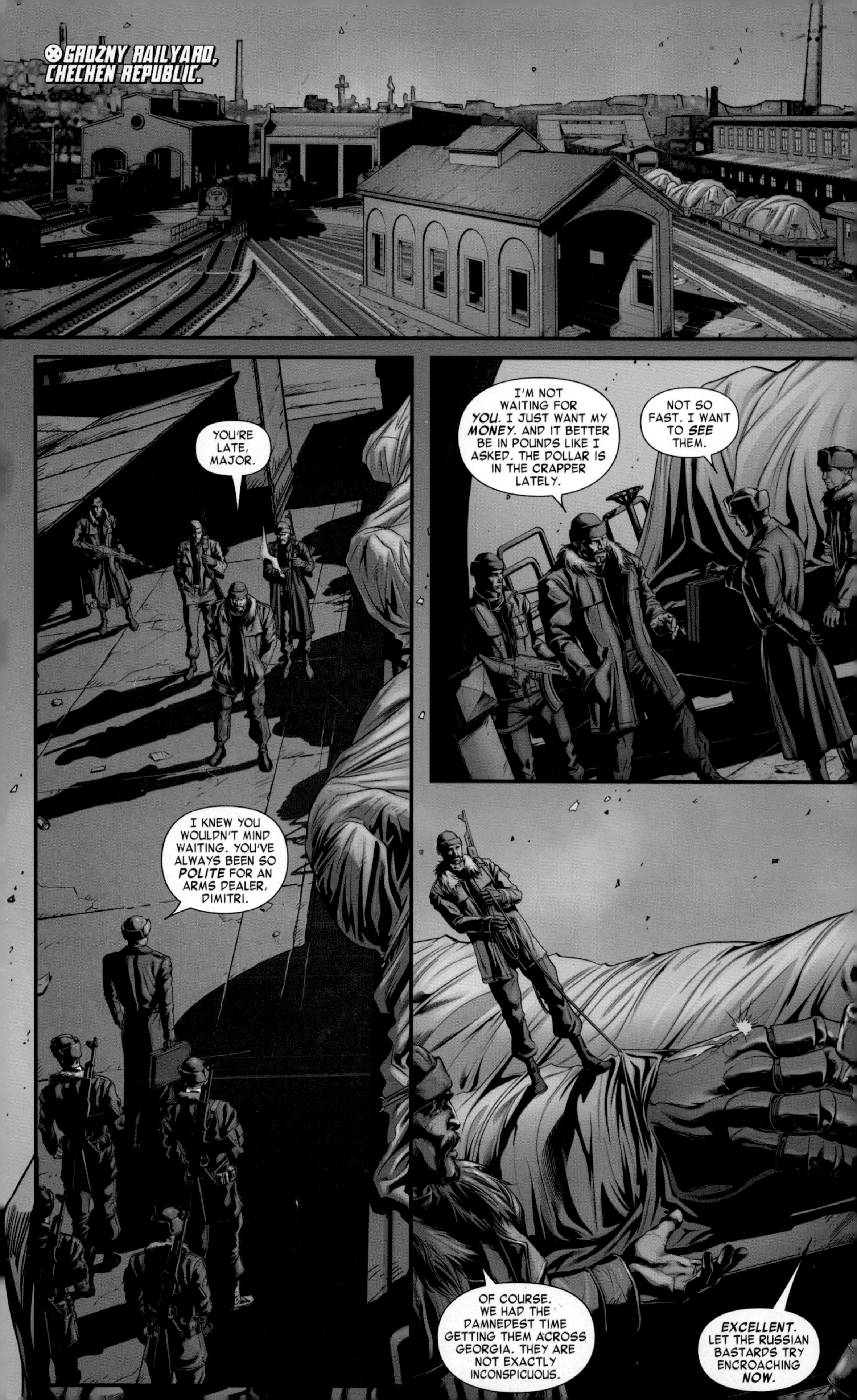
GROZNY RAILYARD, CHECHEN REPUBLIC.
YOU'RE LATE, MAJOR.
I'M NOT WAITING FOR YOU. I JUST WANT MY MONEY. AND IT BETTER BE IN POUNDS LIKE I ASKED. THE DOLLAR IS IN THE CRAPPER LATELY.
NOT SO FAST. I WANT TO SEE THEM.
I KNEW YOU WOULDN'T MIND WAITING. YOU'VE ALWAYS BEEN SO POLITE FOR AN ARMS DEALER, DIMITRI.
OF COURSE. WE HAD THE DAMNEDEST TIME GETTING THEM ACROSS GEORGIA. THEY ARE NOT EXACTLY INCONSPICUOUS.
EXCELLENT. LET THE RUSSIAN BASTARDS TRY ENCROACHING NOW.

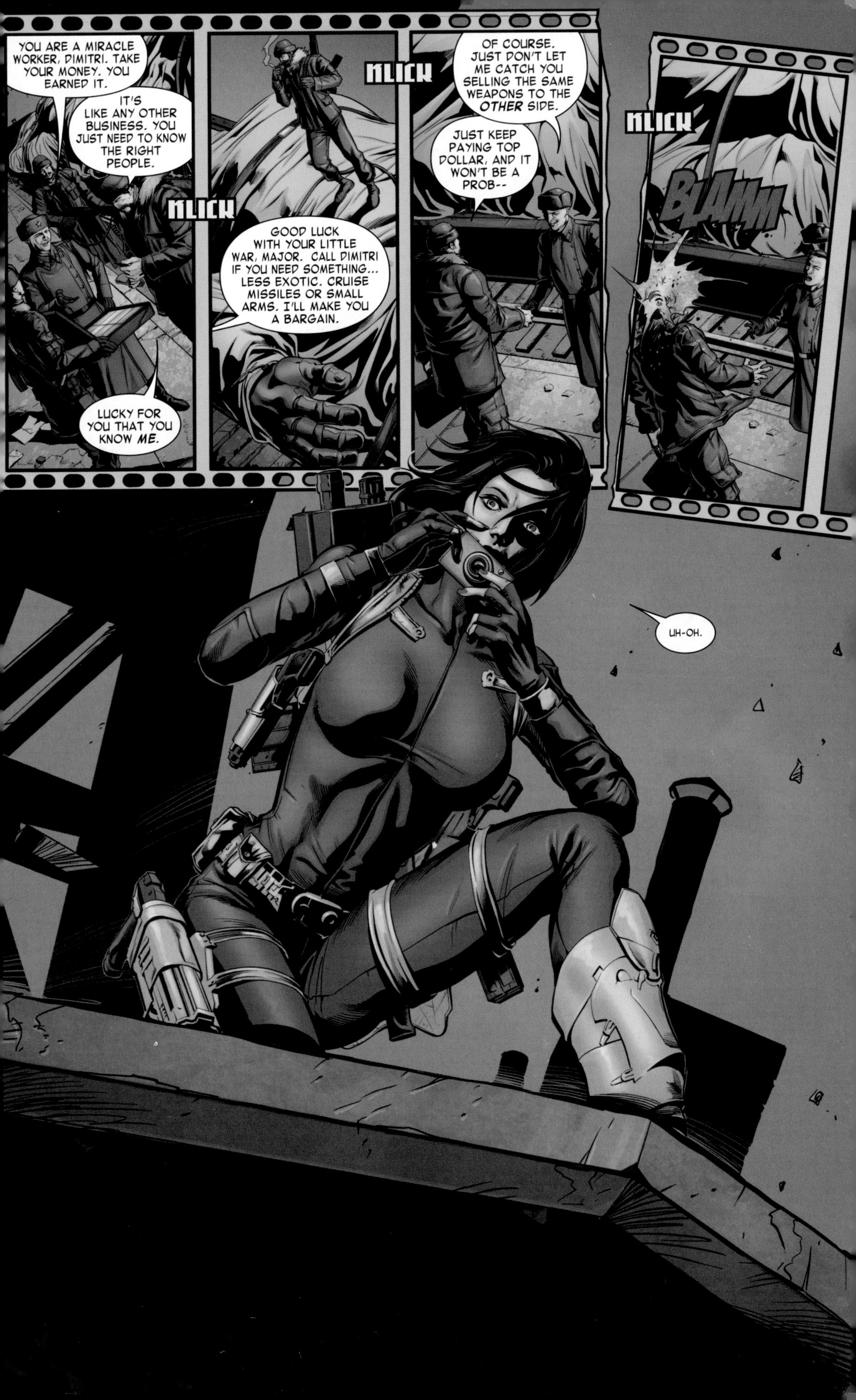
YOU ARE A MIRACLE WORKER, DIMITRI. TAKE YOUR MONEY. YOU EARNED IT.
IT'S LIKE ANY OTHER BUSINESS. YOU JUST NEED TO KNOW THE RIGHT PEOPLE.
LUCKY FOR YOU THAT YOU KNOW *ME*.
KLICK
GOOD LUCK WITH YOUR LITTLE WAR, MAJOR. CALL DIMITRI IF YOU NEED SOMETHING... LESS EXOTIC. CRUISE MISSILES OR SMALL ARMS. I'LL MAKE YOU A BARGAIN.
KLICK
OF COURSE. JUST DON'T LET ME CATCH YOU SELLING THE SAME WEAPONS TO THE *OTHER* SIDE.
JUST KEEP PAYING TOP DOLLAR, AND IT WON'T BE A PROB--
KLICK
BLAMM
UH-OH.

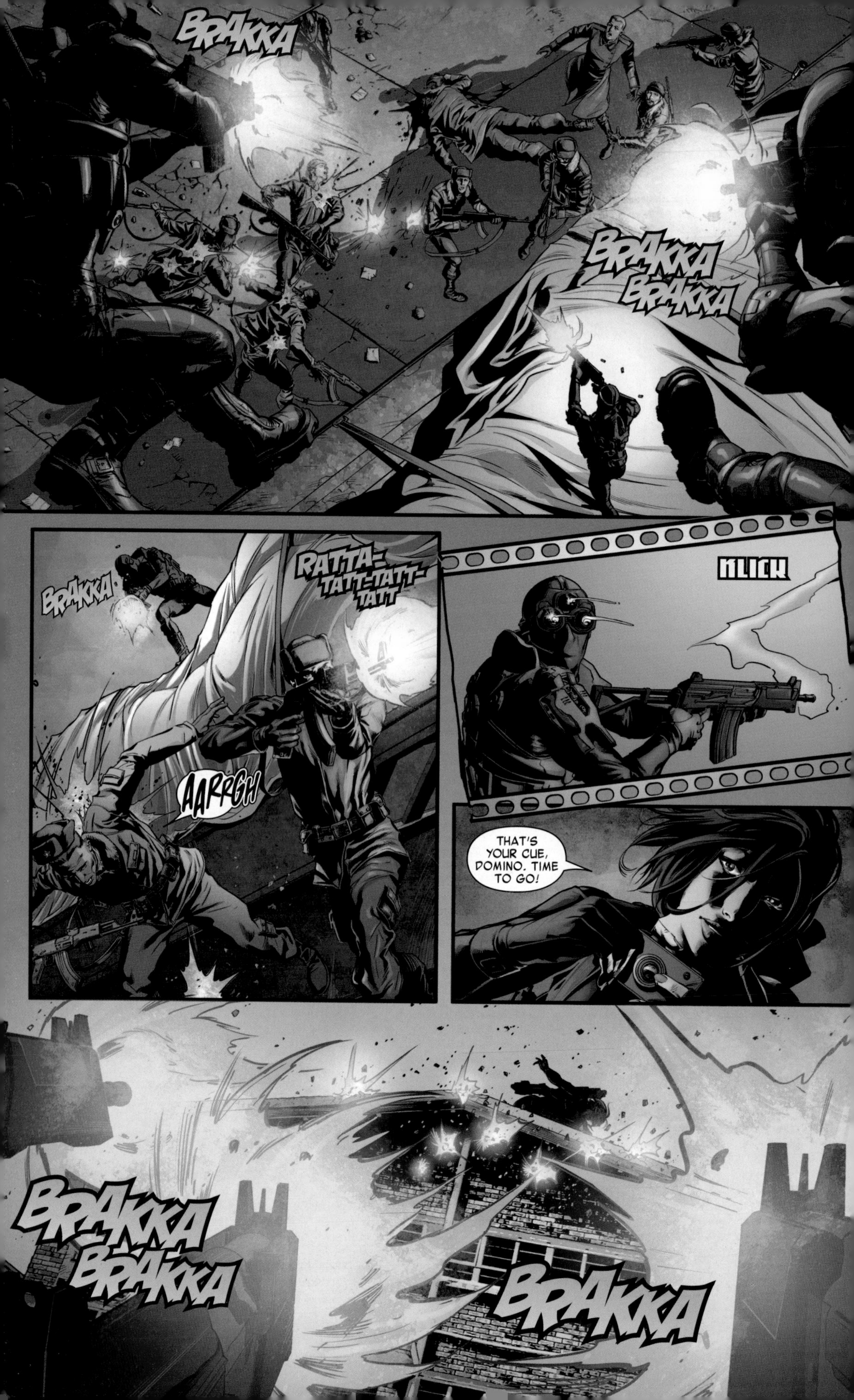
BRAKKA
BRAKKA BRAKKA
BRAKKA
RATTA-TATT-TATT-TATT
AARRGH
KLICK
THAT'S YOUR CUE, DOMINO. TIME TO GO!
BRAKKA BRAKKA
BRAKKA

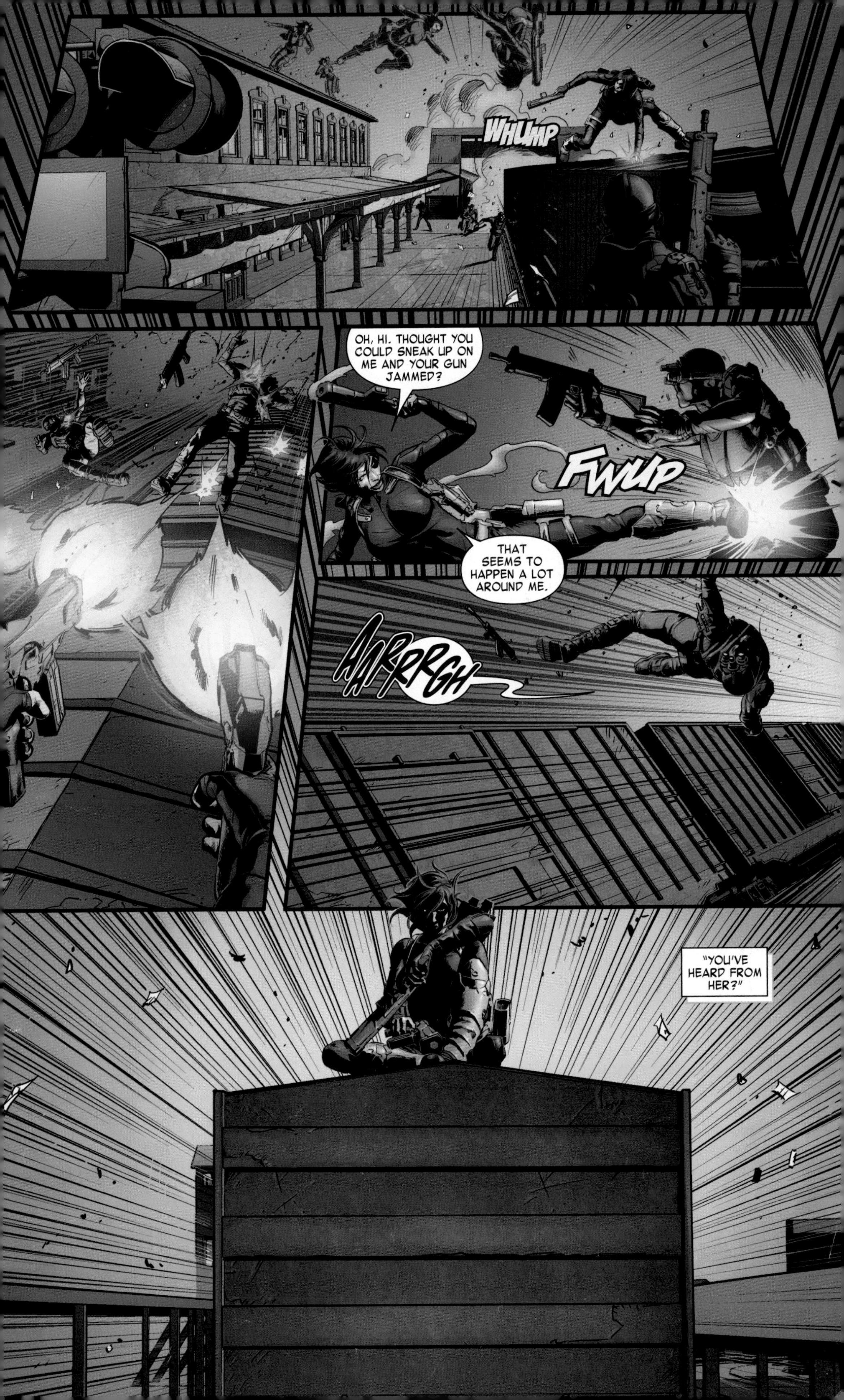
WHUMP
OH, HI. THOUGHT YOU COULD SNEAK UP ON ME AND YOUR GUN JAMMED?
FWUP
THAT SEEMS TO HAPPEN A LOT AROUND ME.
AARRRGH
"YOU'VE HEARD FROM HER?"

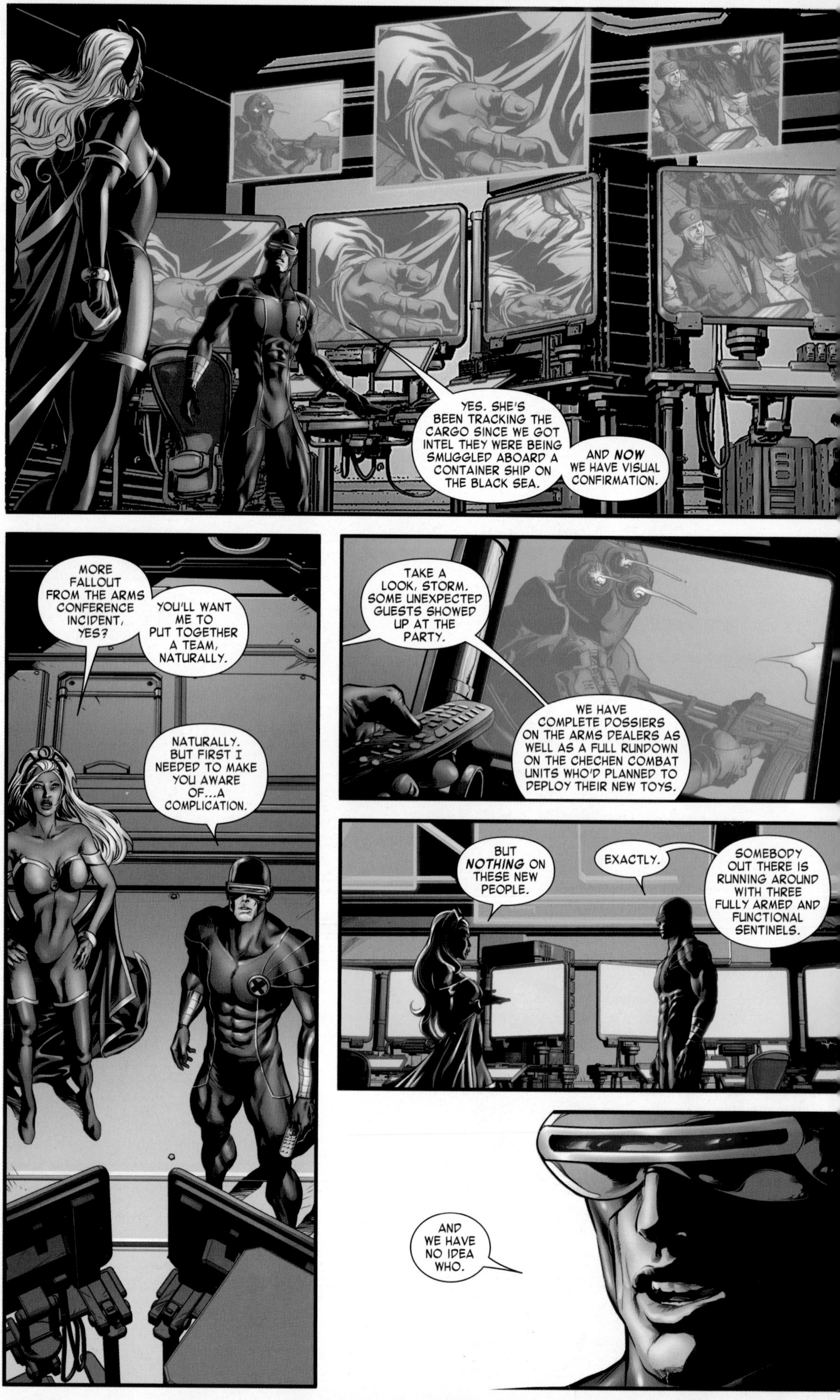

YES. SHE'S BEEN TRACKING THE CARGO SINCE WE GOT INTEL THEY WERE BEING SMUGGLED ABOARD A CONTAINER SHIP ON THE BLACK SEA.
AND NOW WE HAVE VISUAL CONFIRMATION.
MORE FALLOUT FROM THE ARMS CONFERENCE INCIDENT, YES?
YOU'LL WANT ME TO PUT TOGETHER A TEAM, NATURALLY.
NATURALLY. BUT FIRST I NEEDED TO MAKE YOU AWARE OF...A COMPLICATION.
TAKE A LOOK, STORM. SOME UNEXPECTED GUESTS SHOWED UP AT THE PARTY.
WE HAVE COMPLETE DOSSIERS ON THE ARMS DEALERS AS WELL AS A FULL RUNDOWN ON THE CHECHEN COMBAT UNITS WHO'D PLANNED TO DEPLOY THEIR NEW TOYS.
BUT NOTHING ON THESE NEW PEOPLE.
EXACTLY.
SOMEBODY OUT THERE IS RUNNING AROUND WITH THREE FULLY ARMED AND FUNCTIONAL SENTINELS.
AND WE HAVE NO IDEA WHO.

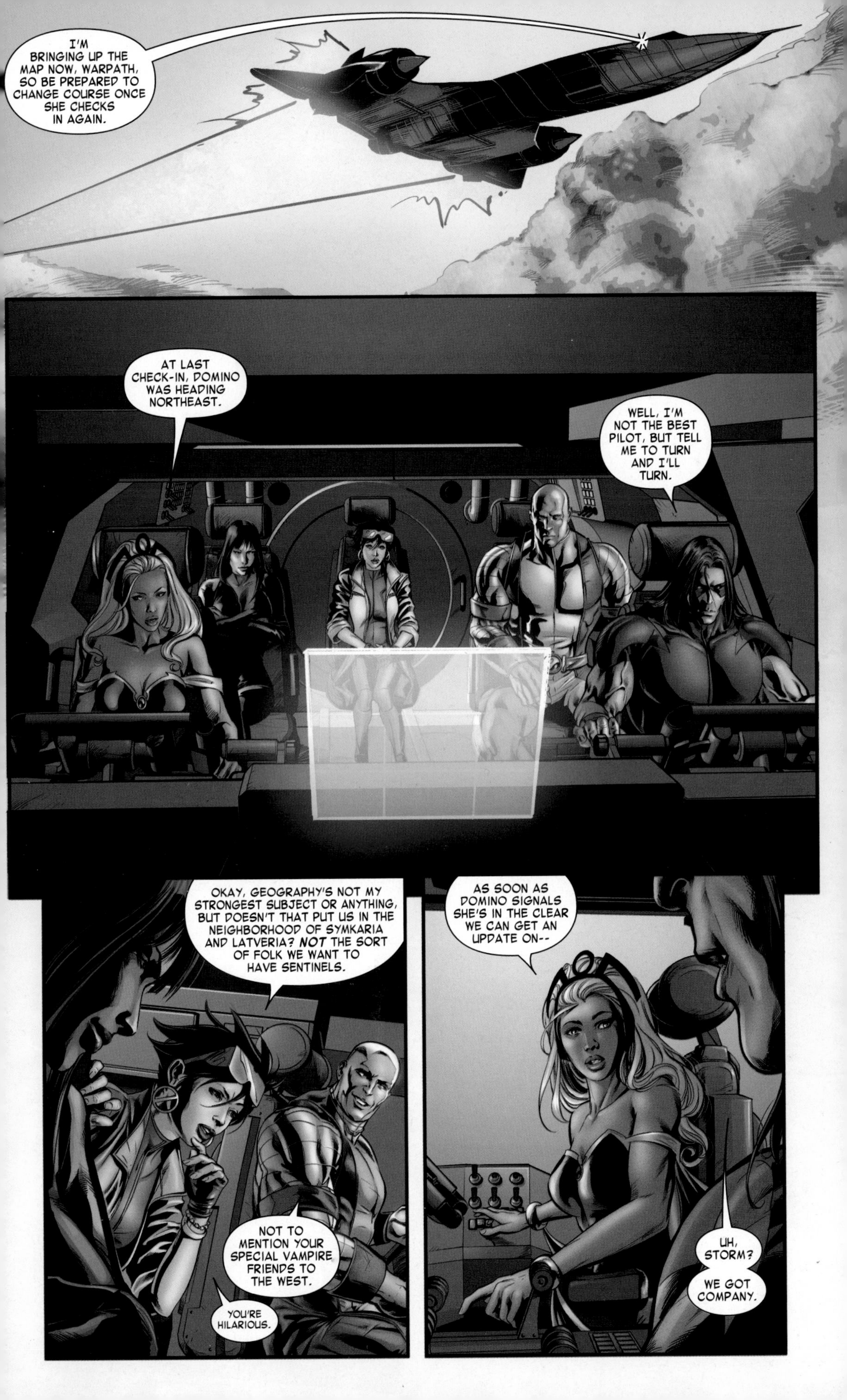
I'M BRINGING UP THE MAP NOW, WARPATH, SO BE PREPARED TO CHANGE COURSE ONCE SHE CHECKS IN AGAIN.
AT LAST CHECK-IN, DOMINO WAS HEADING NORTHEAST.
WELL, I'M NOT THE BEST PILOT, BUT TELL ME TO TURN AND I'LL TURN.
OKAY, GEOGRAPHY'S NOT MY STRONGEST SUBJECT OR ANYTHING, BUT DOESN'T THAT PUT US IN THE NEIGHBORHOOD OF SYMKARIA AND LATVERIA? NOT THE SORT OF FOLK WE WANT TO HAVE SENTINELS.
NOT TO MENTION YOUR SPECIAL VAMPIRE FRIENDS TO THE WEST.
YOU'RE HILARIOUS.
AS SOON AS DOMINO SIGNALS SHE'S IN THE CLEAR WE CAN GET AN UPDATE ON--
UH, STORM?
WE GOT COMPANY.

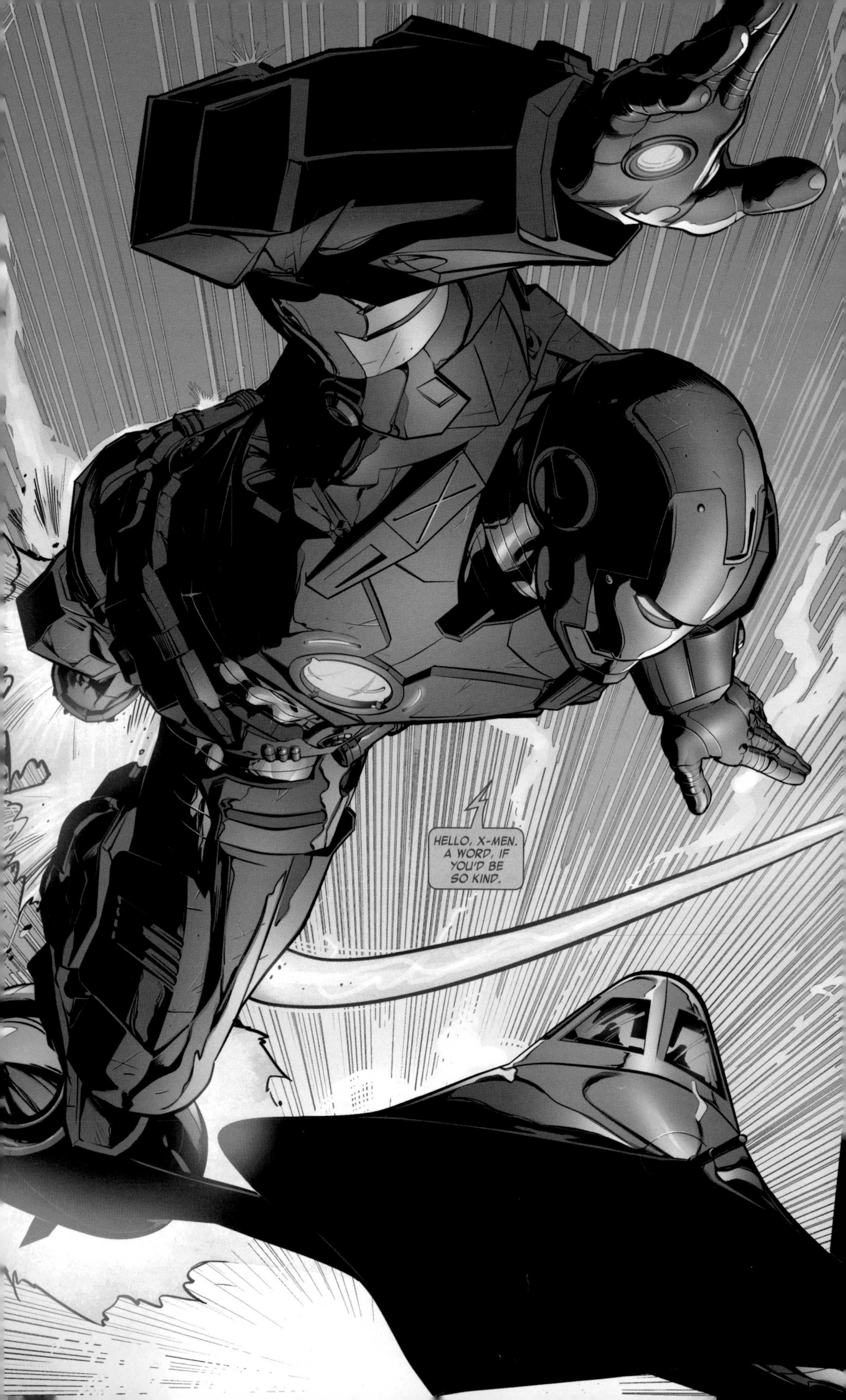
HELLO, X-MEN. A WORD, IF YOU'D BE SO KIND.

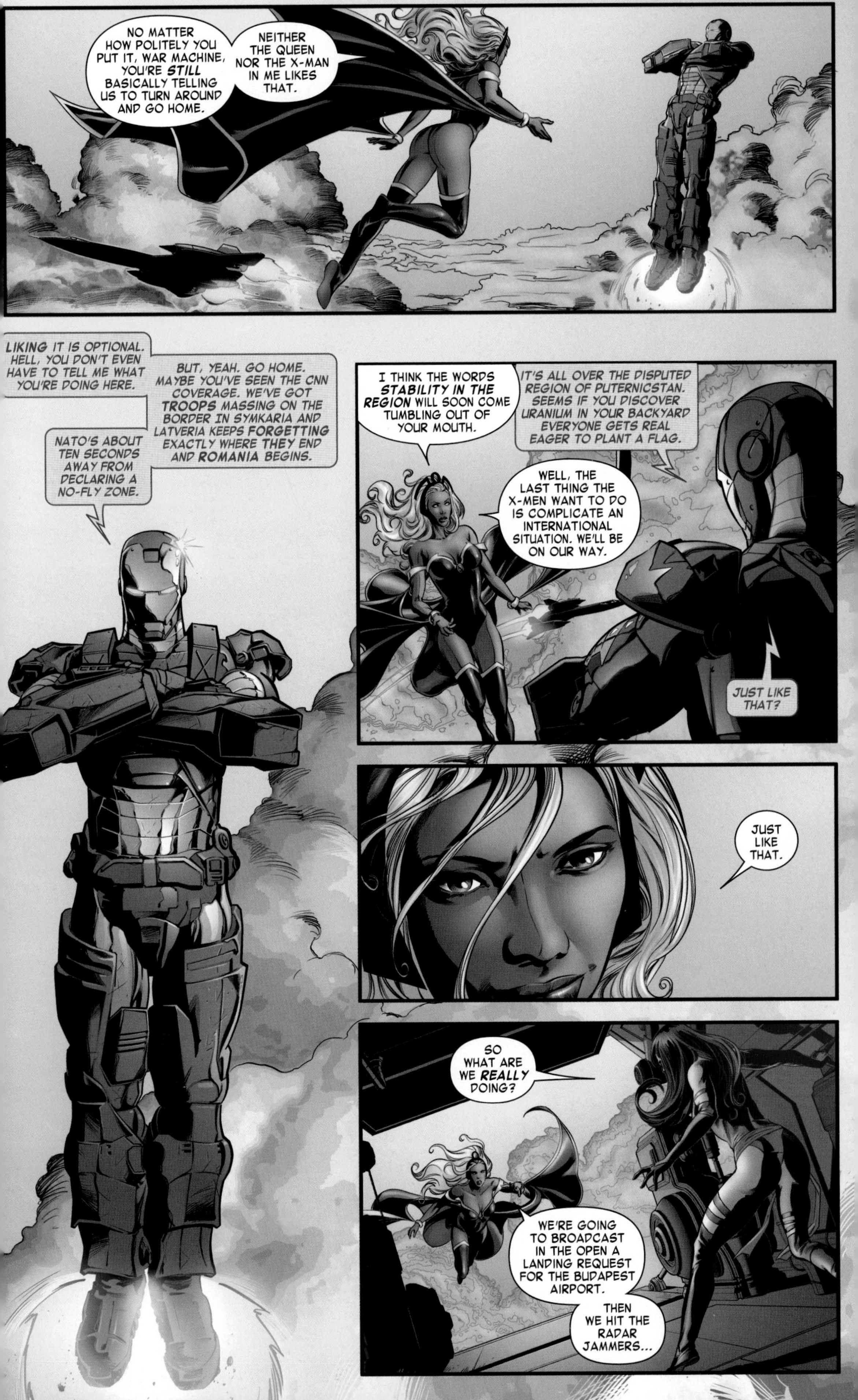
NO MATTER HOW POLITELY YOU PUT IT, WAR MACHINE, YOU'RE STILL BASICALLY TELLING US TO TURN AROUND AND GO HOME.
NEITHER THE QUEEN NOR THE X-MAN IN ME LIKES THAT.
LIKING IT IS OPTIONAL. HELL, YOU DON'T EVEN HAVE TO TELL ME WHAT YOU'RE DOING HERE.
BUT, YEAH. GO HOME. MAYBE YOU'VE SEEN THE CNN COVERAGE. WE'VE GOT TROOPS MASSING ON THE BORDER IN SYMKARIA AND LATVERIA KEEPS FORGETTING EXACTLY WHERE THEY END AND ROMANIA BEGINS.
NATO'S ABOUT TEN SECONDS AWAY FROM DECLARING A NO-FLY ZONE.
I THINK THE WORDS STABILITY IN THE REGION WILL SOON COME TUMBLING OUT OF YOUR MOUTH.
IT'S ALL OVER THE DISPUTED REGION OF PUTERNICSTAN. SEEMS IF YOU DISCOVER URANIUM IN YOUR BACKYARD EVERYONE GETS REAL EAGER TO PLANT A FLAG.
WELL, THE LAST THING THE X-MEN WANT TO DO IS COMPLICATE AN INTERNATIONAL SITUATION. WE'LL BE ON OUR WAY.
JUST LIKE THAT?
JUST LIKE THAT.
SO WHAT ARE WE REALLY DOING?
WE'RE GOING TO BROADCAST IN THE OPEN A LANDING REQUEST FOR THE BUDAPEST AIRPORT.
THEN WE HIT THE RADAR JAMMERS...

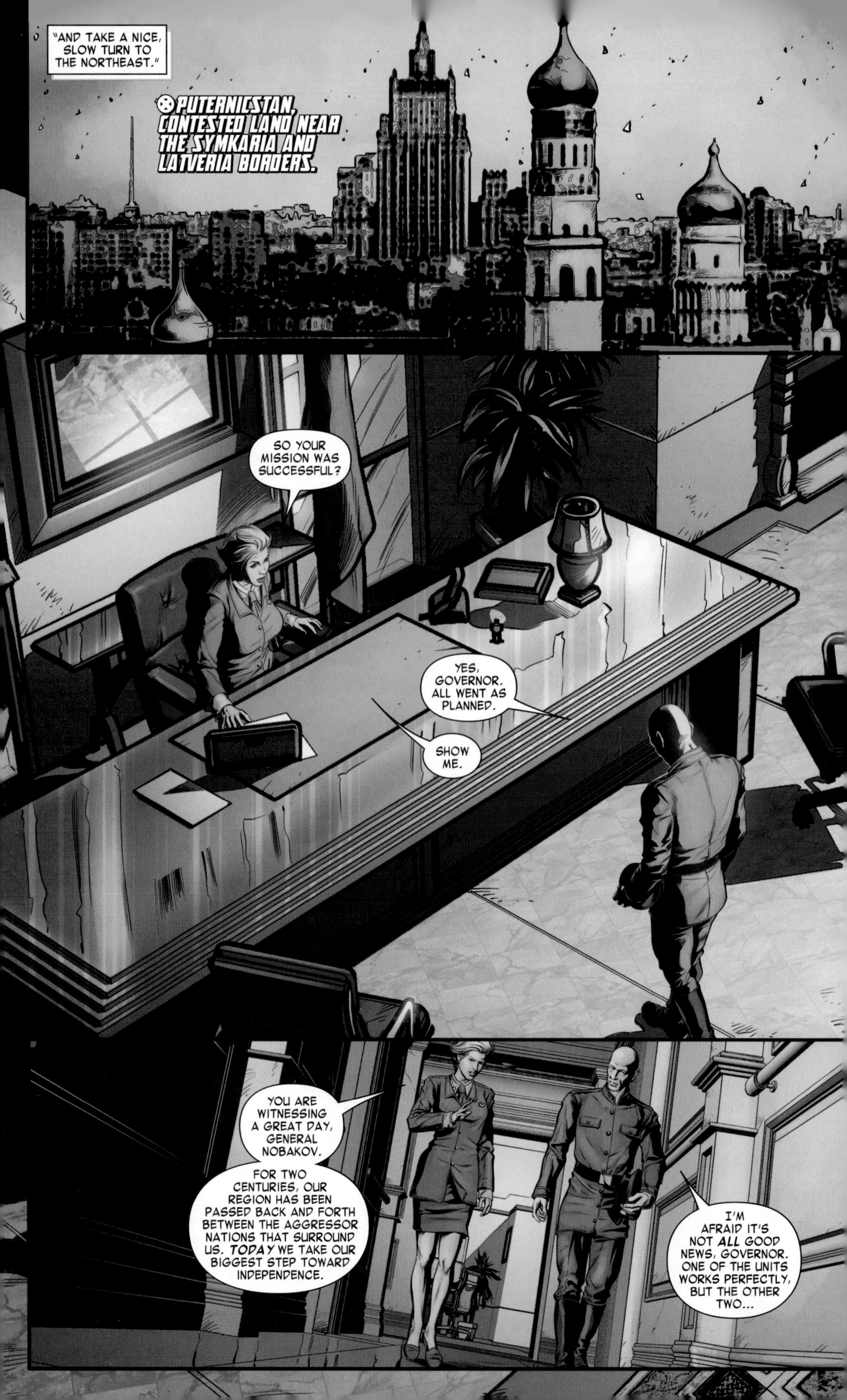
"AND TAKE A NICE, SLOW TURN TO THE NORTHEAST."
PUTERNICSTAN, CONTESTED LAND NEAR THE SYMKARIA AND LATVERIA BORDERS.
SO YOUR MISSION WAS SUCCESSFUL?
YES, GOVERNOR. ALL WENT AS PLANNED.
SHOW ME.
YOU ARE WITNESSING A GREAT DAY, GENERAL NOBAKOV.
FOR TWO CENTURIES, OUR REGION HAS BEEN PASSED BACK AND FORTH BETWEEN THE AGGRESSOR NATIONS THAT SURROUND US. TODAY WE TAKE OUR BIGGEST STEP TOWARD INDEPENDENCE.
I'M AFRAID IT'S NOT ALL GOOD NEWS, GOVERNOR. ONE OF THE UNITS WORKS PERFECTLY, BUT THE OTHER TWO...

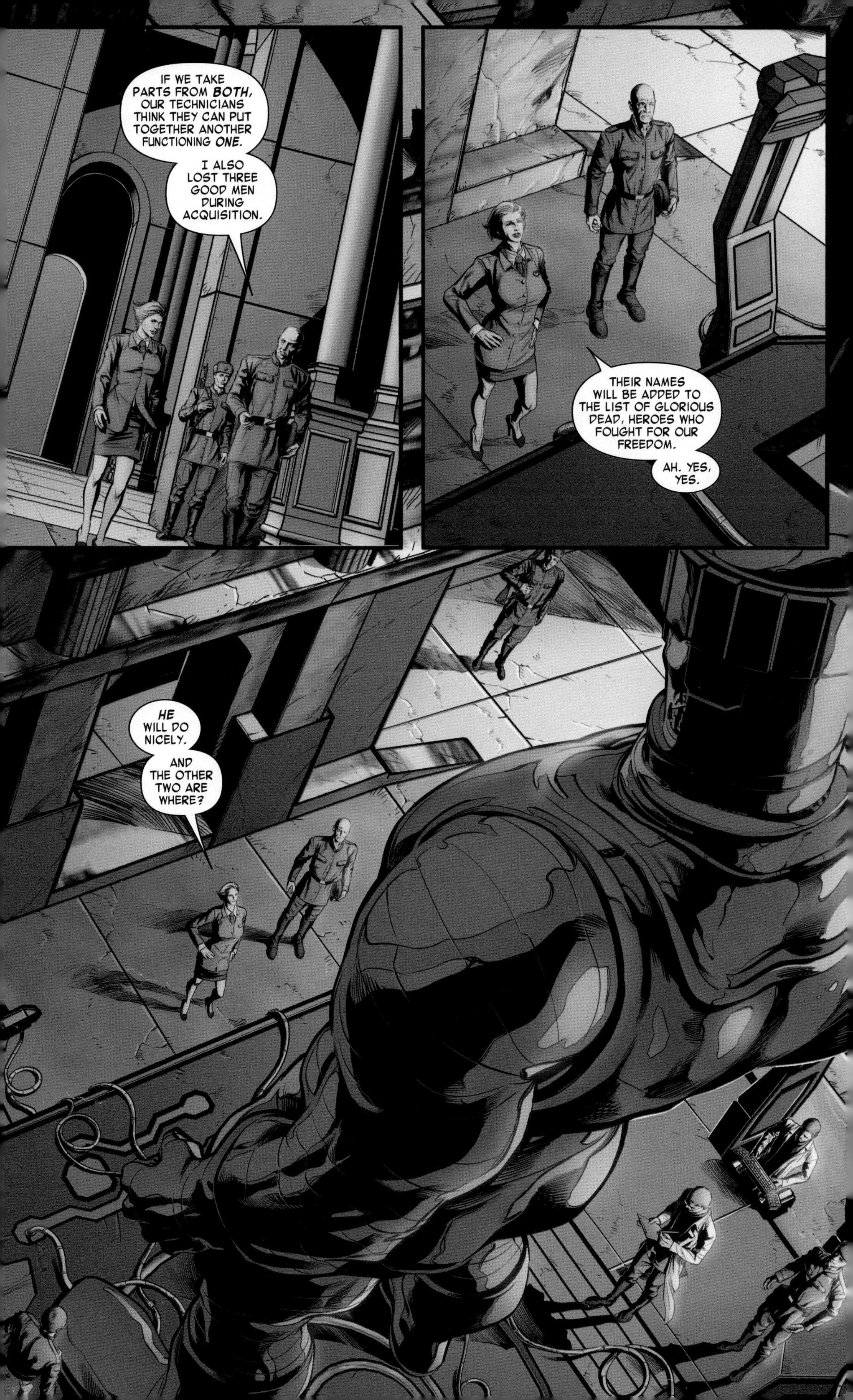
IF WE TAKE PARTS FROM BOTH, OUR TECHNICIANS THINK THEY CAN PUT TOGETHER ANOTHER FUNCTIONING ONE.
I ALSO LOST THREE GOOD MEN DURING ACQUISITION.
THEIR NAMES WILL BE ADDED TO THE LIST OF GLORIOUS DEAD, HEROES WHO FOUGHT FOR OUR FREEDOM.
AH. YES, YES.
HE WILL DO NICELY.
AND THE OTHER TWO ARE WHERE?

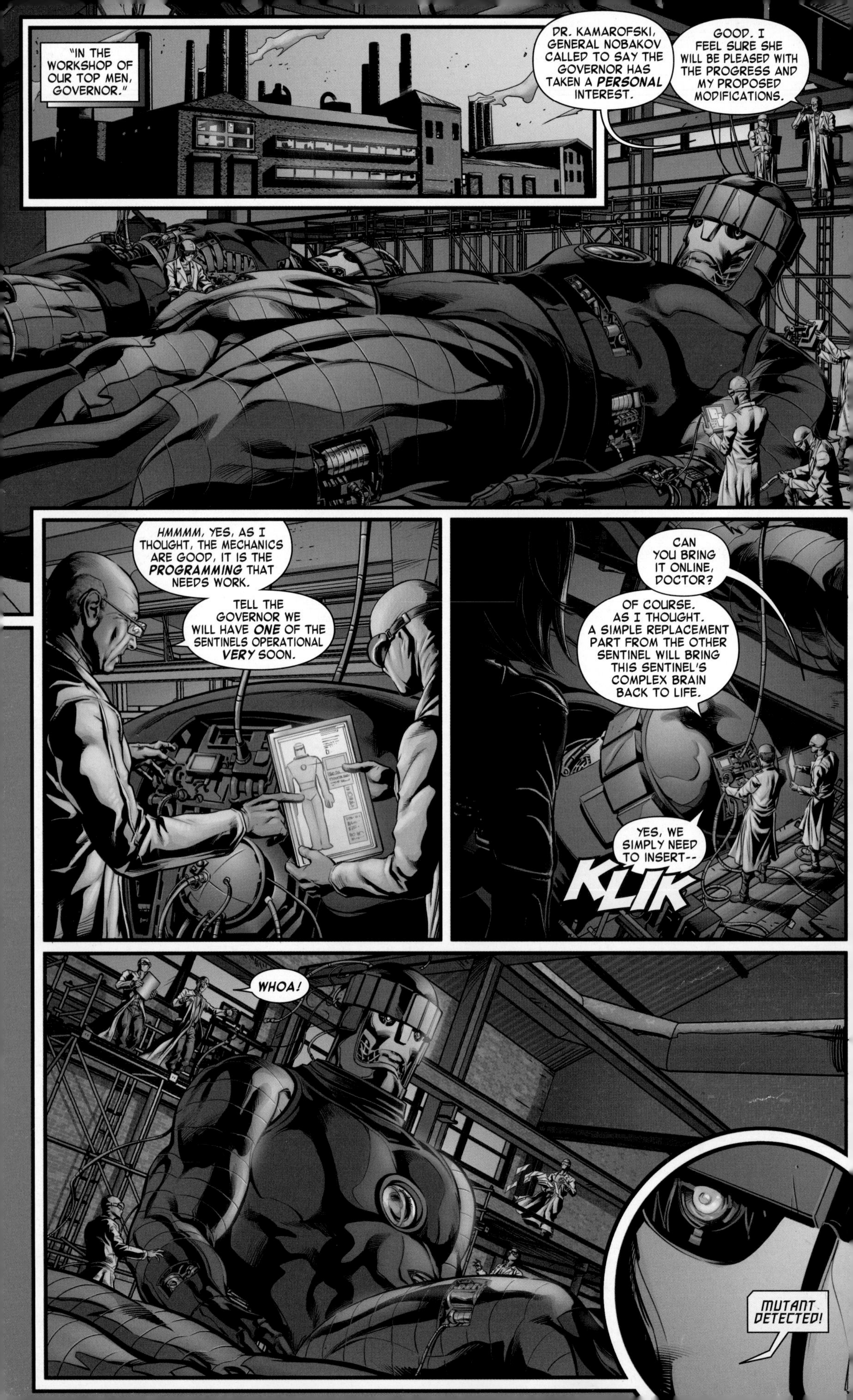
"IN THE WORKSHOP OF OUR TOP MEN, GOVERNOR."
DR. KAMAROFSKI, GENERAL NOBAKOV CALLED TO SAY THE GOVERNOR HAS TAKEN A PERSONAL INTEREST.
GOOD. I FEEL SURE SHE WILL BE PLEASED WITH THE PROGRESS AND MY PROPOSED MODIFICATIONS.
HMMMM, YES, AS I THOUGHT, THE MECHANICS ARE GOOD, IT IS THE PROGRAMMING THAT NEEDS WORK.
TELL THE GOVERNOR WE WILL HAVE ONE OF THE SENTINELS OPERATIONAL VERY SOON.
CAN YOU BRING IT ONLINE, DOCTOR?
OF COURSE. AS I THOUGHT. A SIMPLE REPLACEMENT PART FROM THE OTHER SENTINEL WILL BRING THIS SENTINEL'S COMPLEX BRAIN BACK TO LIFE.
YES, WE SIMPLY NEED TO INSERT--
KLIK
WHOA!
MUTANT DETECTED!

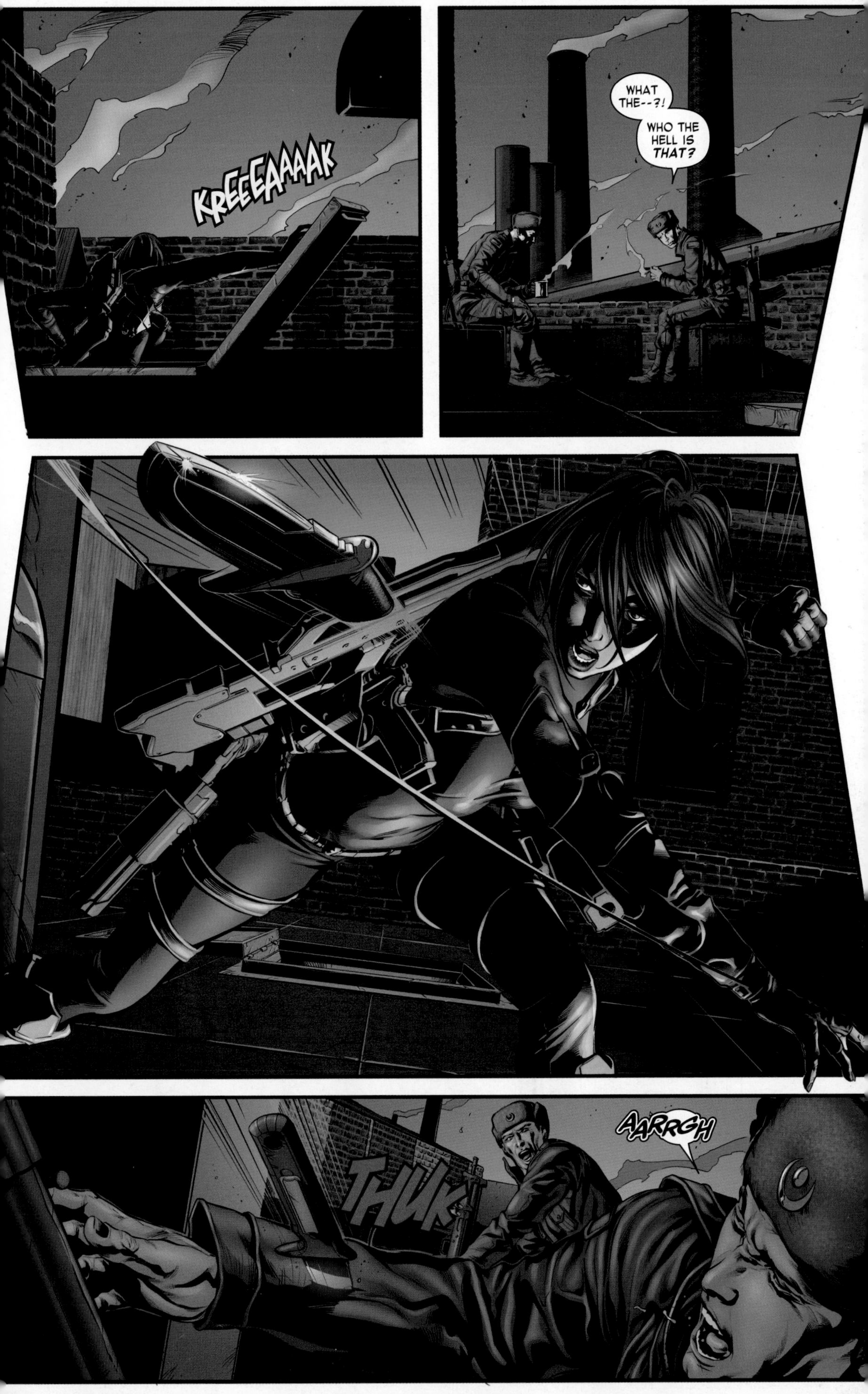
KREEEAAAAK
WHAT THE--?!
WHO THE HELL IS THAT?
THUK
AARRGH

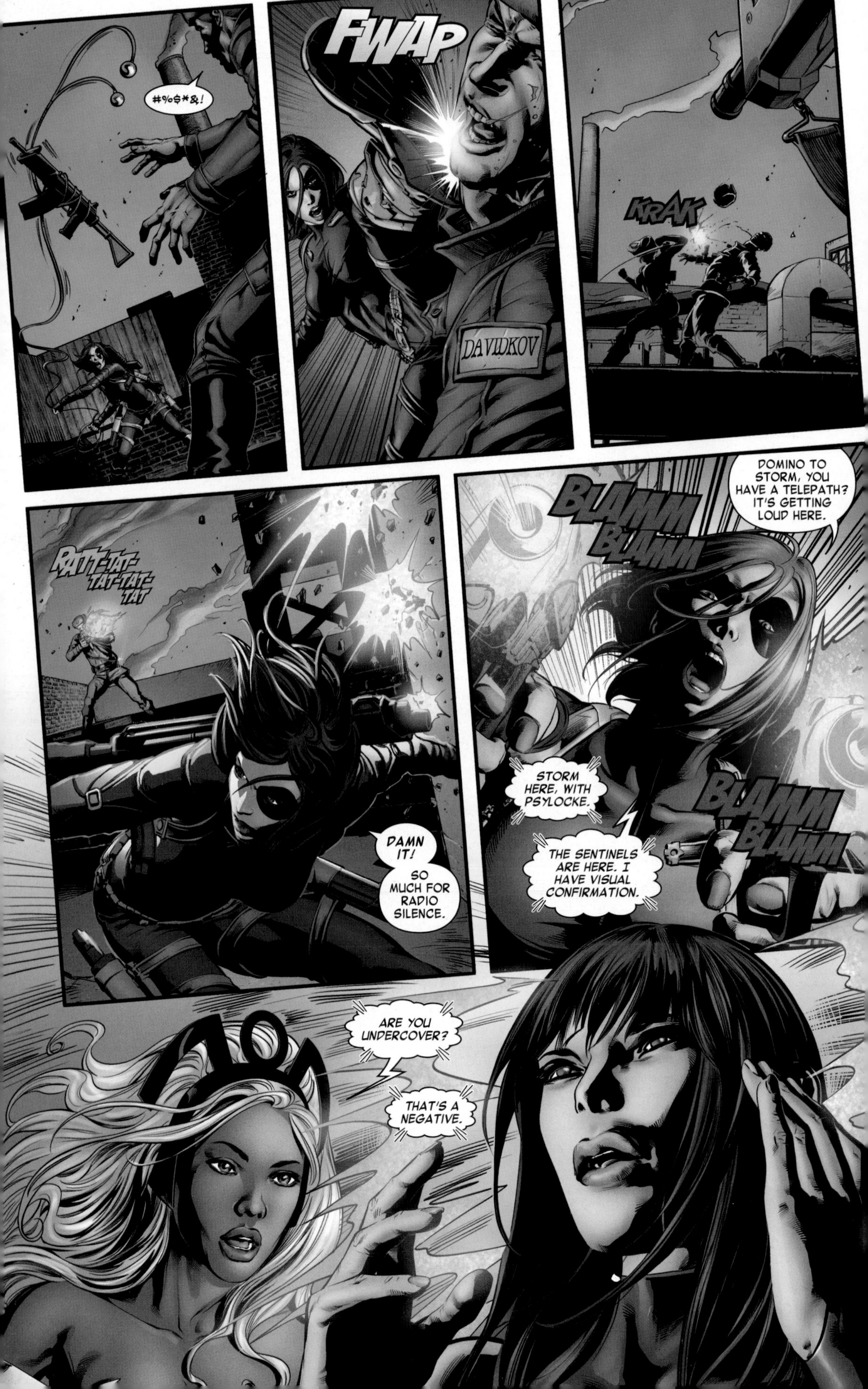

#%$*&!
FWAP
DAVIDKOV
KRAK
RATT-TAT-TAT-TAT-TAT
DAMN IT!
SO MUCH FOR RADIO SILENCE.
BLAMM BLAMM
DOMINO TO STORM, YOU HAVE A TELEPATH? IT'S GETTING LOUD HERE.
STORM HERE, WITH PSYLOCKE.
THE SENTINELS ARE HERE. I HAVE VISUAL CONFIRMATION.
BLAMM BLAMM
ARE YOU UNDERCOVER?
THAT'S A NEGATIVE.

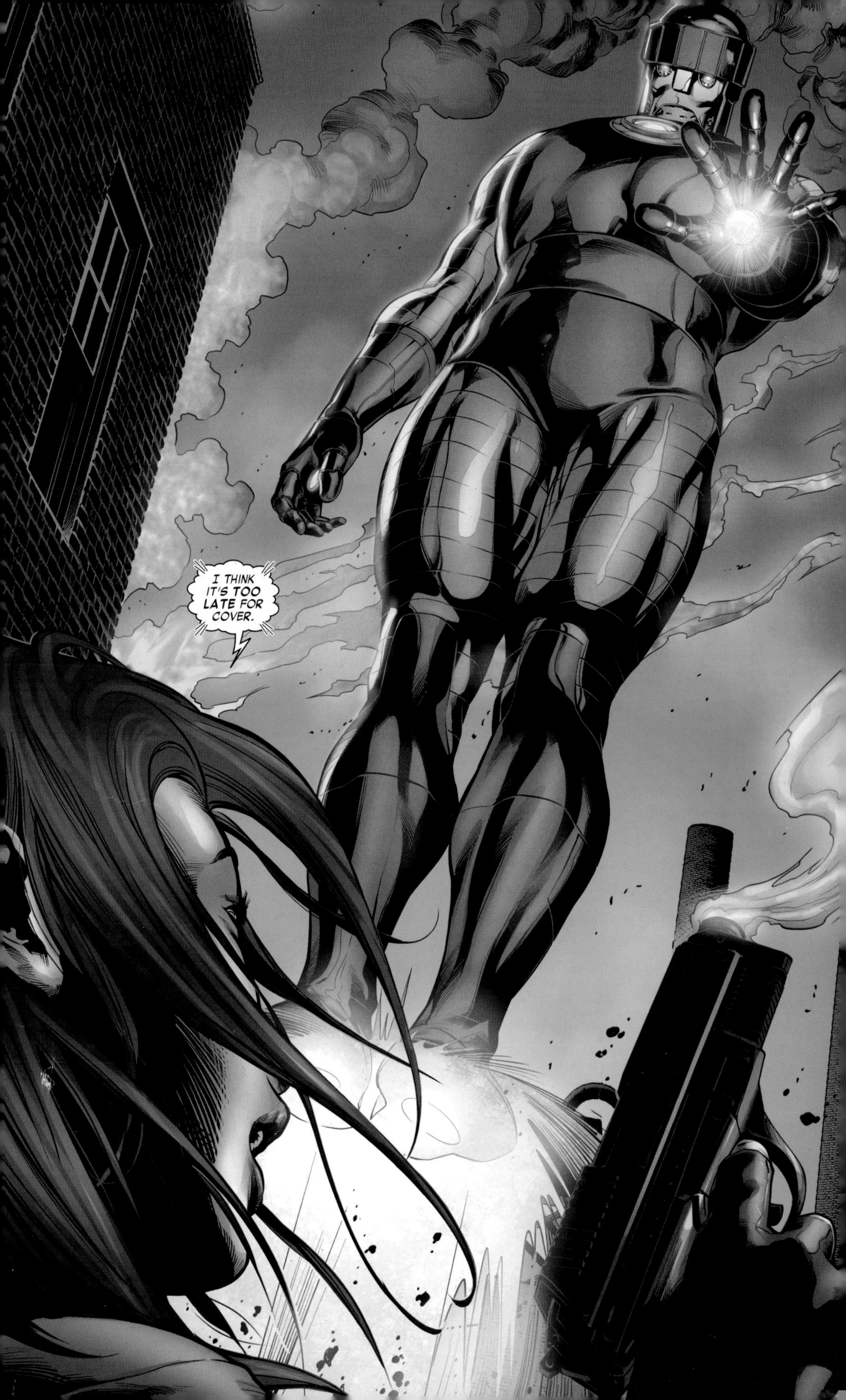
I THINK IT'S TOO LATE FOR COVER.

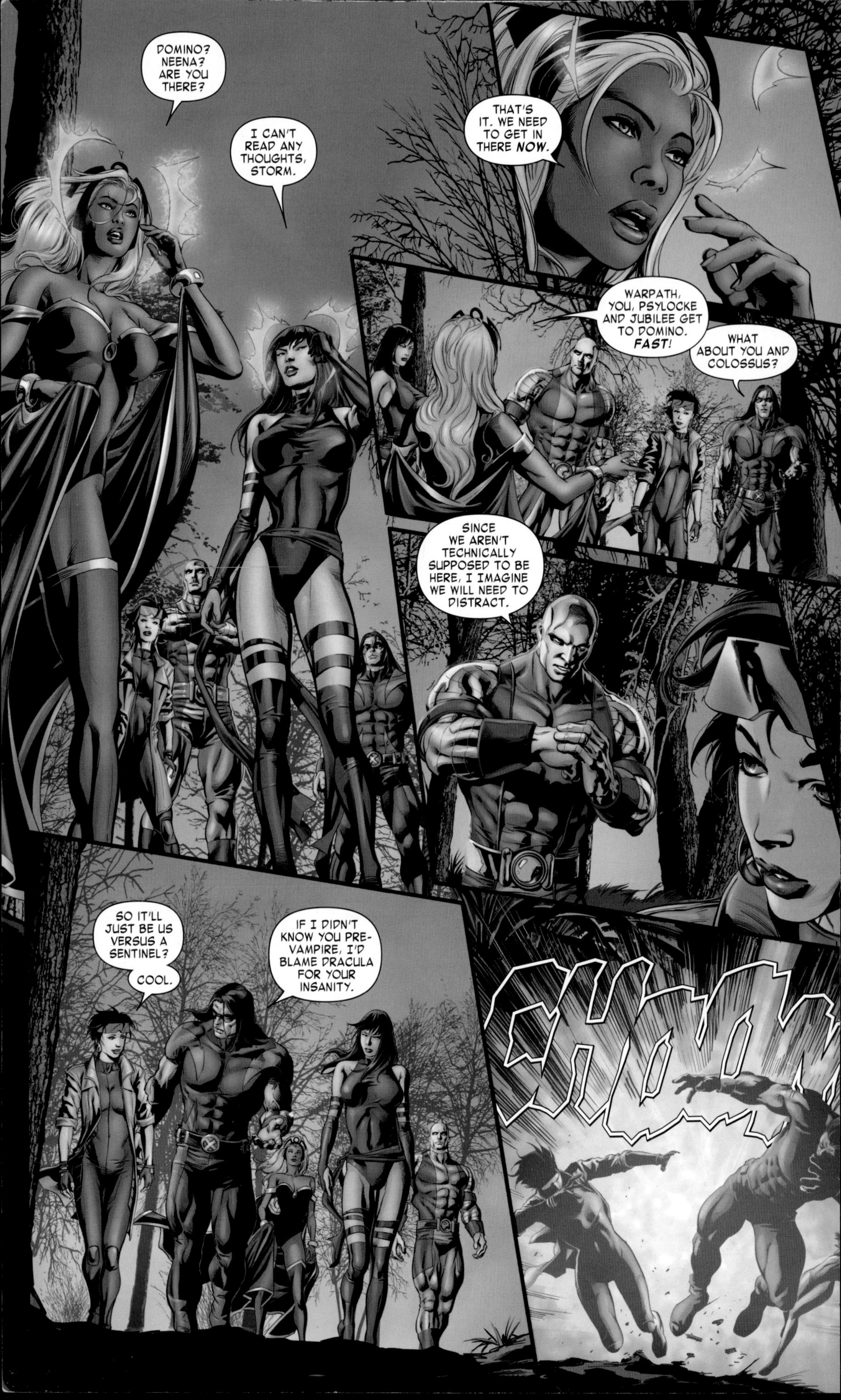
DOMINO? NEENA? ARE YOU THERE?
I CAN'T READ ANY THOUGHTS, STORM.
THAT'S IT. WE NEED TO GET IN THERE NOW.
WARPATH, YOU, PSYLOCKE AND JUBILEE GET TO DOMINO. FAST!
WHAT ABOUT YOU AND COLOSSUS?
SINCE WE AREN'T TECHNICALLY SUPPOSED TO BE HERE, I IMAGINE WE WILL NEED TO DISTRACT.
SO IT'LL JUST BE US VERSUS A SENTINEL?
COOL.
IF I DIDN'T KNOW YOU PRE-VAMPIRE, I'D BLAME DRACULA FOR YOUR INSANITY.

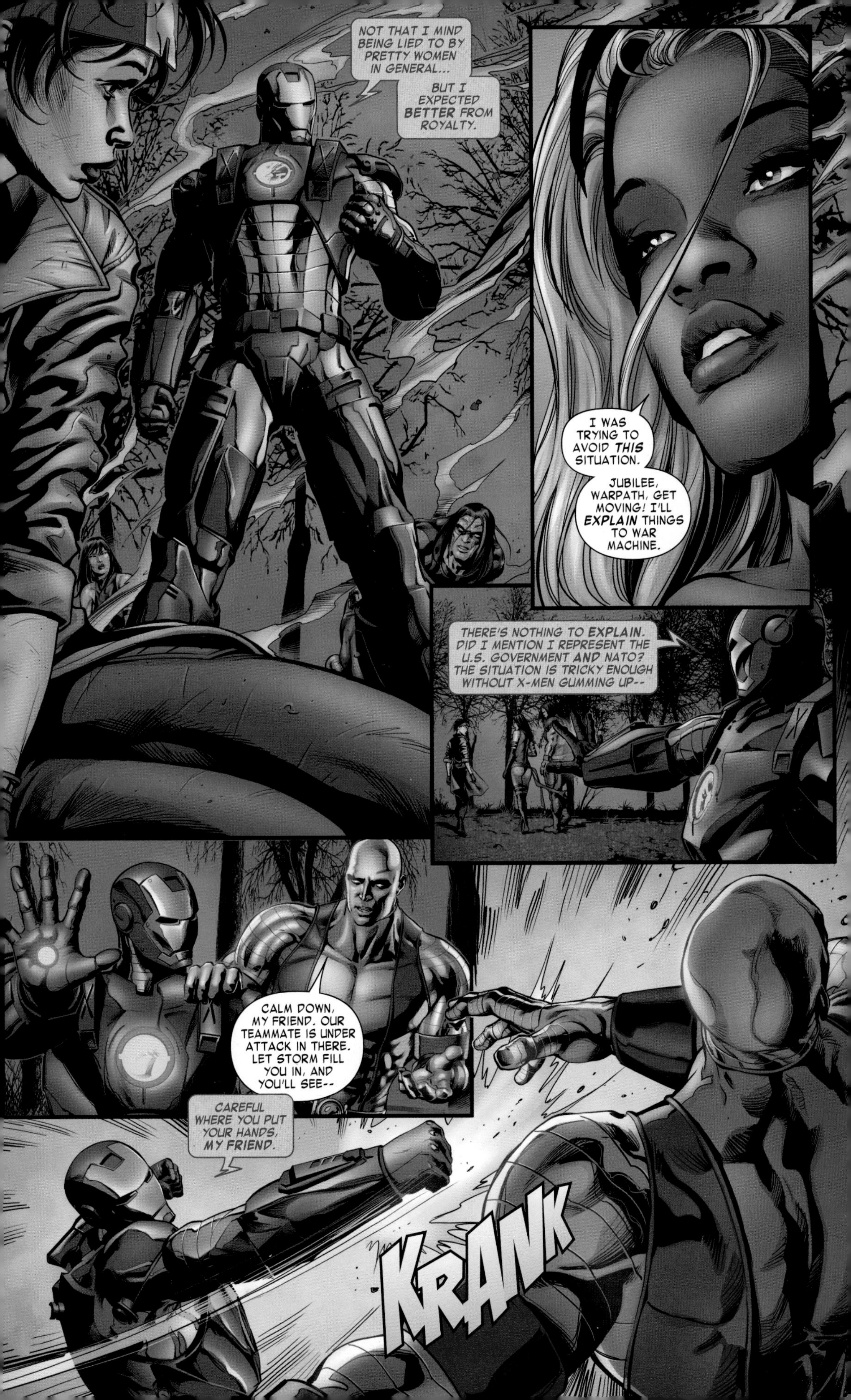
NOT THAT I MIND BEING LIED TO BY PRETTY WOMEN IN GENERAL...
BUT I EXPECTED BETTER FROM ROYALTY.
I WAS TRYING TO AVOID THIS SITUATION.
JUBILEE, WARPATH, GET MOVING! I'LL EXPLAIN THINGS TO WAR MACHINE.
THERE'S NOTHING TO EXPLAIN. DID I MENTION I REPRESENT THE U.S. GOVERNMENT AND NATO? THE SITUATION IS TRICKY ENOUGH WITHOUT X-MEN GUMMING UP--
CALM DOWN, MY FRIEND. OUR TEAMMATE IS UNDER ATTACK IN THERE. LET STORM FILL YOU IN, AND YOU'LL SEE--
CAREFUL WHERE YOU PUT YOUR HANDS, MY FRIEND.
KRANK

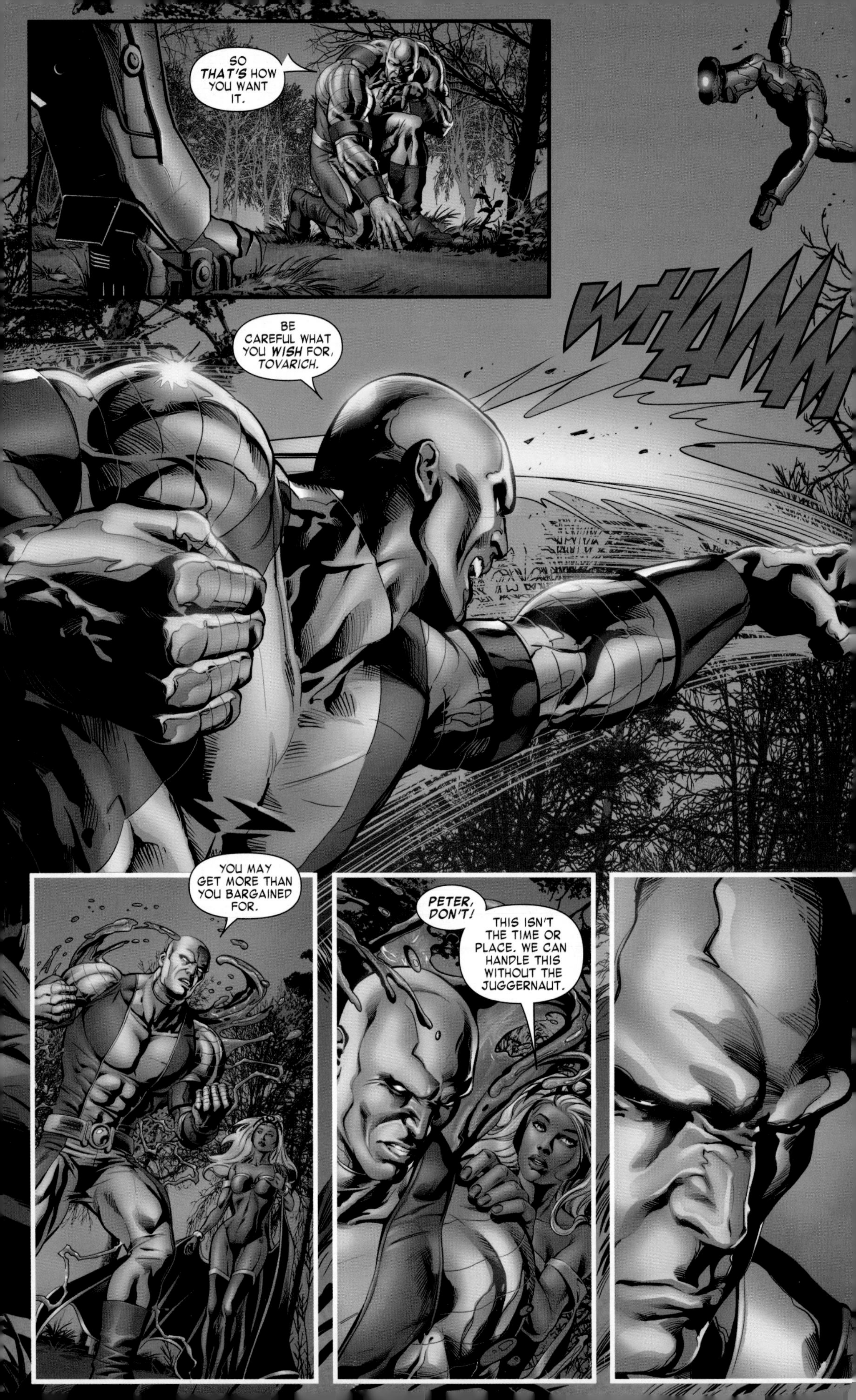
SO THAT'S HOW YOU WANT IT.
WHAMM
BE CAREFUL WHAT YOU WISH FOR, TOVARICH.
YOU MAY GET MORE THAN YOU BARGAINED FOR.
PETER, DON'T!
THIS ISN'T THE TIME OR PLACE. WE CAN HANDLE THIS WITHOUT THE JUGGERNAUT.

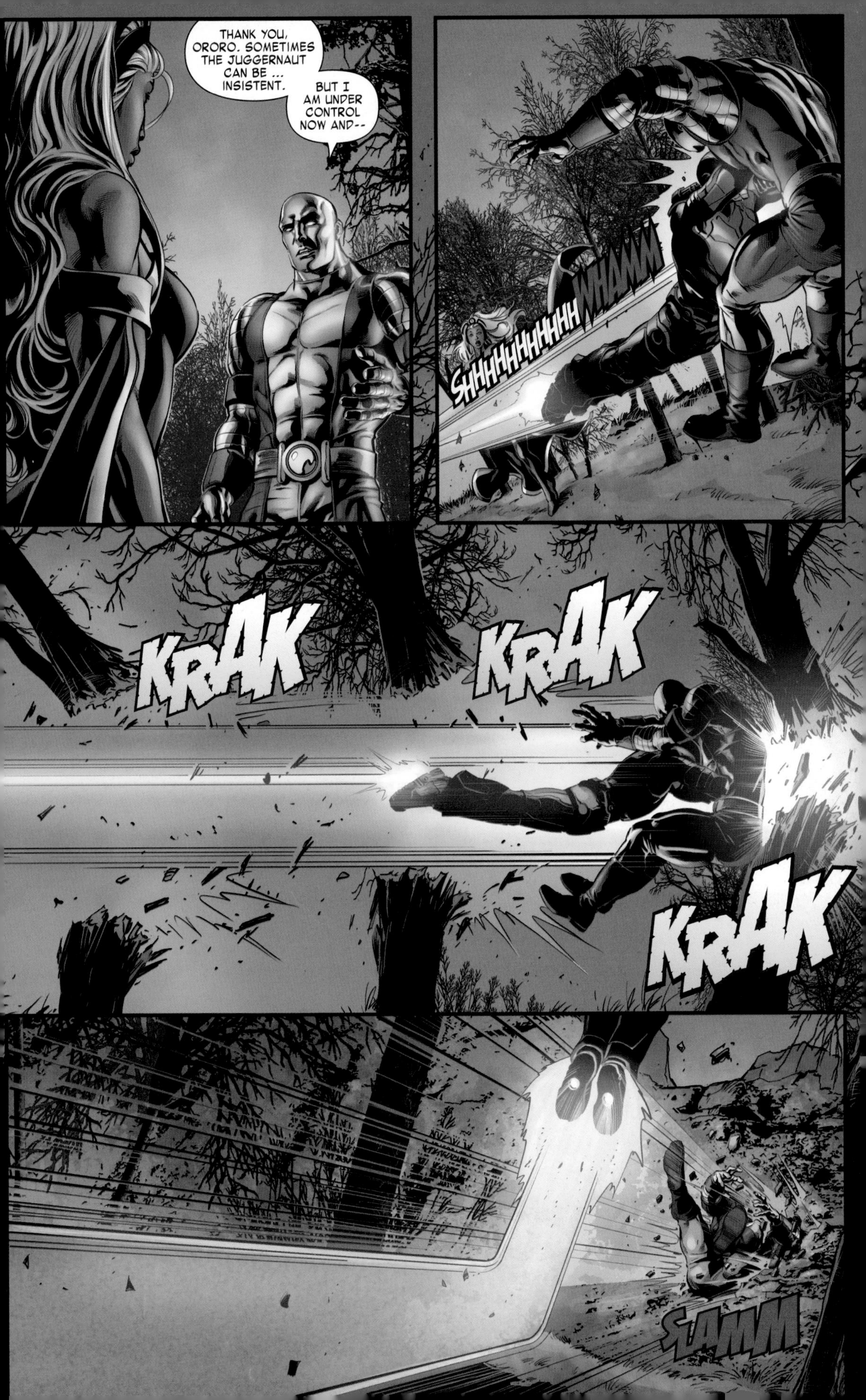
THANK YOU, ORORO. SOMETIMES THE JUGGERNAUT CAN BE ... INSISTENT.
BUT I AM UNDER CONTROL NOW AND--
SHHHHHHHHHHHHWHAMM
KRAK
KRAK
KRAK
SLAMM

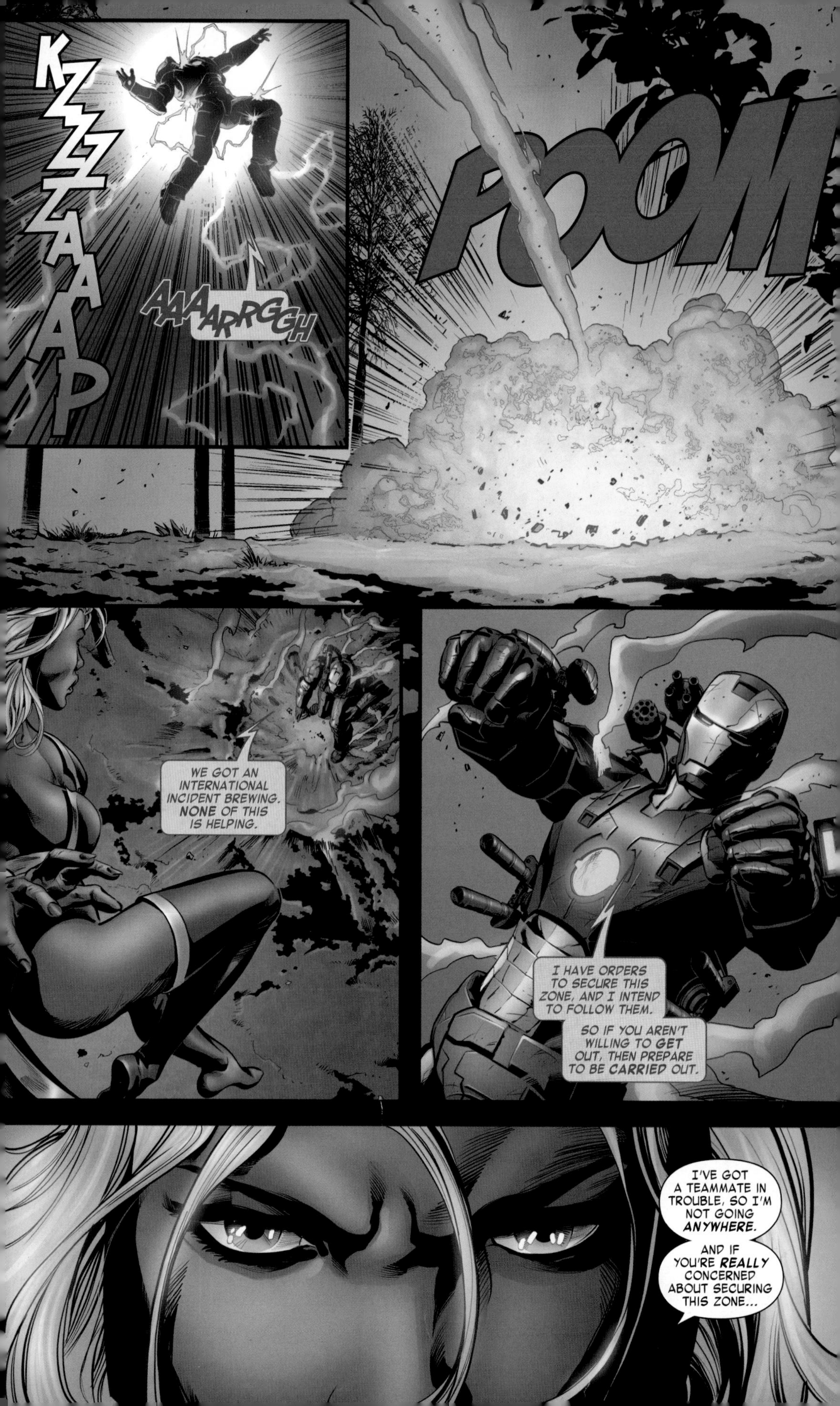
KZZZZAAAAP
AAAARRGGH
POOM
WE GOT AN INTERNATIONAL INCIDENT BREWING. NONE OF THIS IS HELPING.
I HAVE ORDERS TO SECURE THIS ZONE, AND I INTEND TO FOLLOW THEM.
SO IF YOU AREN'T WILLING TO GET OUT, THEN PREPARE TO BE CARRIED OUT.
I'VE GOT A TEAMMATE IN TROUBLE, SO I'M NOT GOING ANYWHERE.
AND IF YOU'RE REALLY CONCERNED ABOUT SECURING THIS ZONE...

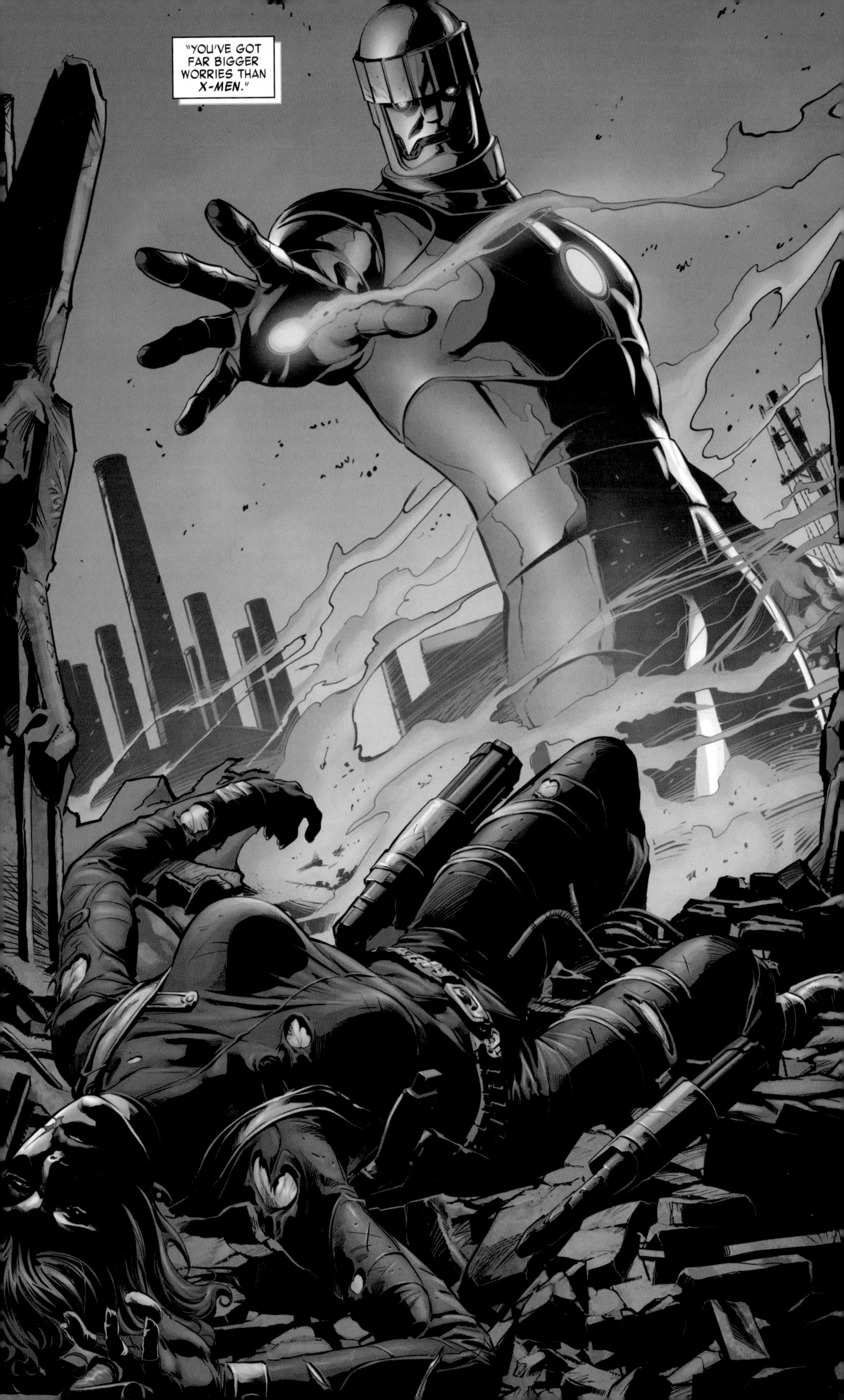
"YOU'VE GOT FAR BIGGER WORRIES THAN *X-MEN*."

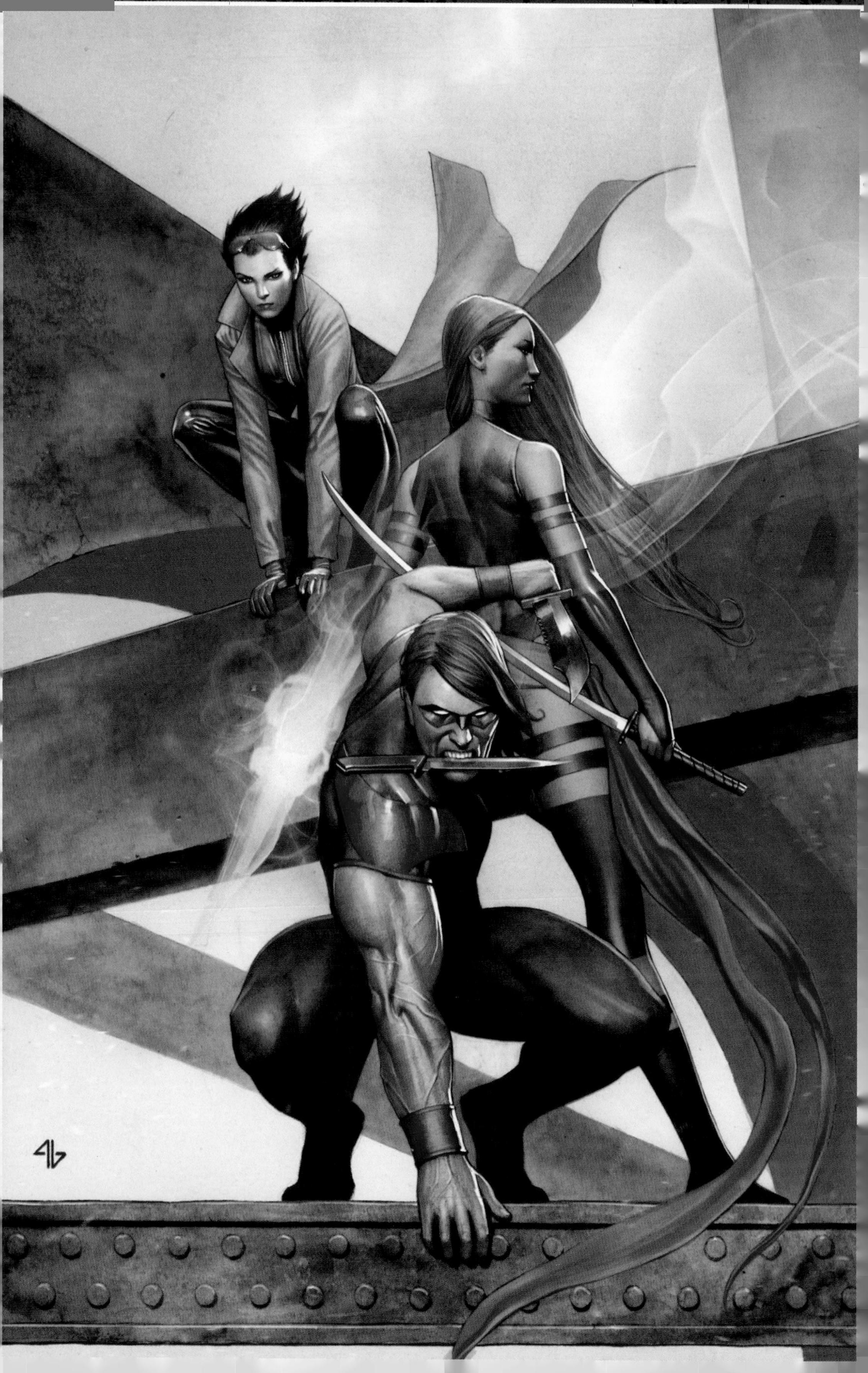

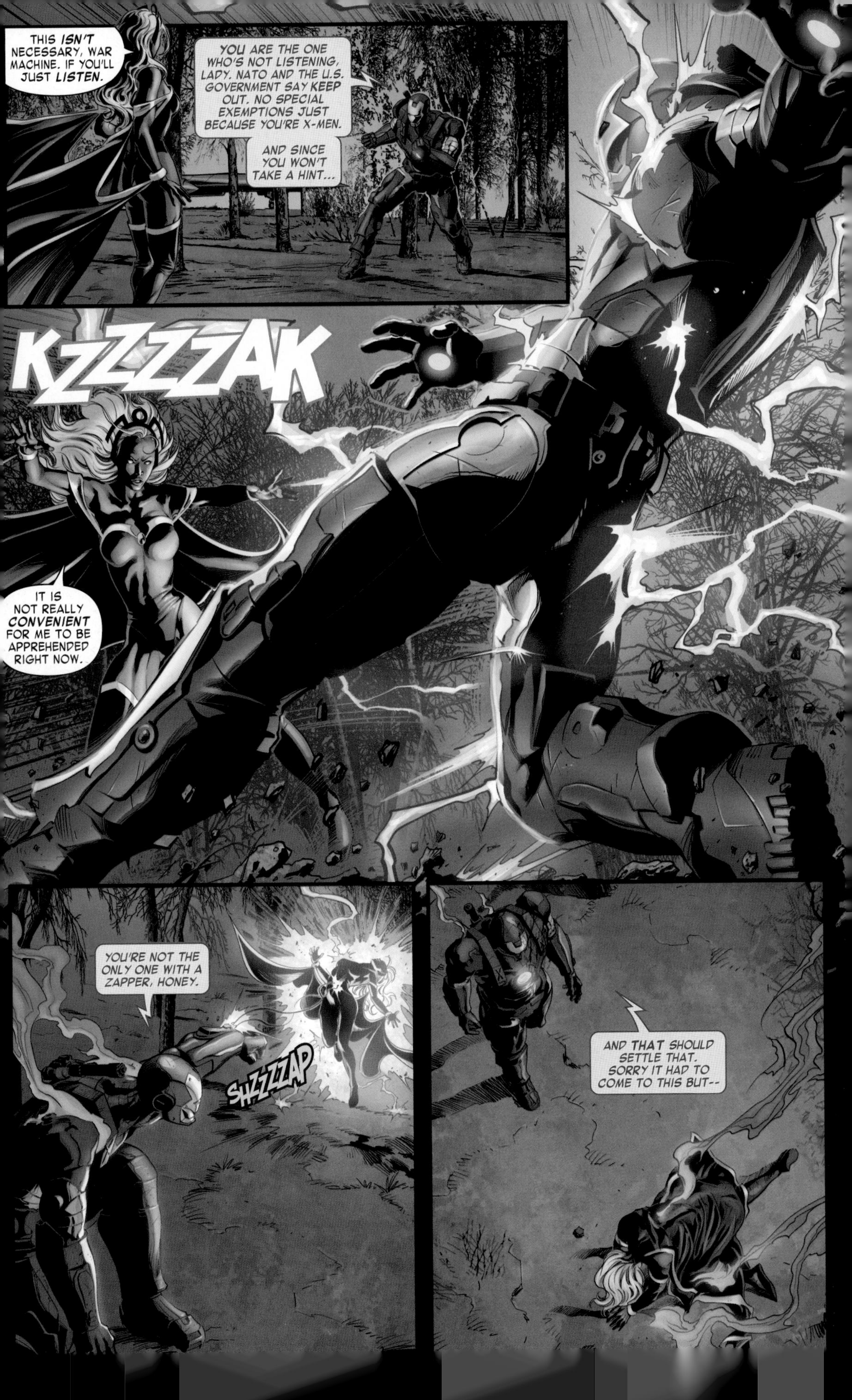
THIS ISN'T NECESSARY, WAR MACHINE. IF YOU'LL JUST LISTEN.
YOU ARE THE ONE WHO'S NOT LISTENING, LADY. NATO AND THE U.S. GOVERNMENT SAY KEEP OUT. NO SPECIAL EXEMPTIONS JUST BECAUSE YOU'RE X-MEN.
AND SINCE YOU WON'T TAKE A HINT...
KZZZZZAK
IT IS NOT REALLY CONVENIENT FOR ME TO BE APPREHENDED RIGHT NOW.
YOU'RE NOT THE ONLY ONE WITH A ZAPPER, HONEY.
SHZZZZAP
AND THAT SHOULD SETTLE THAT. SORRY IT HAD TO COME TO THIS BUT--

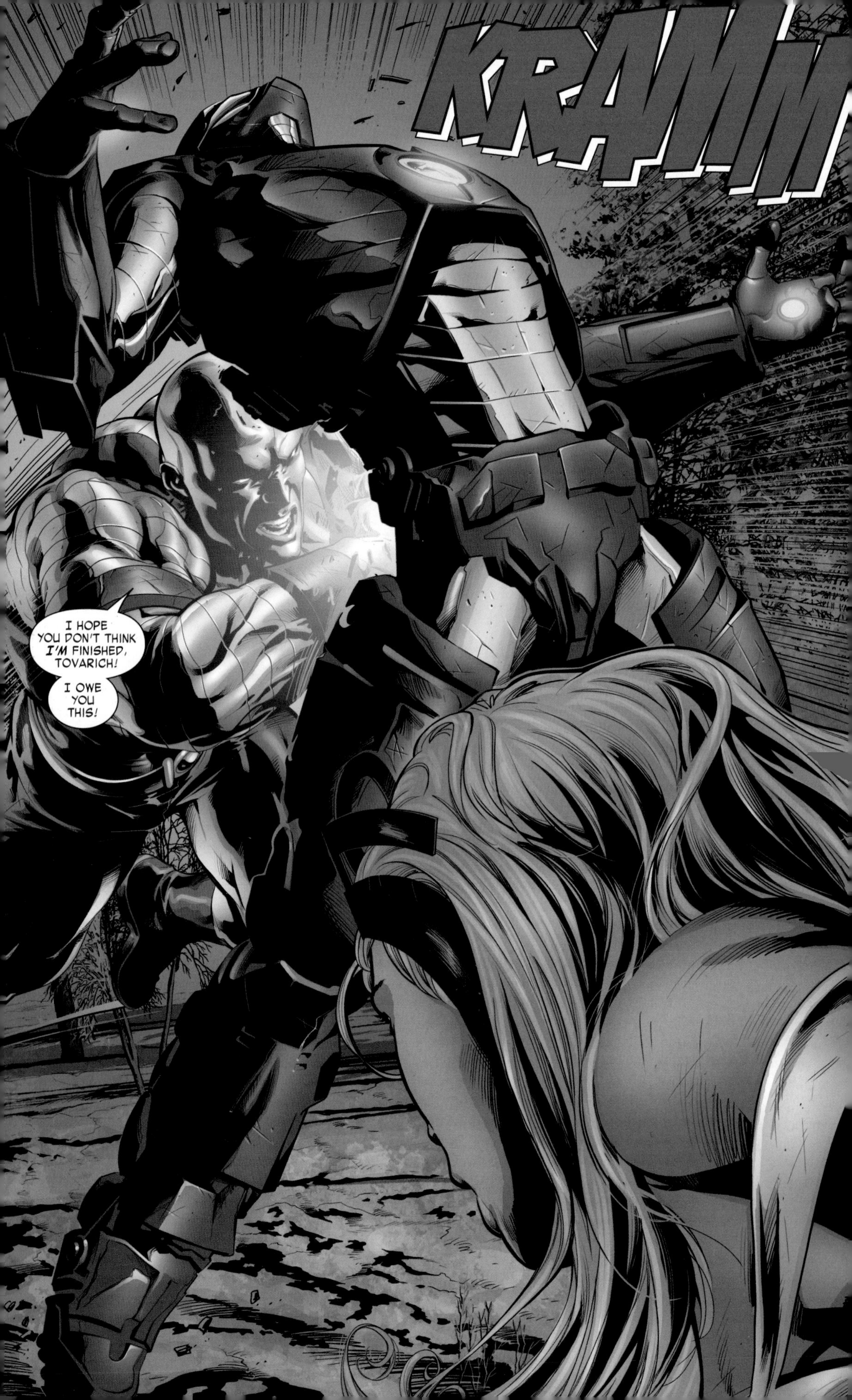
KRAMM
I HOPE YOU DON'T THINK ***I'M*** FINISHED, TOVARICH!
I OWE YOU THIS!

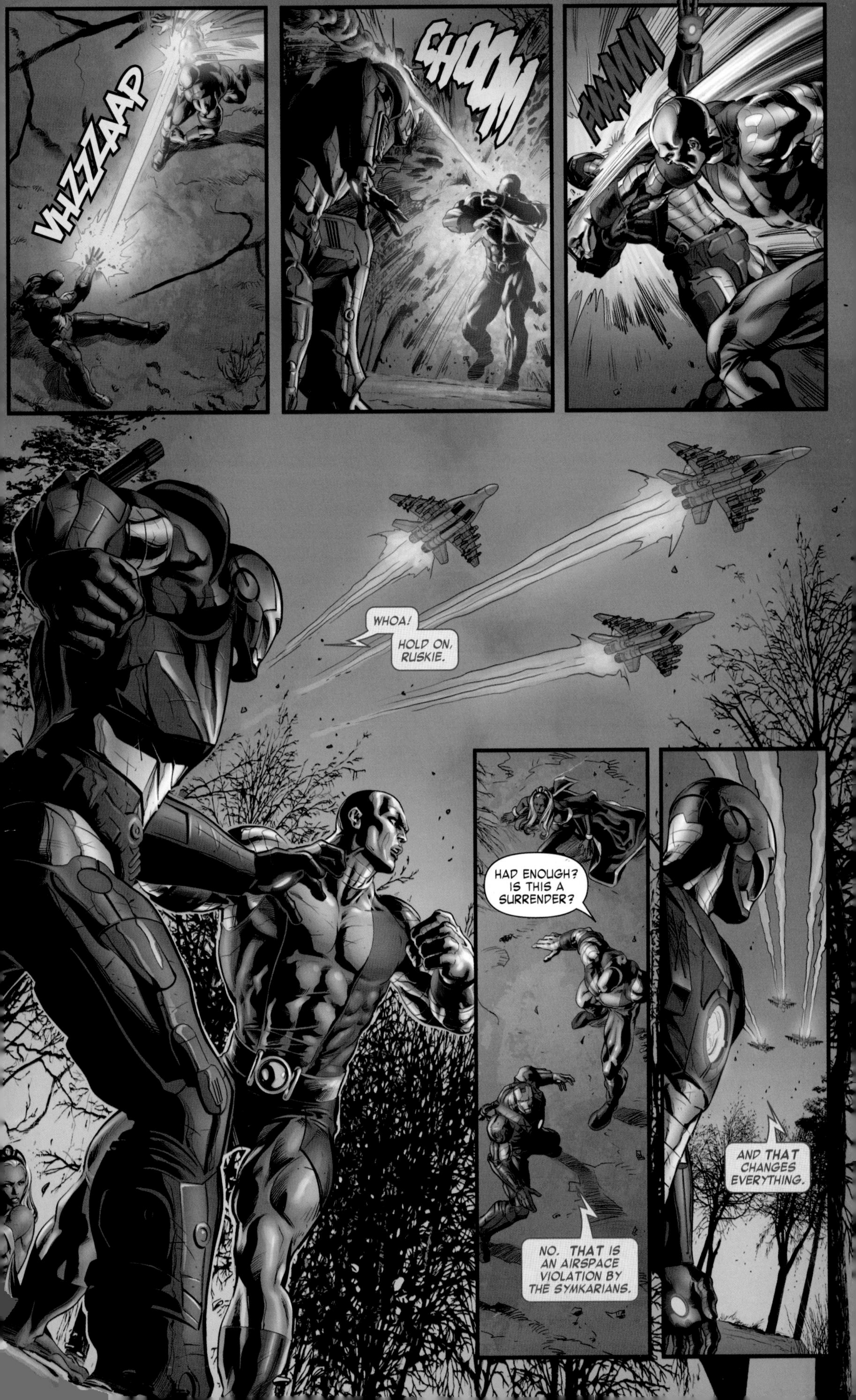
VHZZZAAP
CHOOM
FWAMM
WHOA!
HOLD ON, RUSKIE.
HAD ENOUGH? IS THIS A SURRENDER?
NO. THAT IS AN AIRSPACE VIOLATION BY THE SYMKARIANS.
AND THAT CHANGES EVERYTHING.

PUTERNICSTAN.

THE INTRUDER HAS BEEN TAKEN CARE OF, GOVERNOR.

OBVIOUSLY SHE WAS A *MUTANT* SINCE THE SENTINEL DETECTED HER.

I REACHED OUT TO SOME OF MY OLD KGB CONTACTS WHO ARE STILL PLUGGED IN. THEY SAY HER NAME WAS *DOMINO.* AN AGENT OF SOME TALENT APPARENTLY.

NOT ANYMORE.

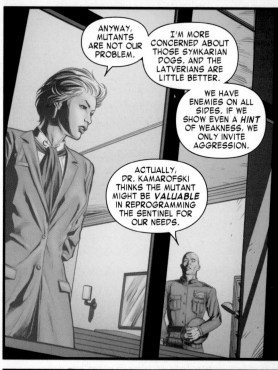

ANYWAY, MUTANTS ARE NOT OUR PROBLEM.

I'M MORE CONCERNED ABOUT THOSE SYMKARIAN DOGS. AND THE LATVERIANS ARE LITTLE BETTER.

WE HAVE ENEMIES ON ALL SIDES. IF WE SHOW EVEN A *HINT* OF WEAKNESS, WE ONLY INVITE AGGRESSION.

ACTUALLY, DR. KAMAROFSKI THINKS THE MUTANT MIGHT BE *VALUABLE* IN REPROGRAMMING THE SENTINEL FOR OUR NEEDS.

EXCELLENT. ANYTHING THAT ACCELERATES THE TIMETABLE IS GOOD NEWS.

TIMETABLE, GOVERNOR?

Hungary

Puternicstan *Latveria* *Romania*

Croatia

Symkaria

Serbia

Bulgaria

FORGIVE ME, GENERAL NOBAKOV, BUT UNTIL NOW, IT HAS BEEN NECESSARY TO KEEP YOU IN THE DARK ABOUT CERTAIN...PLANS.

AMBITIOUS PLANS.

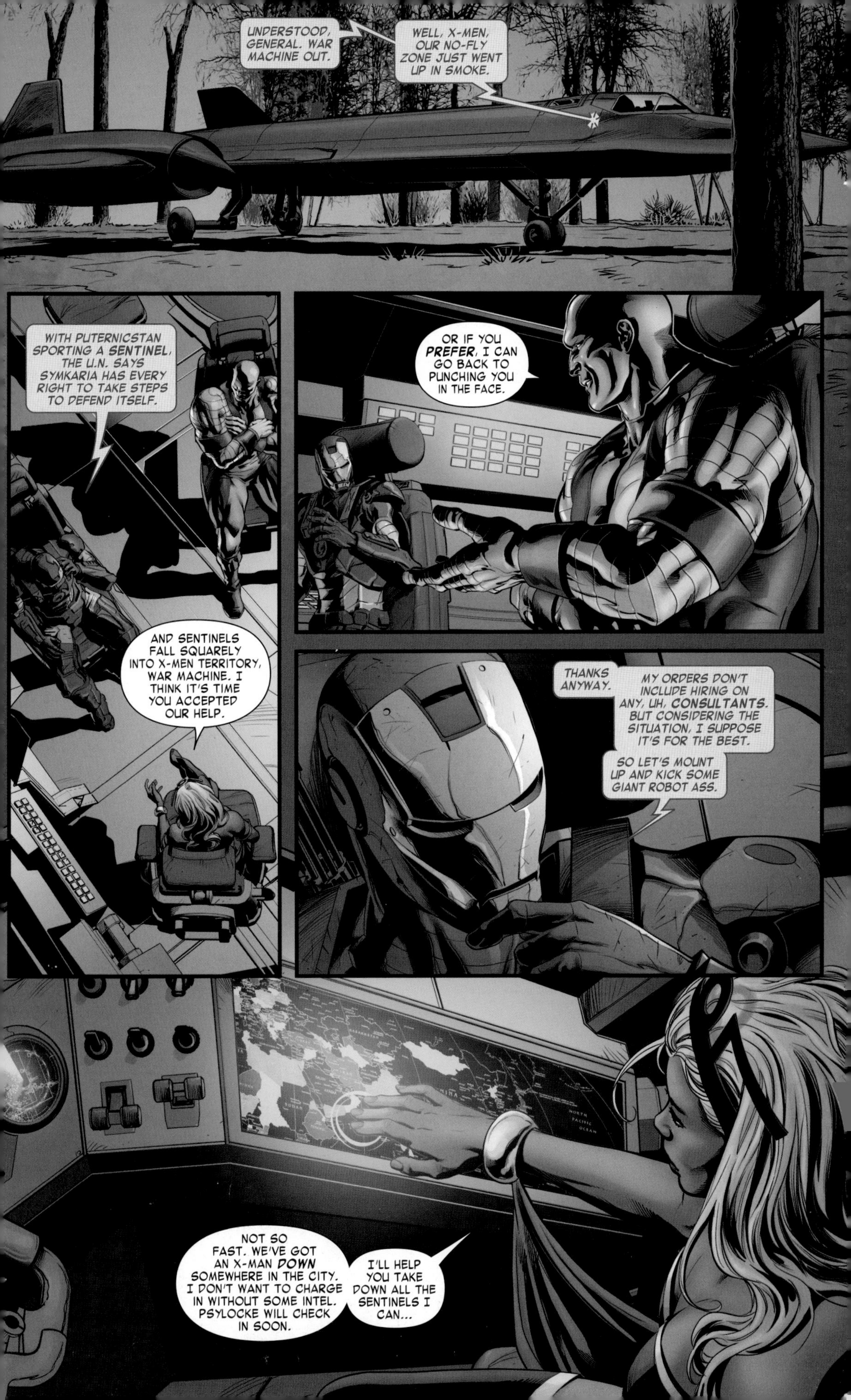

UNDERSTOOD, GENERAL. WAR MACHINE OUT.
WELL, X-MEN, OUR NO-FLY ZONE JUST WENT UP IN SMOKE.
WITH PUTERNICSTAN SPORTING A SENTINEL, THE U.N. SAYS SYMKARIA HAS EVERY RIGHT TO TAKE STEPS TO DEFEND ITSELF.
AND SENTINELS FALL SQUARELY INTO X-MEN TERRITORY, WAR MACHINE. I THINK IT'S TIME YOU ACCEPTED OUR HELP.
OR IF YOU PREFER, I CAN GO BACK TO PUNCHING YOU IN THE FACE.
THANKS ANYWAY.
MY ORDERS DON'T INCLUDE HIRING ON ANY, UH, CONSULTANTS. BUT CONSIDERING THE SITUATION, I SUPPOSE IT'S FOR THE BEST.
SO LET'S MOUNT UP AND KICK SOME GIANT ROBOT ASS.
I'LL HELP YOU TAKE DOWN ALL THE SENTINELS I CAN...
NOT SO FAST. WE'VE GOT AN X-MAN DOWN SOMEWHERE IN THE CITY. I DON'T WANT TO CHARGE IN WITHOUT SOME INTEL. PSYLOCKE WILL CHECK IN SOON.

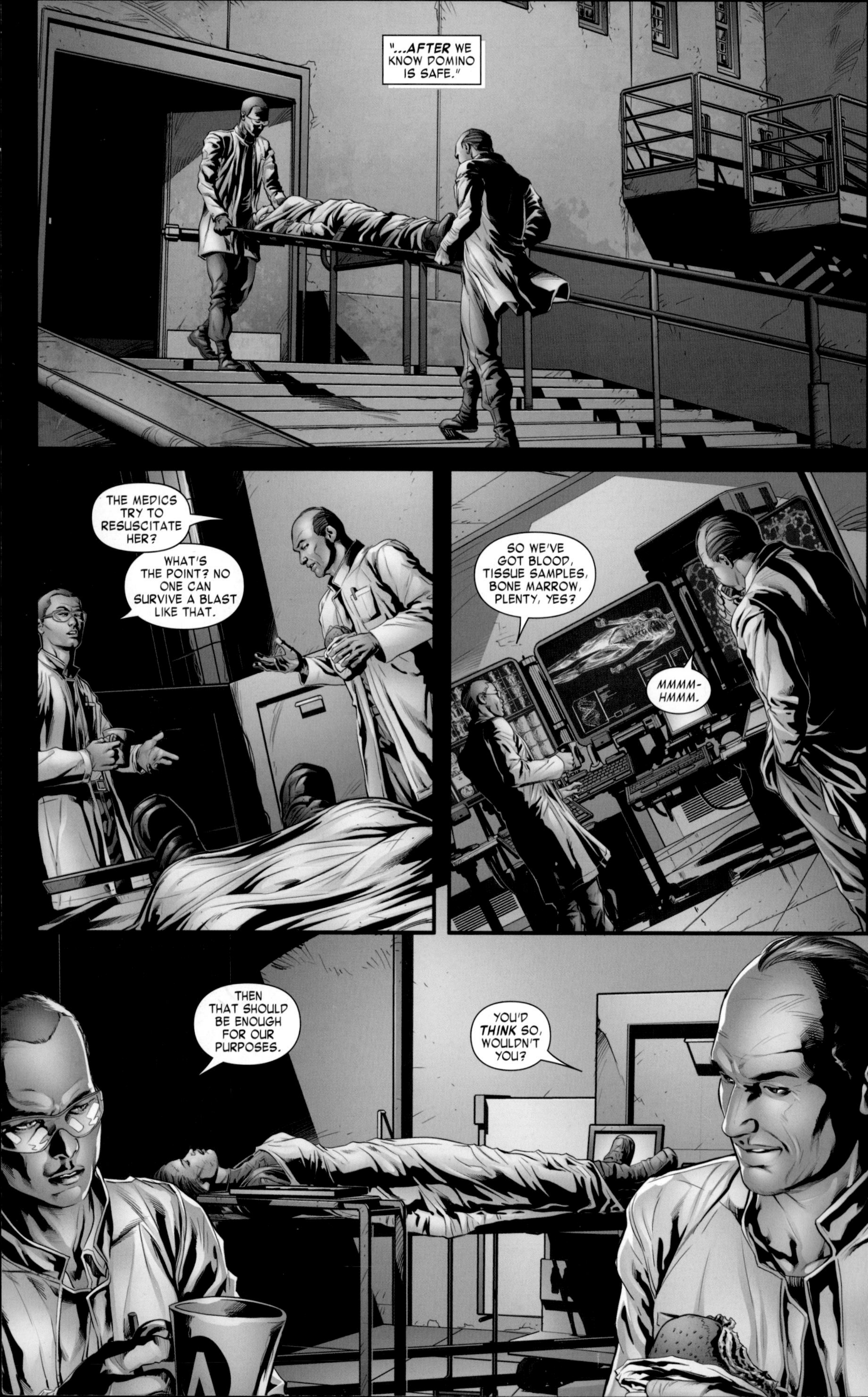
"...AFTER WE KNOW DOMINO IS SAFE."
THE MEDICS TRY TO RESUSCITATE HER?
WHAT'S THE POINT? NO ONE CAN SURVIVE A BLAST LIKE THAT.
SO WE'VE GOT BLOOD, TISSUE SAMPLES, BONE MARROW, PLENTY, YES?
MMMM-HMMM.
THEN THAT SHOULD BE ENOUGH FOR OUR PURPOSES.
YOU'D THINK SO, WOULDN'T YOU?

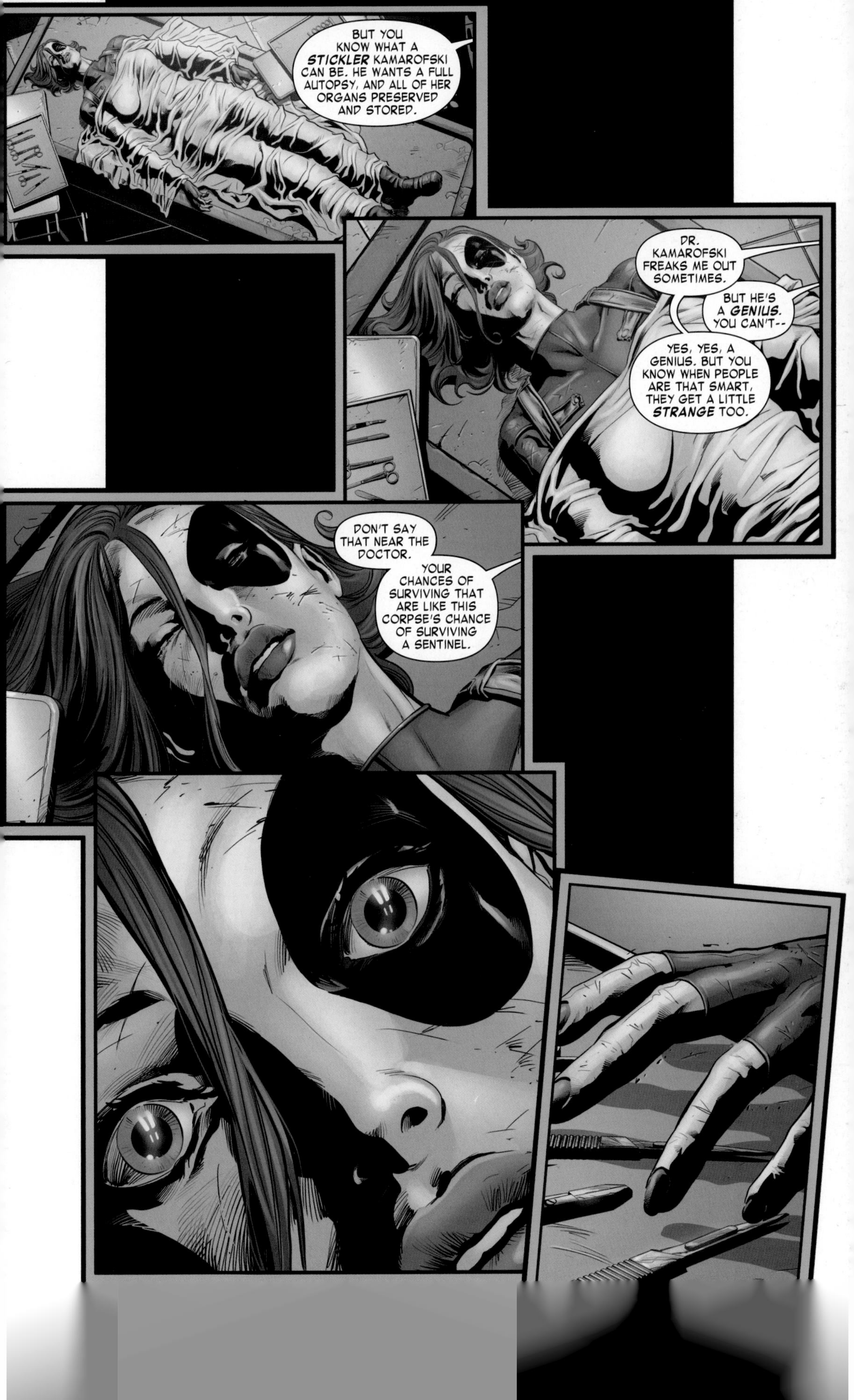

BUT YOU KNOW WHAT A STICKLER KAMAROFSKI CAN BE. HE WANTS A FULL AUTOPSY, AND ALL OF HER ORGANS PRESERVED AND STORED.
DR. KAMAROFSKI FREAKS ME OUT SOMETIMES.
BUT HE'S A GENIUS. YOU CAN'T--
YES, YES, A GENIUS. BUT YOU KNOW WHEN PEOPLE ARE THAT SMART, THEY GET A LITTLE STRANGE TOO.
DON'T SAY THAT NEAR THE DOCTOR.
YOUR CHANCES OF SURVIVING THAT ARE LIKE THIS CORPSE'S CHANCE OF SURVIVING A SENTINEL.

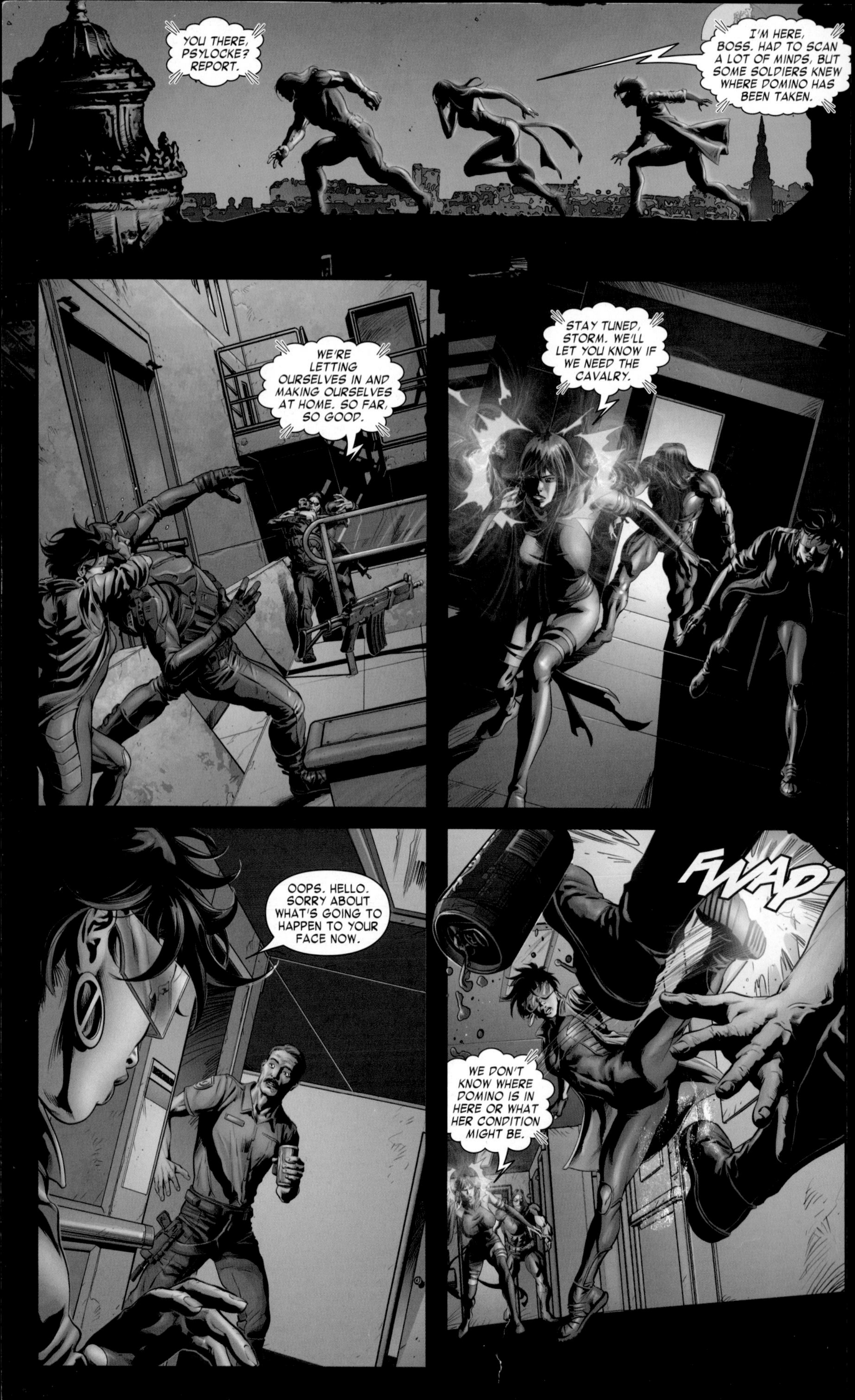
YOU THERE, PSYLOCKE? REPORT.
I'M HERE, BOSS. HAD TO SCAN A LOT OF MINDS, BUT SOME SOLDIERS KNEW WHERE DOMINO HAS BEEN TAKEN.
WE'RE LETTING OURSELVES IN AND MAKING OURSELVES AT HOME. SO FAR, SO GOOD.
STAY TUNED, STORM. WE'LL LET YOU KNOW IF WE NEED THE CAVALRY.
OOPS. HELLO. SORRY ABOUT WHAT'S GOING TO HAPPEN TO YOUR FACE NOW.
FWAP
WE DON'T KNOW WHERE DOMINO IS IN HERE OR WHAT HER CONDITION MIGHT BE.

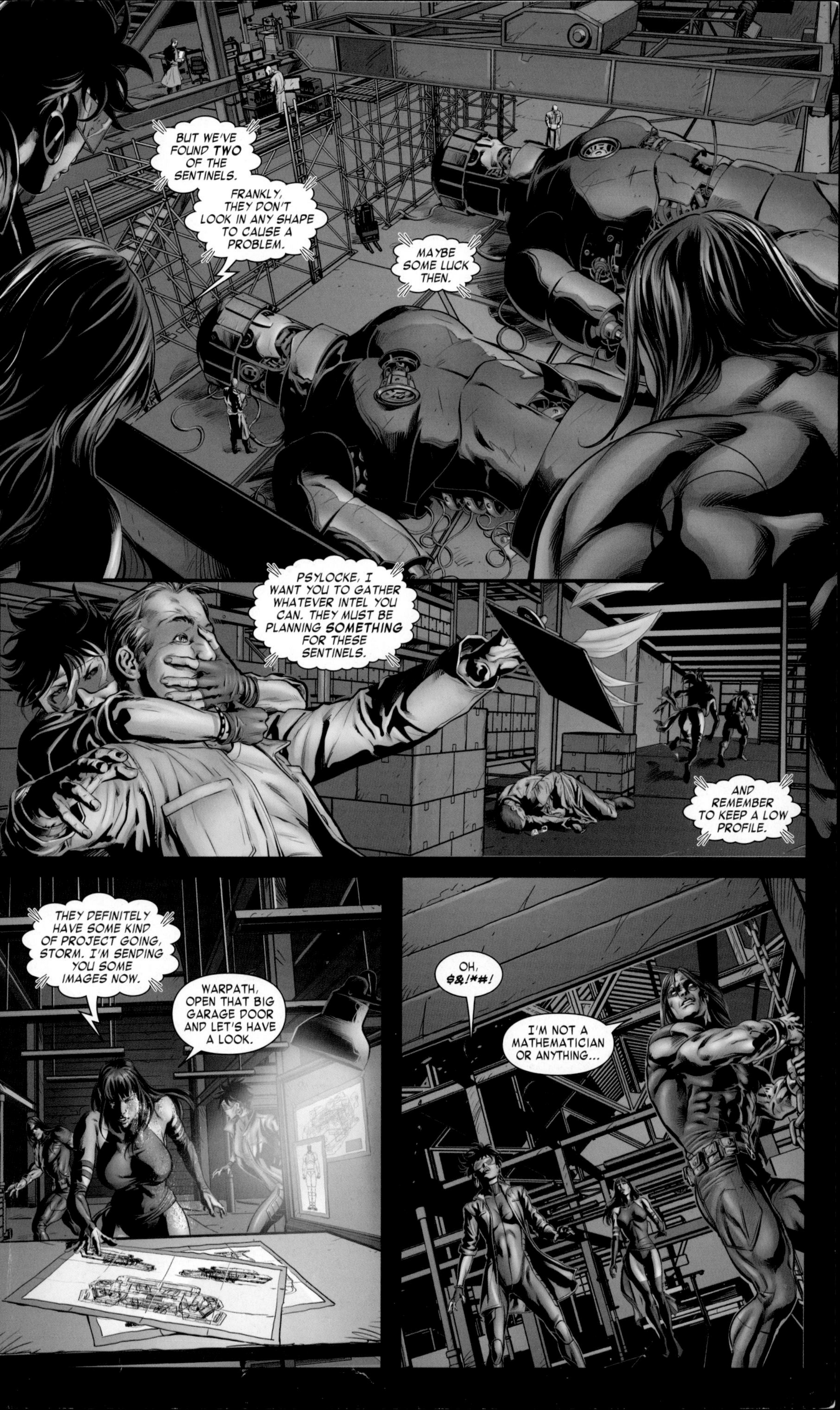

BUT WE'VE FOUND **TWO** OF THE SENTINELS.
FRANKLY, THEY DON'T LOOK IN ANY SHAPE TO CAUSE A PROBLEM.
MAYBE SOME LUCK THEN.
PSYLOCKE, I WANT YOU TO GATHER WHATEVER INTEL YOU CAN. THEY MUST BE PLANNING **SOMETHING** FOR THESE SENTINELS.
AND REMEMBER TO KEEP A LOW PROFILE.
THEY DEFINITELY HAVE SOME KIND OF PROJECT GOING, STORM. I'M SENDING YOU SOME IMAGES NOW.
WARPATH, OPEN THAT BIG GARAGE DOOR AND LET'S HAVE A LOOK.
OH, $&!*#!
I'M NOT A MATHEMATICIAN OR ANYTHING...

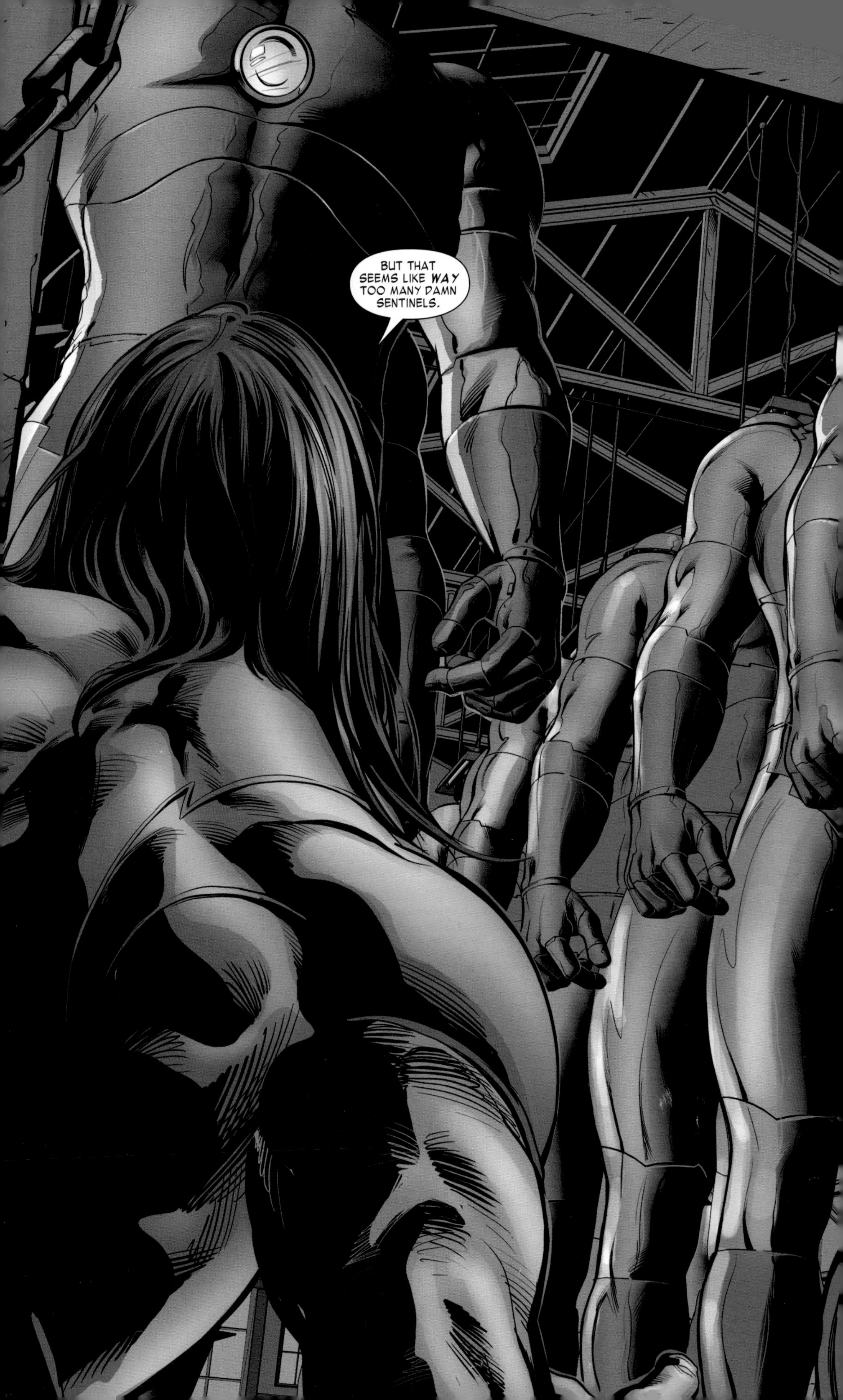
BUT THAT SEEMS LIKE WAY TOO MANY DAMN SENTINELS.

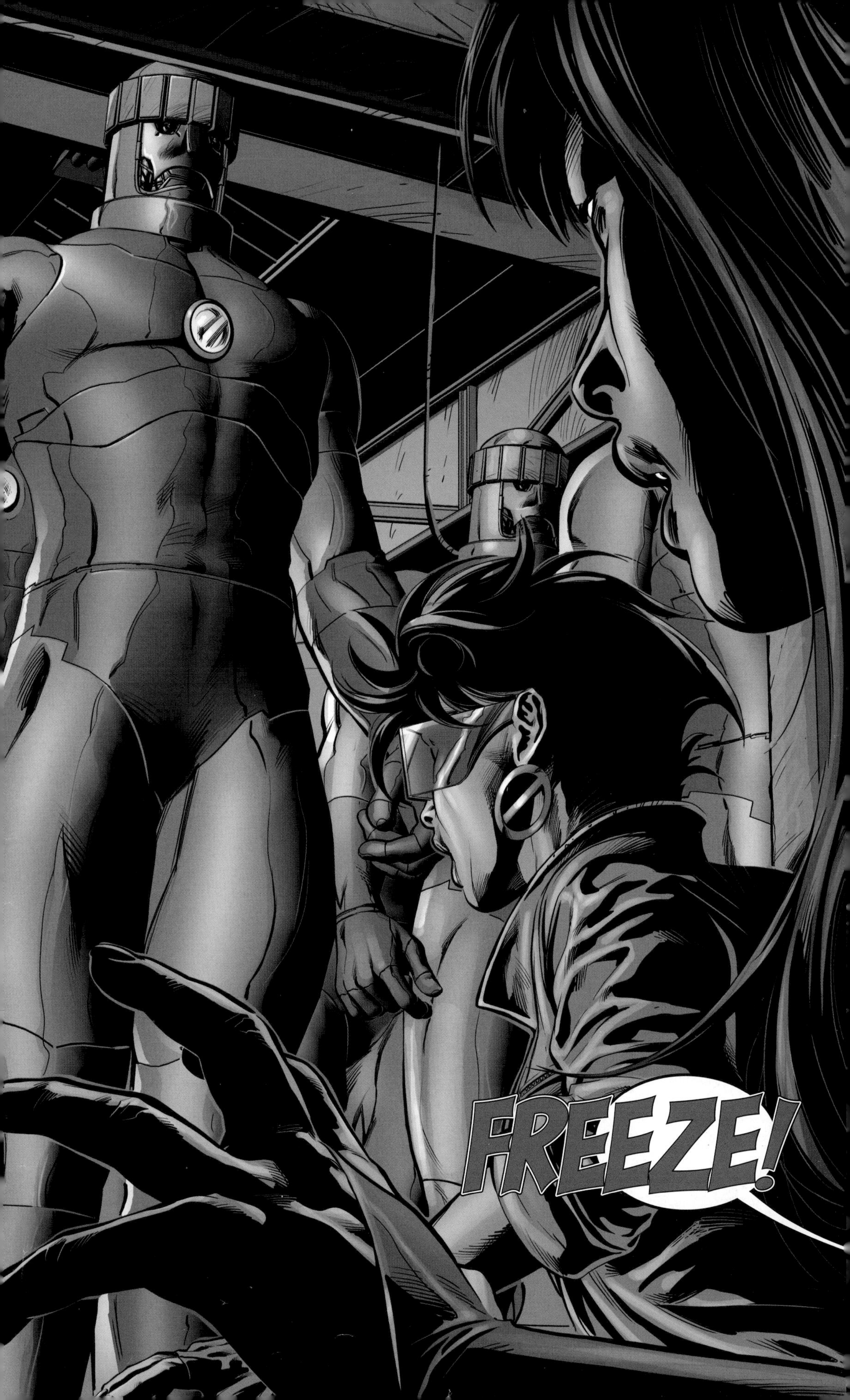
FREEZE!

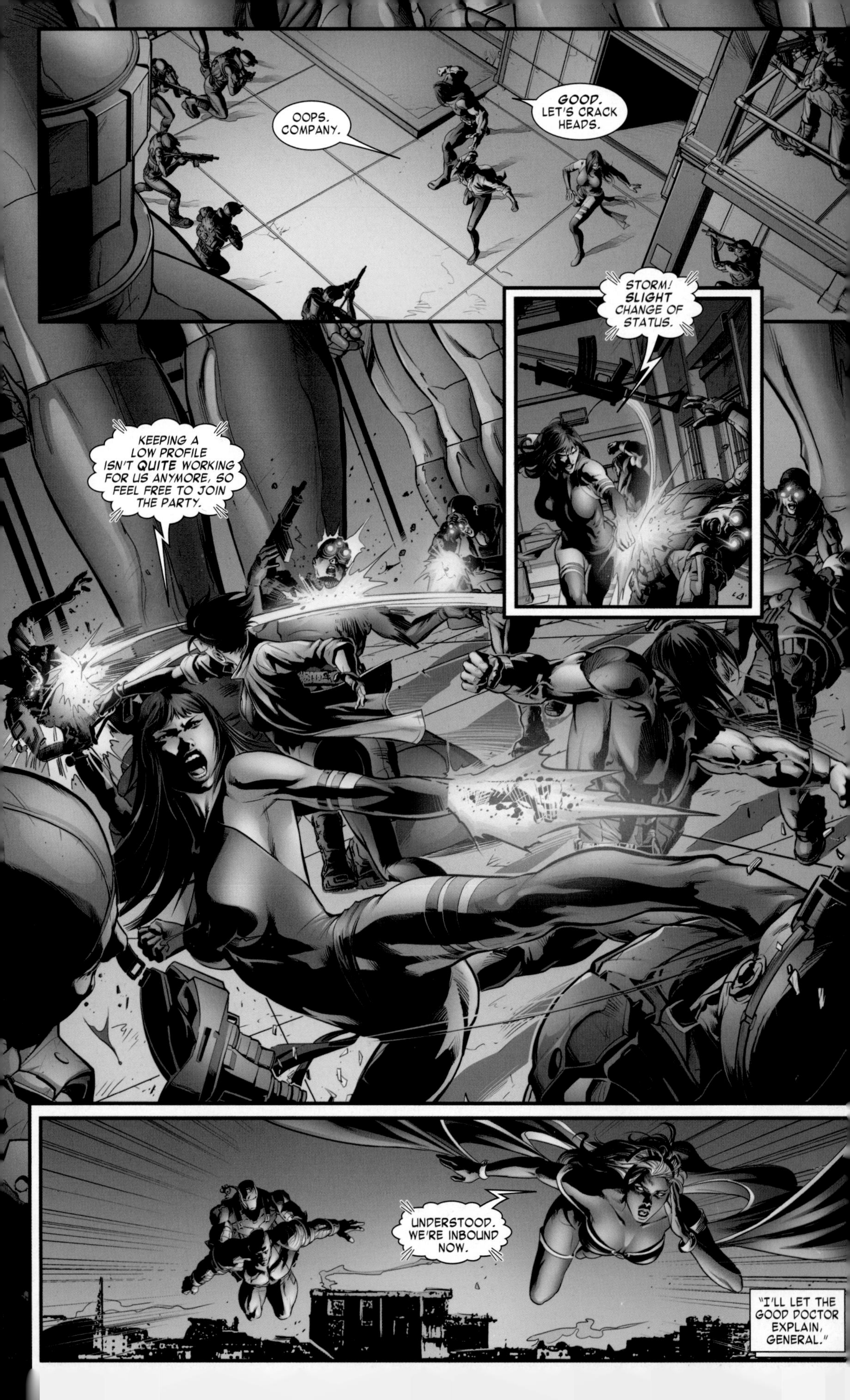
OOPS. COMPANY.
GOOD. LET'S CRACK HEADS.
KEEPING A LOW PROFILE ISN'T QUITE WORKING FOR US ANYMORE, SO FEEL FREE TO JOIN THE PARTY.
STORM! SLIGHT CHANGE OF STATUS.
UNDERSTOOD. WE'RE INBOUND NOW.
"I'LL LET THE GOOD DOCTOR EXPLAIN, GENERAL."

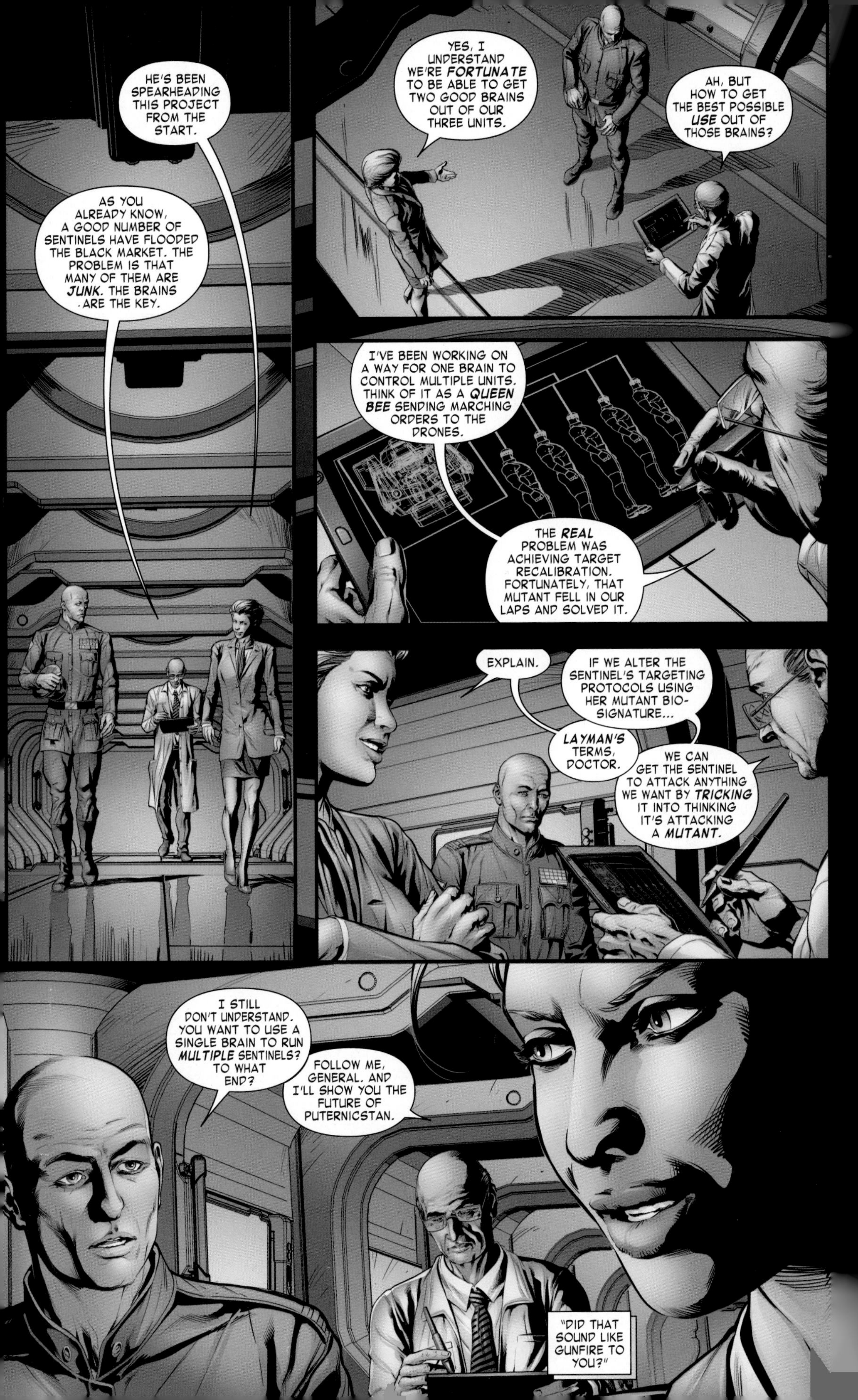
HE'S BEEN SPEARHEADING THIS PROJECT FROM THE START.
AS YOU ALREADY KNOW, A GOOD NUMBER OF SENTINELS HAVE FLOODED THE BLACK MARKET. THE PROBLEM IS THAT MANY OF THEM ARE JUNK. THE BRAINS ARE THE KEY.
YES, I UNDERSTAND WE'RE FORTUNATE TO BE ABLE TO GET TWO GOOD BRAINS OUT OF OUR THREE UNITS.
AH, BUT HOW TO GET THE BEST POSSIBLE USE OUT OF THOSE BRAINS?
I'VE BEEN WORKING ON A WAY FOR ONE BRAIN TO CONTROL MULTIPLE UNITS. THINK OF IT AS A QUEEN BEE SENDING MARCHING ORDERS TO THE DRONES.
THE REAL PROBLEM WAS ACHIEVING TARGET RECALIBRATION. FORTUNATELY, THAT MUTANT FELL IN OUR LAPS AND SOLVED IT.
EXPLAIN.
IF WE ALTER THE SENTINEL'S TARGETING PROTOCOLS USING HER MUTANT BIO-SIGNATURE...
LAYMAN'S TERMS, DOCTOR.
WE CAN GET THE SENTINEL TO ATTACK ANYTHING WE WANT BY TRICKING IT INTO THINKING IT'S ATTACKING A MUTANT.
I STILL DON'T UNDERSTAND. YOU WANT TO USE A SINGLE BRAIN TO RUN MULTIPLE SENTINELS? TO WHAT END?
FOLLOW ME, GENERAL. AND I'LL SHOW YOU THE FUTURE OF PUTERNICSTAN.
"DID THAT SOUND LIKE GUNFIRE TO YOU?"

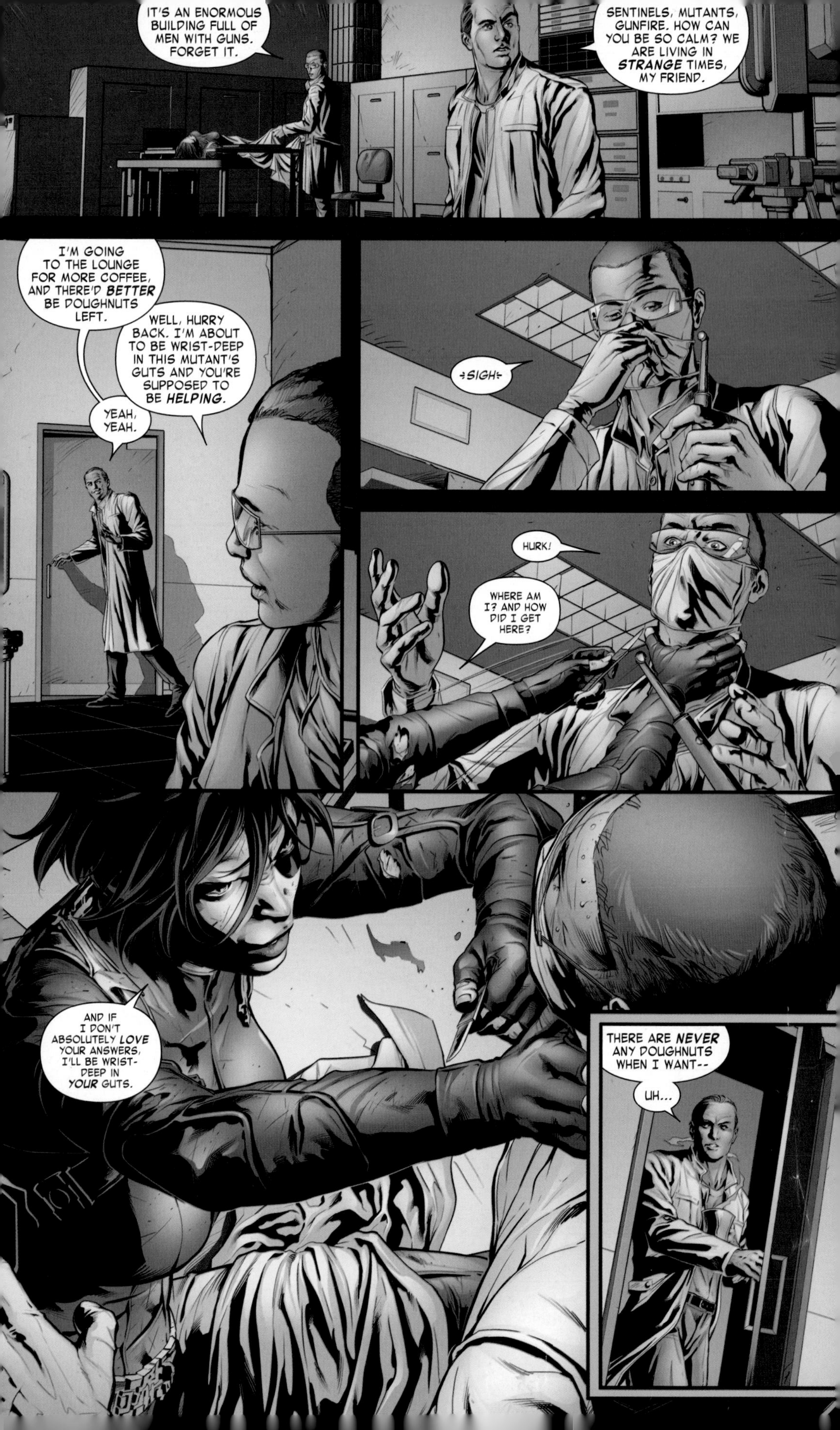
IT'S AN ENORMOUS BUILDING FULL OF MEN WITH GUNS. FORGET IT.
SENTINELS, MUTANTS, GUNFIRE. HOW CAN YOU BE SO CALM? WE ARE LIVING IN STRANGE TIMES, MY FRIEND.
I'M GOING TO THE LOUNGE FOR MORE COFFEE, AND THERE'D BETTER BE DOUGHNUTS LEFT.
WELL, HURRY BACK. I'M ABOUT TO BE WRIST-DEEP IN THIS MUTANT'S GUTS AND YOU'RE SUPPOSED TO BE HELPING.
YEAH, YEAH.
SIGH
HURK!
WHERE AM I? AND HOW DID I GET HERE?
AND IF I DON'T ABSOLUTELY LOVE YOUR ANSWERS, I'LL BE WRIST-DEEP IN YOUR GUTS.
THERE ARE NEVER ANY DOUGHNUTS WHEN I WANT--
UH...

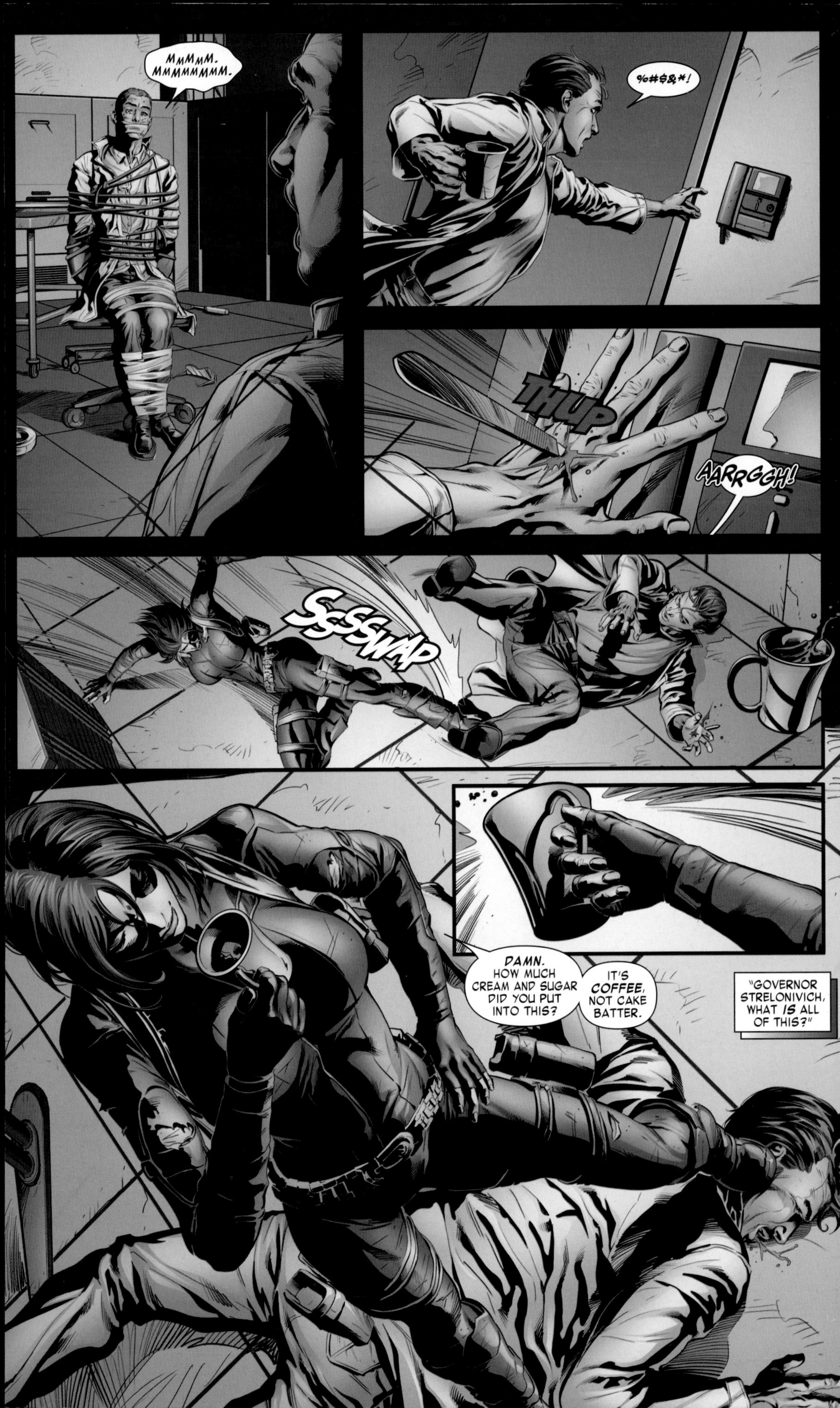
MMMMM.
MMMMMMMM.
%#$&*!
THUP
AARRGGH!
SSSSWAP
DAMN.
HOW MUCH CREAM AND SUGAR DID YOU PUT INTO THIS?
IT'S COFFEE, NOT CAKE BATTER.
"GOVERNOR STRELONIVICH, WHAT IS ALL OF THIS?"

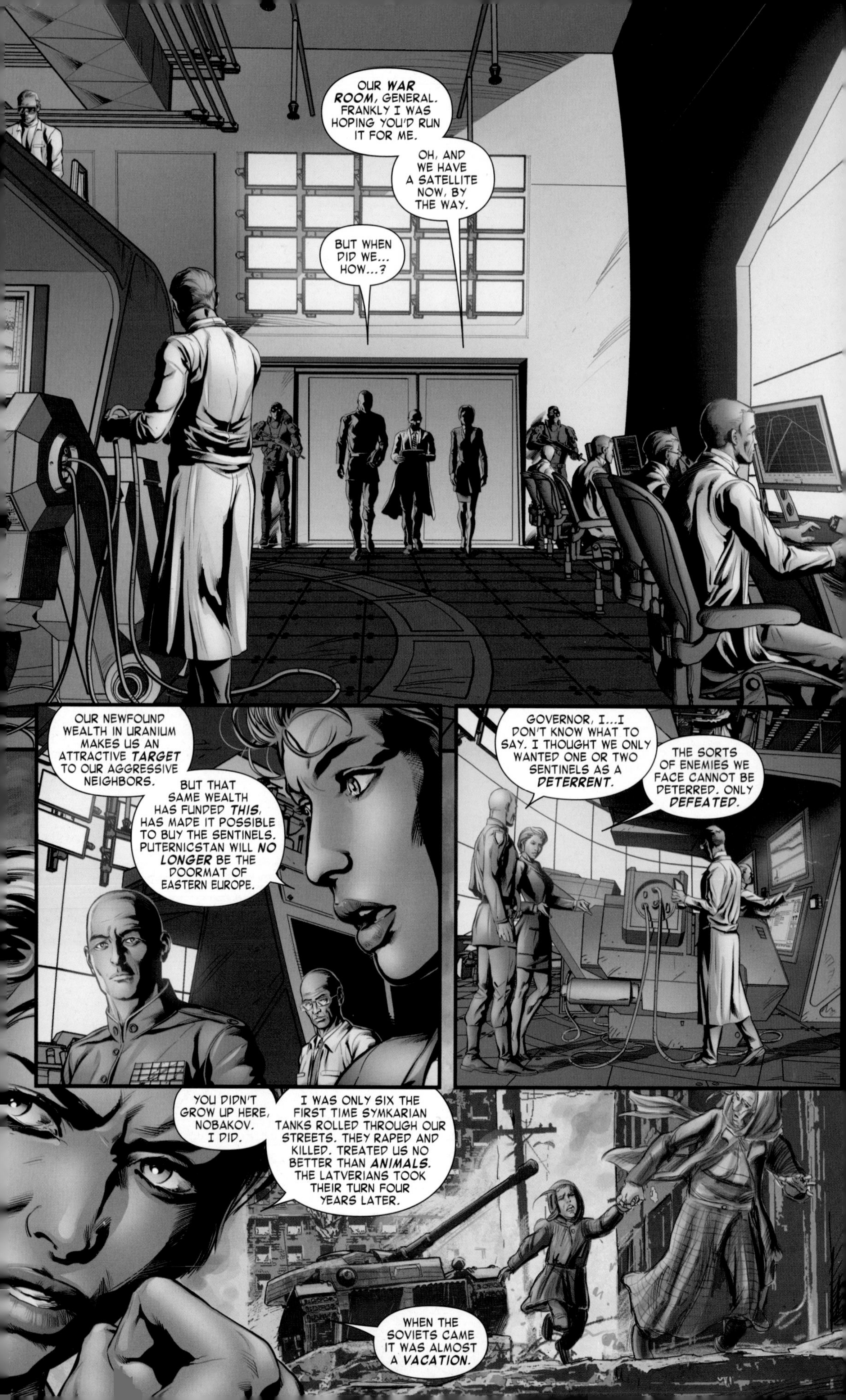
OUR WAR ROOM, GENERAL. FRANKLY I WAS HOPING YOU'D RUN IT FOR ME.
OH, AND WE HAVE A SATELLITE NOW, BY THE WAY.
BUT WHEN DID WE... HOW...?
OUR NEWFOUND WEALTH IN URANIUM MAKES US AN ATTRACTIVE TARGET TO OUR AGGRESSIVE NEIGHBORS.
BUT THAT SAME WEALTH HAS FUNDED THIS, HAS MADE IT POSSIBLE TO BUY THE SENTINELS. PUTERNICSTAN WILL NO LONGER BE THE DOORMAT OF EASTERN EUROPE.
GOVERNOR, I...I DON'T KNOW WHAT TO SAY. I THOUGHT WE ONLY WANTED ONE OR TWO SENTINELS AS A DETERRENT.
THE SORTS OF ENEMIES WE FACE CANNOT BE DETERRED. ONLY DEFEATED.
YOU DIDN'T GROW UP HERE, NOBAKOV. I DID.
I WAS ONLY SIX THE FIRST TIME SYMKARIAN TANKS ROLLED THROUGH OUR STREETS. THEY RAPED AND KILLED. TREATED US NO BETTER THAN ANIMALS. THE LATVERIANS TOOK THEIR TURN FOUR YEARS LATER.
WHEN THE SOVIETS CAME IT WAS ALMOST A VACATION.

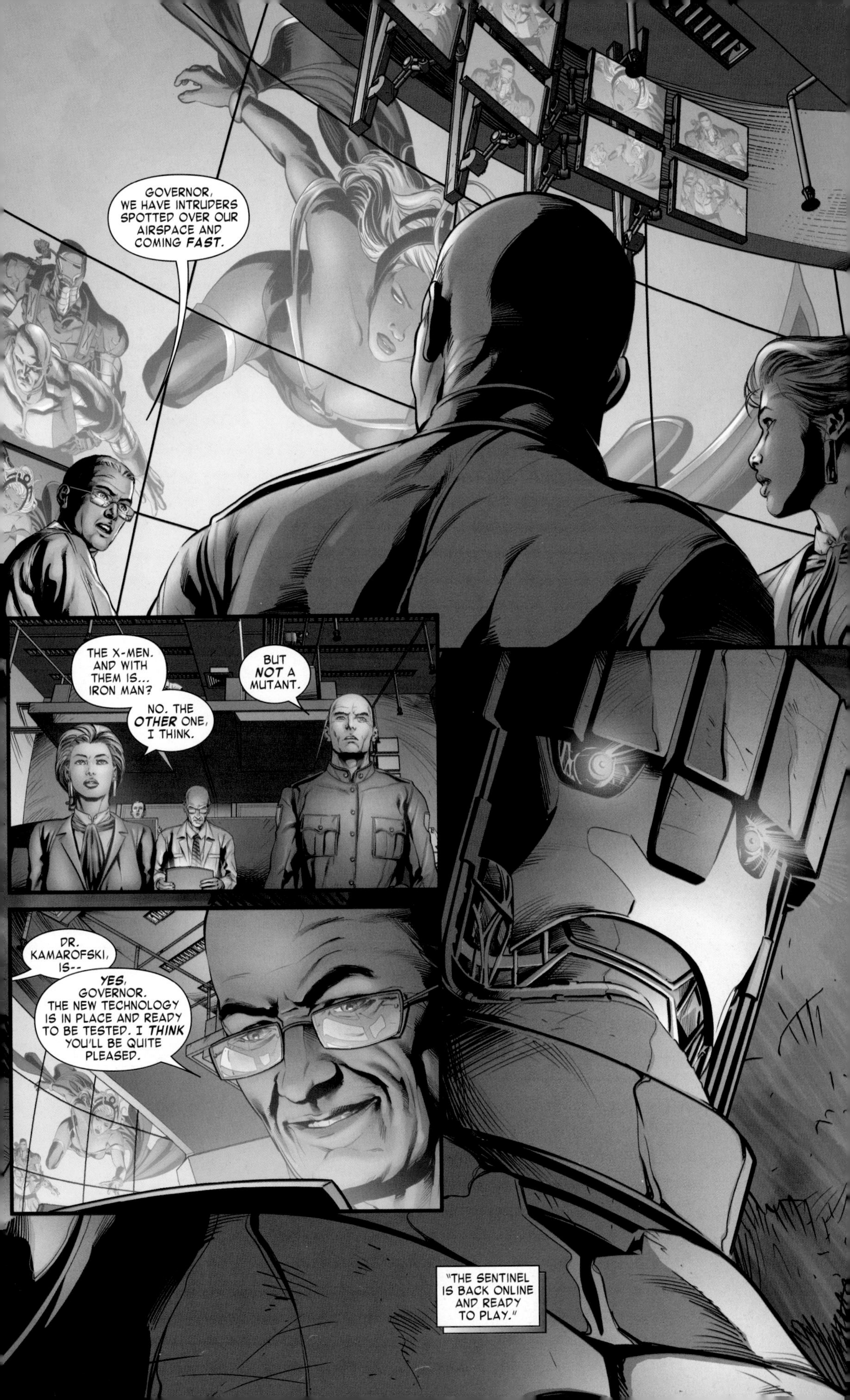

GOVERNOR, WE HAVE INTRUDERS SPOTTED OVER OUR AIRSPACE AND COMING FAST.
THE X-MEN. AND WITH THEM IS... IRON MAN?
NO. THE OTHER ONE, I THINK.
BUT NOT A MUTANT.
DR. KAMAROFSKI, IS--
YES, GOVERNOR. THE NEW TECHNOLOGY IS IN PLACE AND READY TO BE TESTED. I THINK YOU'LL BE QUITE PLEASED.
"THE SENTINEL IS BACK ONLINE AND READY TO PLAY."

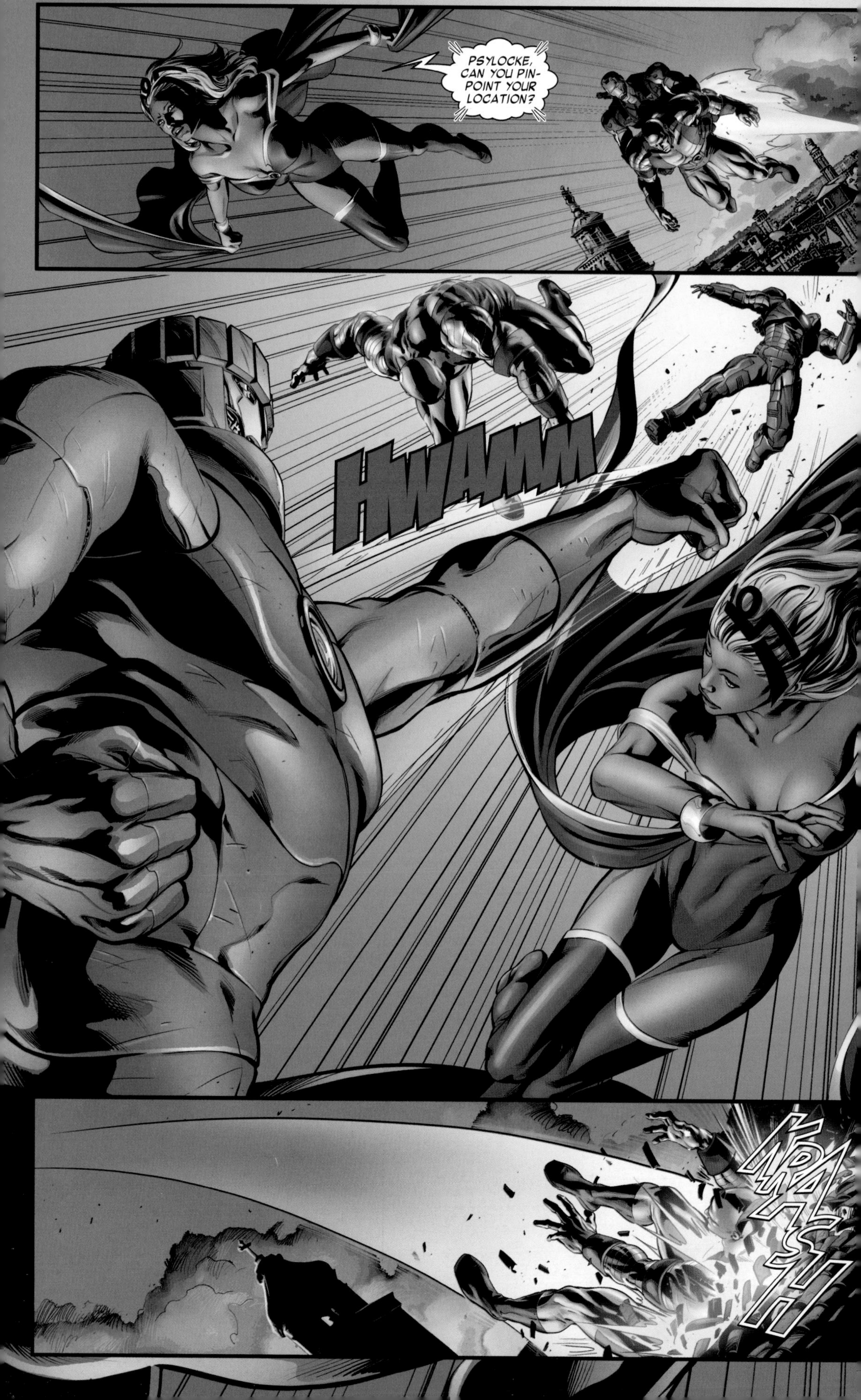
PSYLOCKE, CAN YOU PIN-POINT YOUR LOCATION?
HWAMM
KRAASH

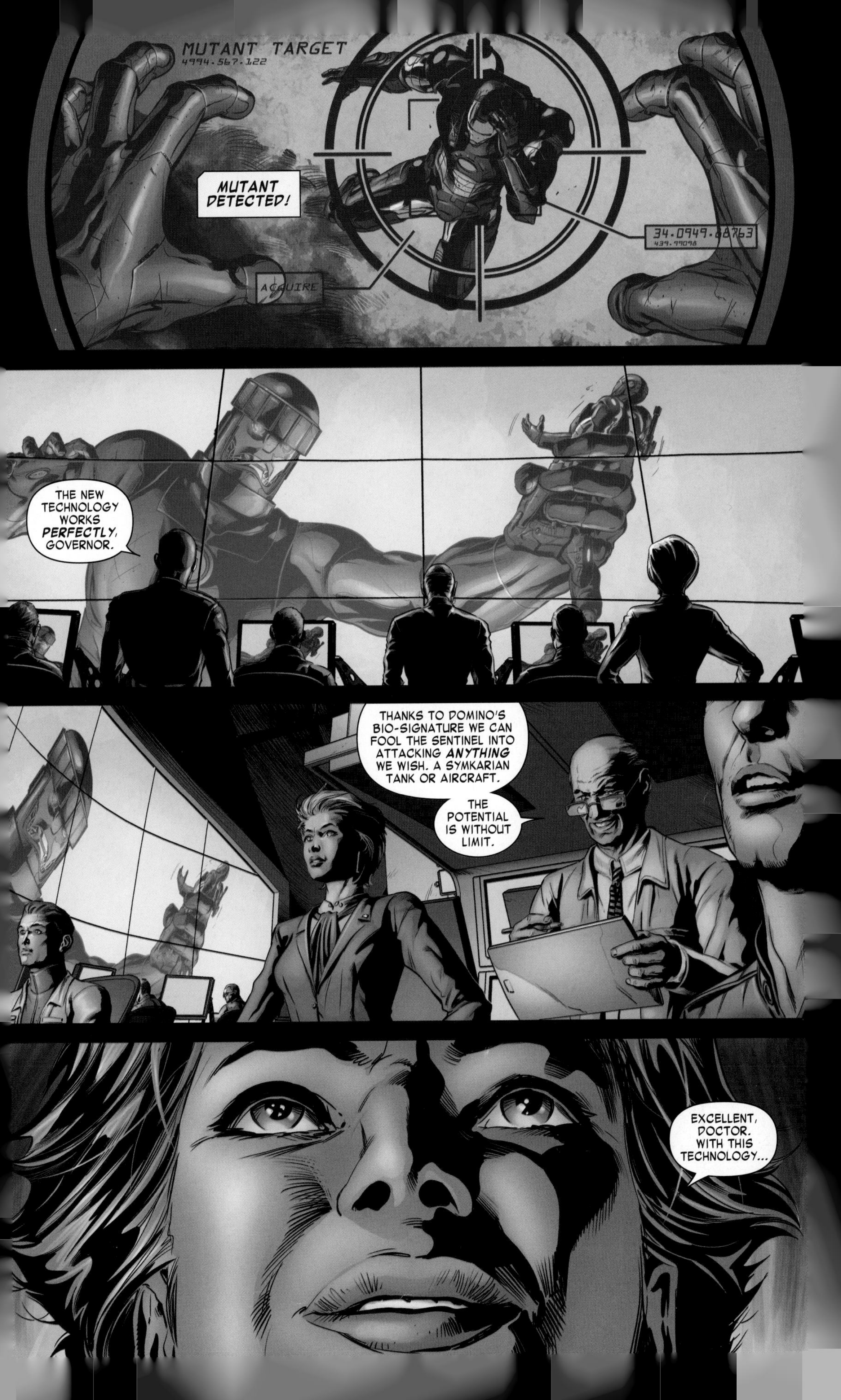
MUTANT TARGET
4994.567.122
MUTANT DETECTED!
34.0949.68763
439.99098
ACQUIRE
THE NEW TECHNOLOGY WORKS PERFECTLY, GOVERNOR.
THANKS TO DOMINO'S BIO-SIGNATURE WE CAN FOOL THE SENTINEL INTO ATTACKING ANYTHING WE WISH. A SYMKARIAN TANK OR AIRCRAFT.
THE POTENTIAL IS WITHOUT LIMIT.
EXCELLENT, DOCTOR. WITH THIS TECHNOLOGY...

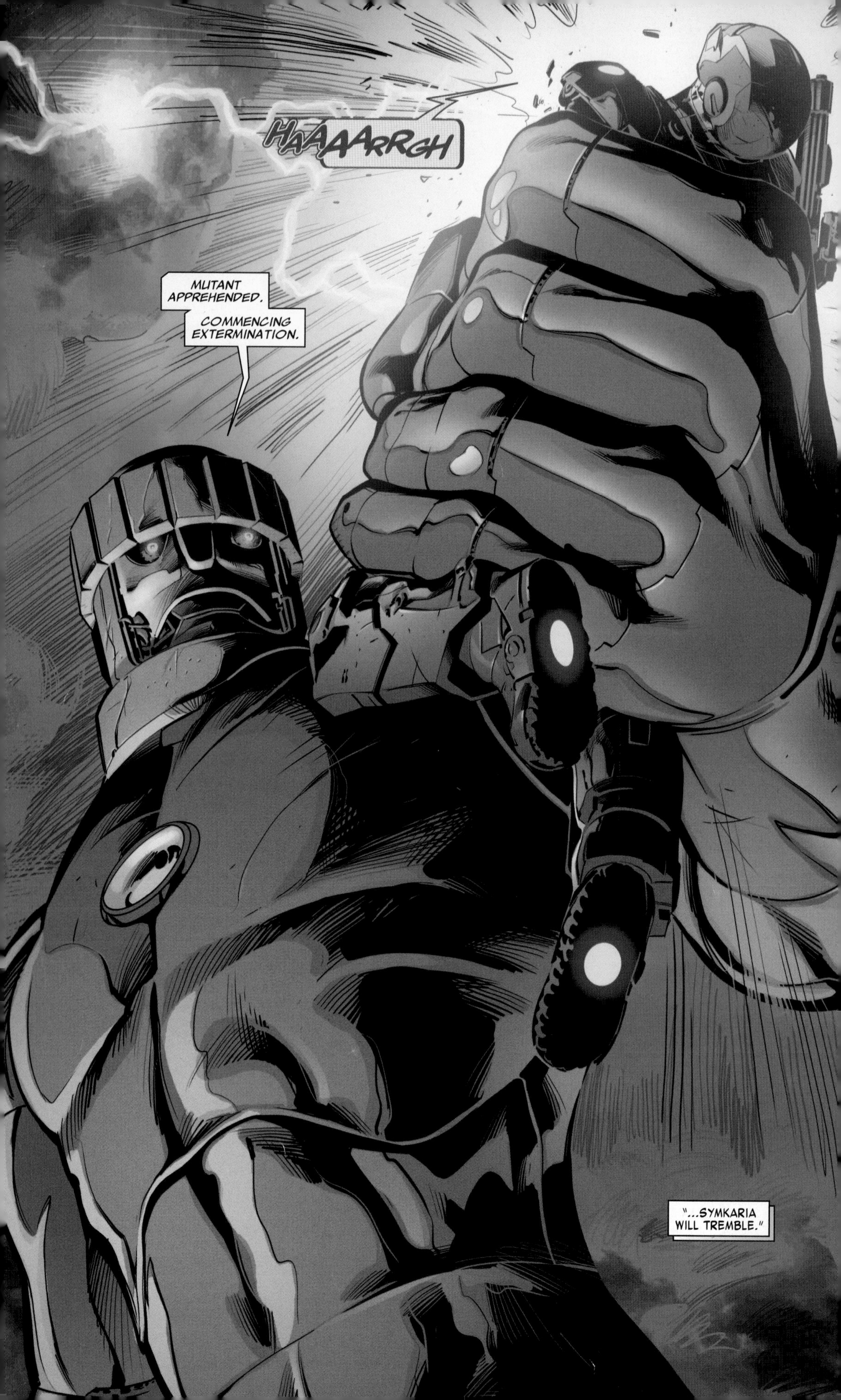
HAAAARRGH
MUTANT APPREHENDED.
COMMENCING EXTERMINATION.
"...SYMKARIA WILL TREMBLE."

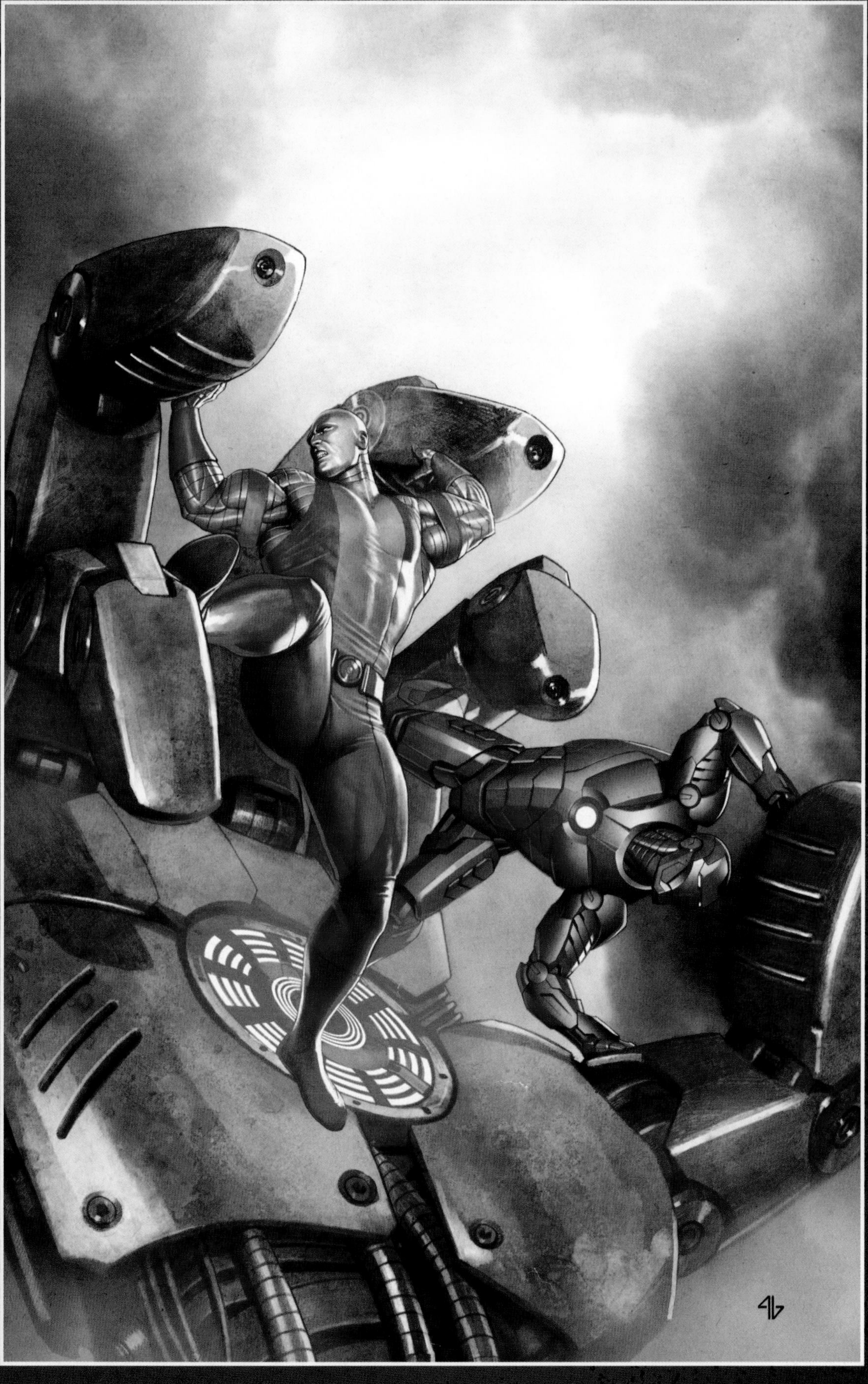

TWENTY-TWO

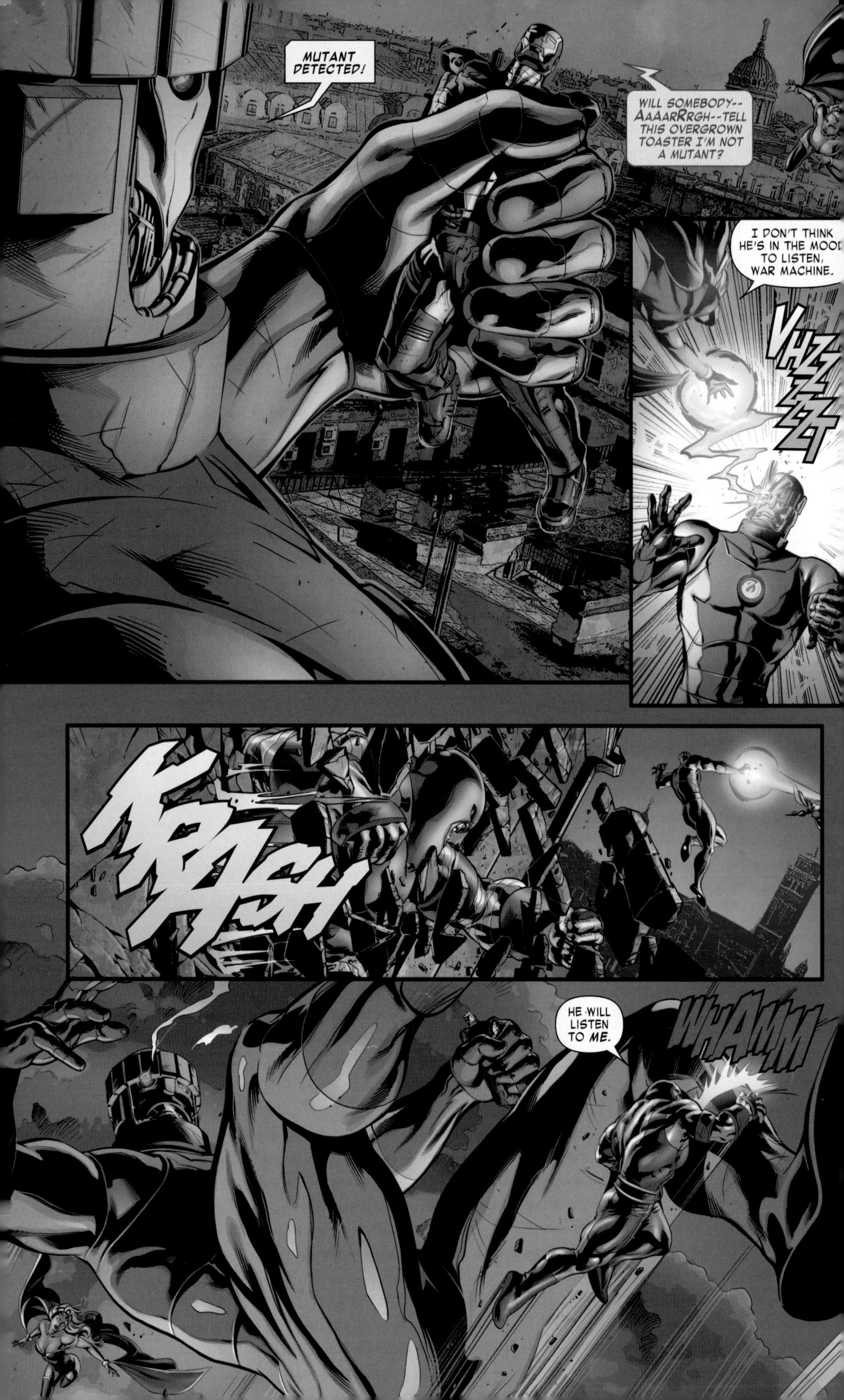
MUTANT DETECTED!
WILL SOMEBODY-- AAAARRRGH--TELL THIS OVERGROWN TOASTER I'M NOT A MUTANT?
I DON'T THINK HE'S IN THE MOOD TO LISTEN, WAR MACHINE.
VHZZZZT
KRASH
HE WILL LISTEN TO ME.
WHAMM

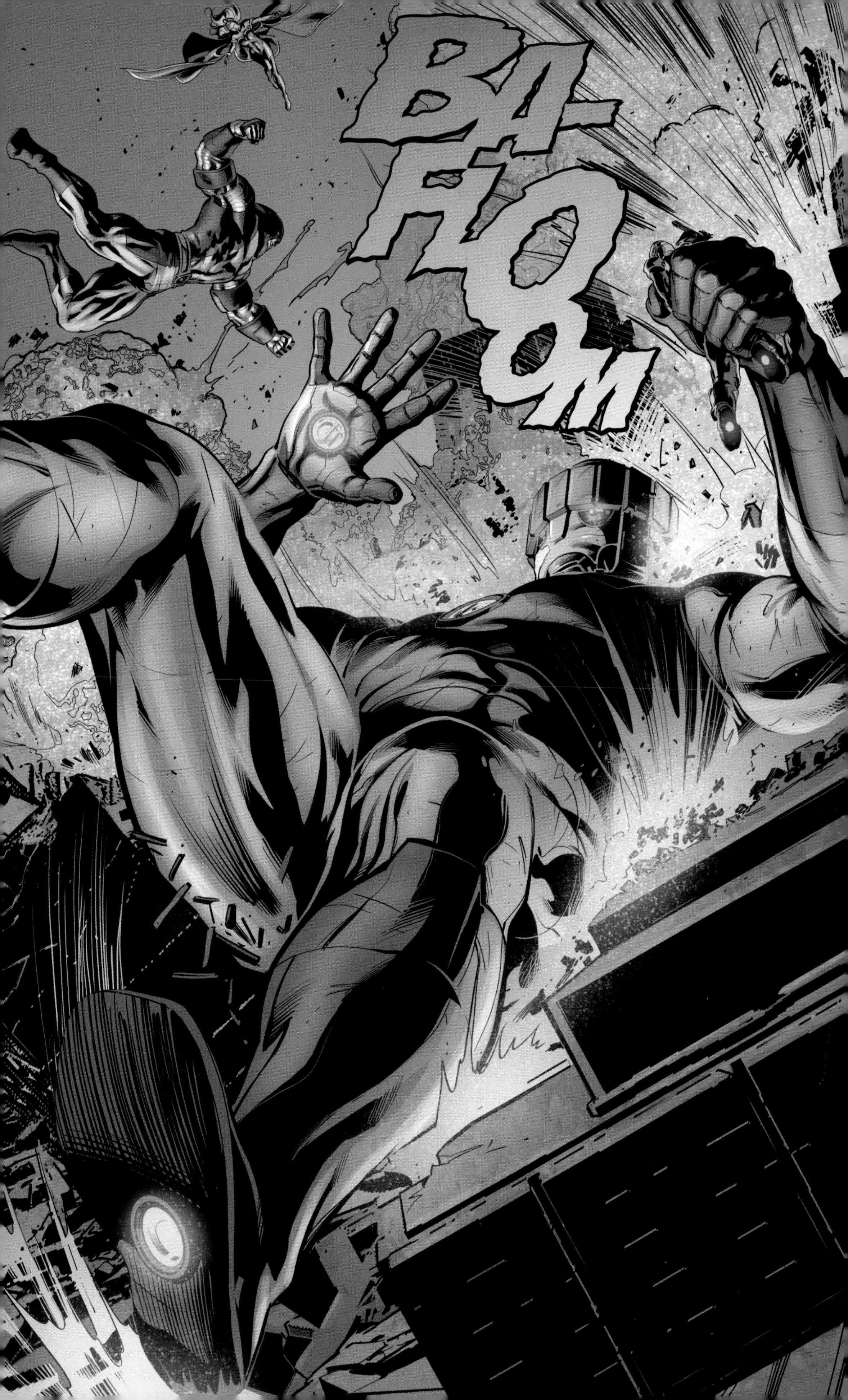
BA-BOOM

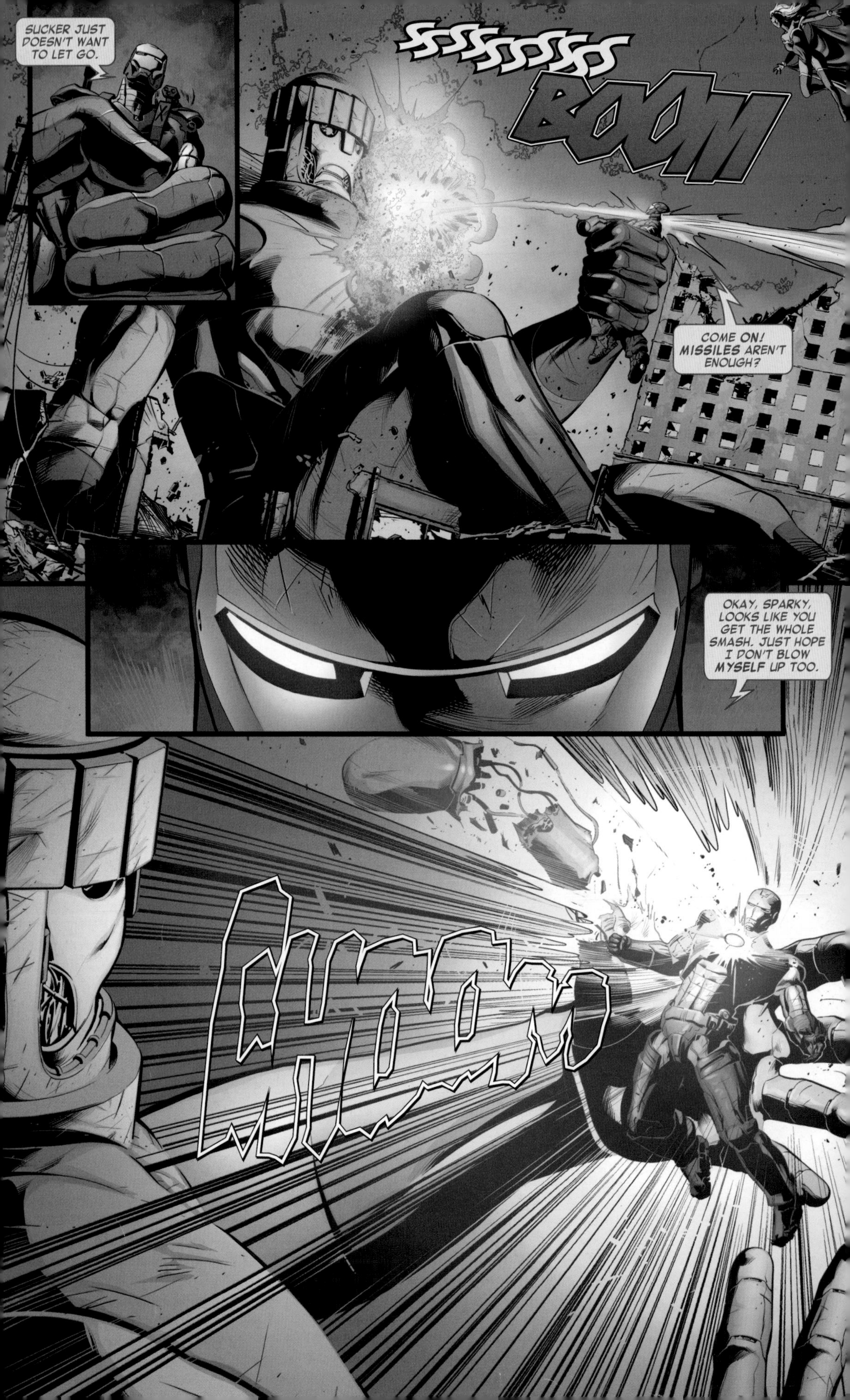
SUCKER JUST DOESN'T WANT TO LET GO.
SSSSSSSS
BOOM
COME ON! MISSILES AREN'T ENOUGH?
OKAY, SPARKY, LOOKS LIKE YOU GET THE WHOLE SMASH. JUST HOPE I DON'T BLOW MYSELF UP TOO.

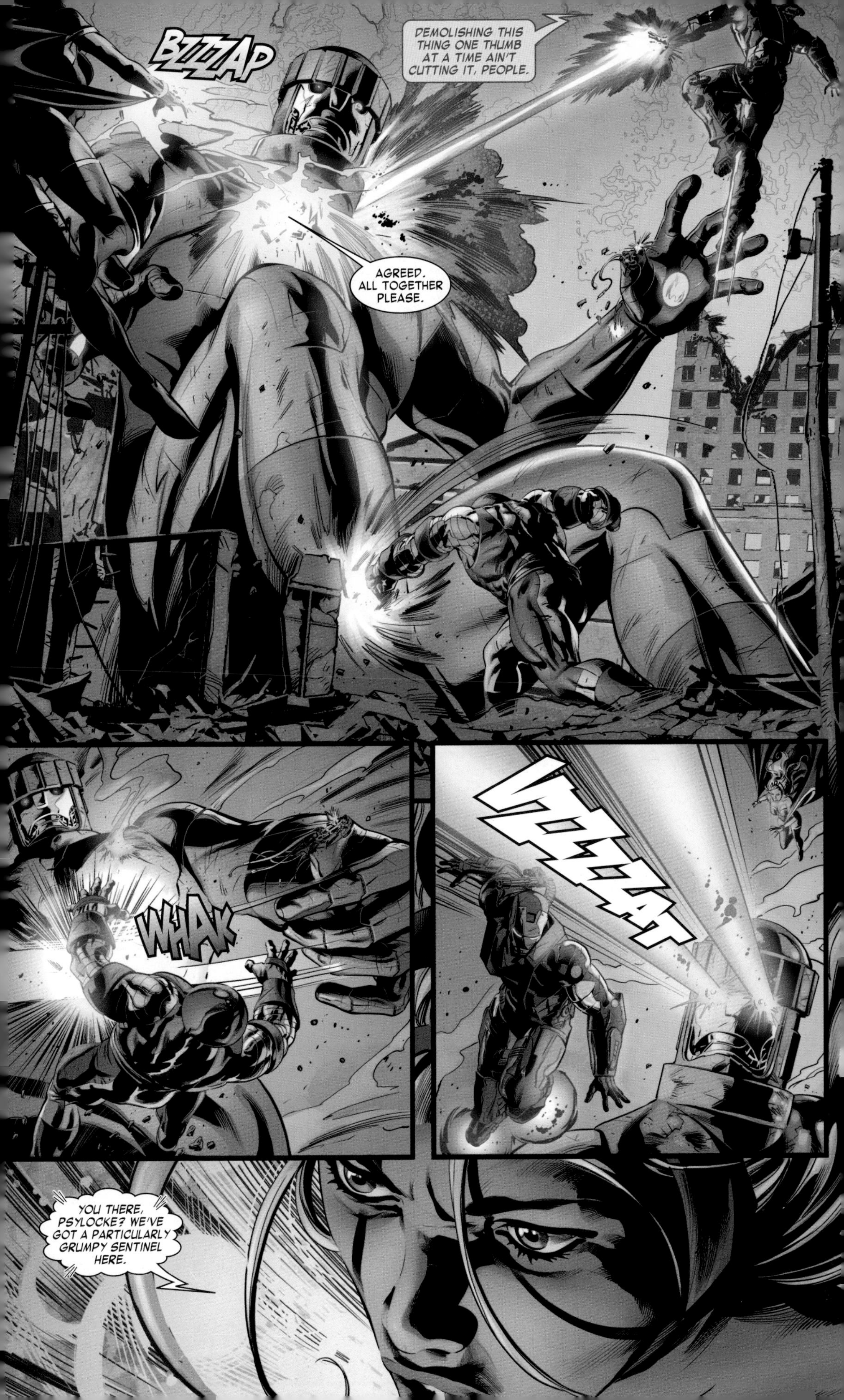
BZZZAP
DEMOLISHING THIS THING ONE THUMB AT A TIME AIN'T CUTTING IT, PEOPLE.
AGREED. ALL TOGETHER PLEASE.
WHAK
VZZZAT
YOU THERE, PSYLOCKE? WE'VE GOT A PARTICULARLY GRUMPY SENTINEL HERE.

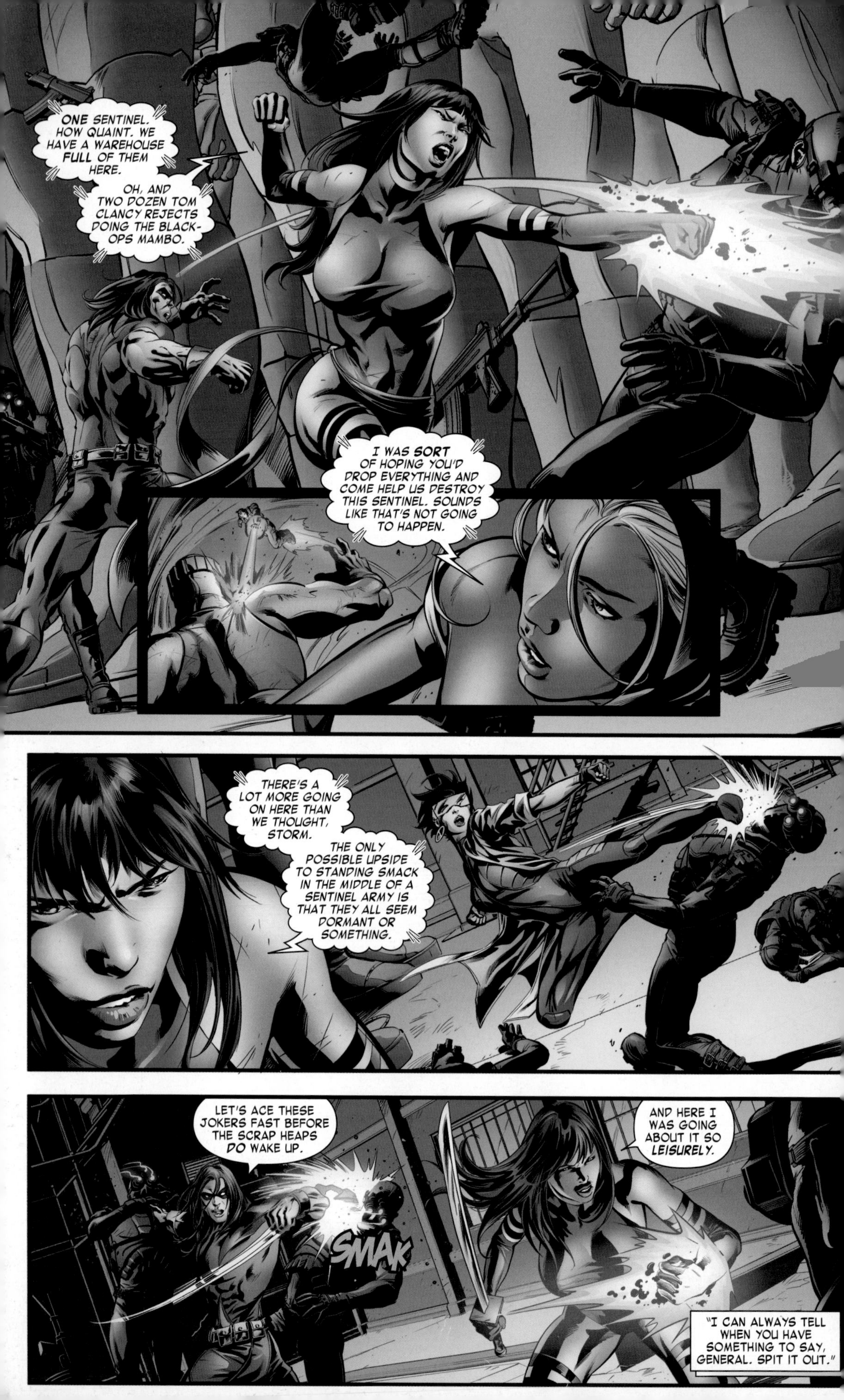
ONE SENTINEL. HOW QUAINT. WE HAVE A WAREHOUSE FULL OF THEM HERE.
OH, AND TWO DOZEN TOM CLANCY REJECTS DOING THE BLACK-OPS MAMBO.
I WAS SORT OF HOPING YOU'D DROP EVERYTHING AND COME HELP US DESTROY THIS SENTINEL. SOUNDS LIKE THAT'S NOT GOING TO HAPPEN.
THERE'S A LOT MORE GOING ON HERE THAN WE THOUGHT, STORM.
THE ONLY POSSIBLE UPSIDE TO STANDING SMACK IN THE MIDDLE OF A SENTINEL ARMY IS THAT THEY ALL SEEM DORMANT OR SOMETHING.
LET'S ACE THESE JOKERS FAST BEFORE THE SCRAP HEAPS DO WAKE UP.
SMAK
AND HERE I WAS GOING ABOUT IT SO LEISURELY.
"I CAN ALWAYS TELL WHEN YOU HAVE SOMETHING TO SAY, GENERAL. SPIT IT OUT."

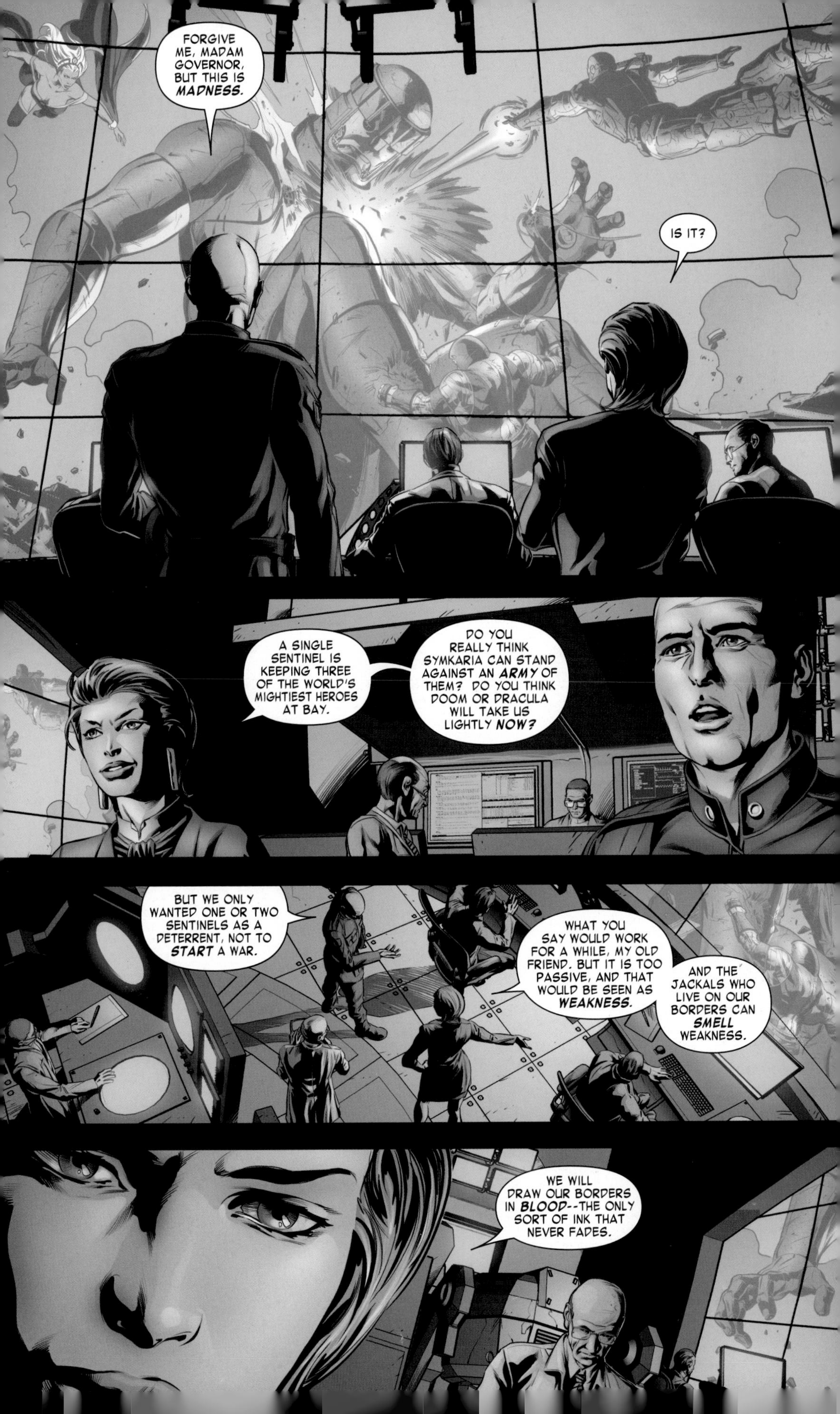
FORGIVE ME, MADAM GOVERNOR, BUT THIS IS MADNESS.
IS IT?
A SINGLE SENTINEL IS KEEPING THREE OF THE WORLD'S MIGHTIEST HEROES AT BAY.
DO YOU REALLY THINK SYMKARIA CAN STAND AGAINST AN ARMY OF THEM? DO YOU THINK DOOM OR DRACULA WILL TAKE US LIGHTLY NOW?
BUT WE ONLY WANTED ONE OR TWO SENTINELS AS A DETERRENT, NOT TO START A WAR.
WHAT YOU SAY WOULD WORK FOR A WHILE, MY OLD FRIEND. BUT IT IS TOO PASSIVE, AND THAT WOULD BE SEEN AS WEAKNESS.
AND THE JACKALS WHO LIVE ON OUR BORDERS CAN SMELL WEAKNESS.
WE WILL DRAW OUR BORDERS IN BLOOD--THE ONLY SORT OF INK THAT NEVER FADES.

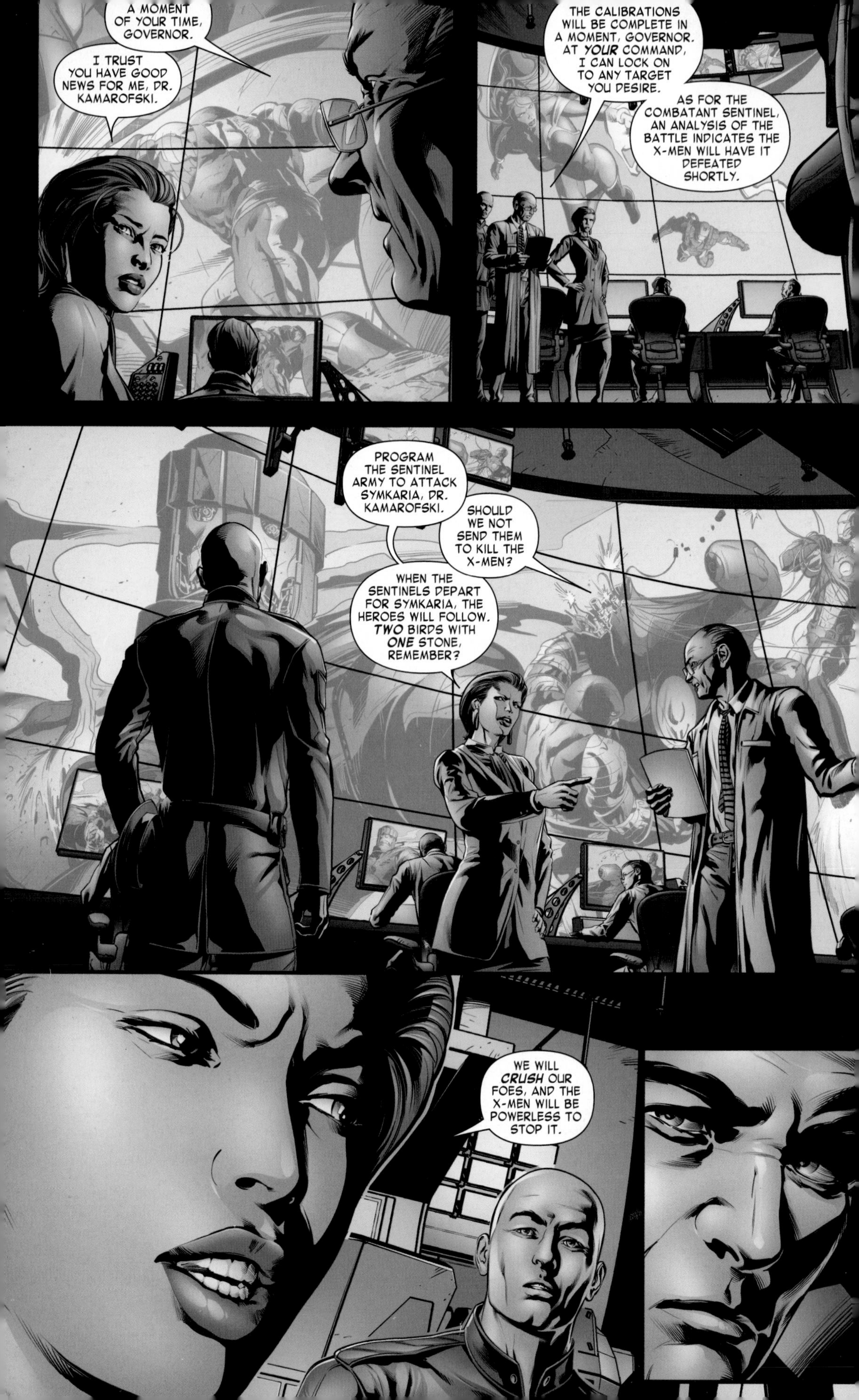

A MOMENT OF YOUR TIME, GOVERNOR.
I TRUST YOU HAVE GOOD NEWS FOR ME, DR. KAMAROFSKI.
THE CALIBRATIONS WILL BE COMPLETE IN A MOMENT, GOVERNOR. AT YOUR COMMAND, I CAN LOCK ON TO ANY TARGET YOU DESIRE.
AS FOR THE COMBATANT SENTINEL, AN ANALYSIS OF THE BATTLE INDICATES THE X-MEN WILL HAVE IT DEFEATED SHORTLY.
PROGRAM THE SENTINEL ARMY TO ATTACK SYMKARIA, DR. KAMAROFSKI.
SHOULD WE NOT SEND THEM TO KILL THE X-MEN?
WHEN THE SENTINELS DEPART FOR SYMKARIA, THE HEROES WILL FOLLOW. TWO BIRDS WITH ONE STONE, REMEMBER?
WE WILL CRUSH OUR FOES, AND THE X-MEN WILL BE POWERLESS TO STOP IT.

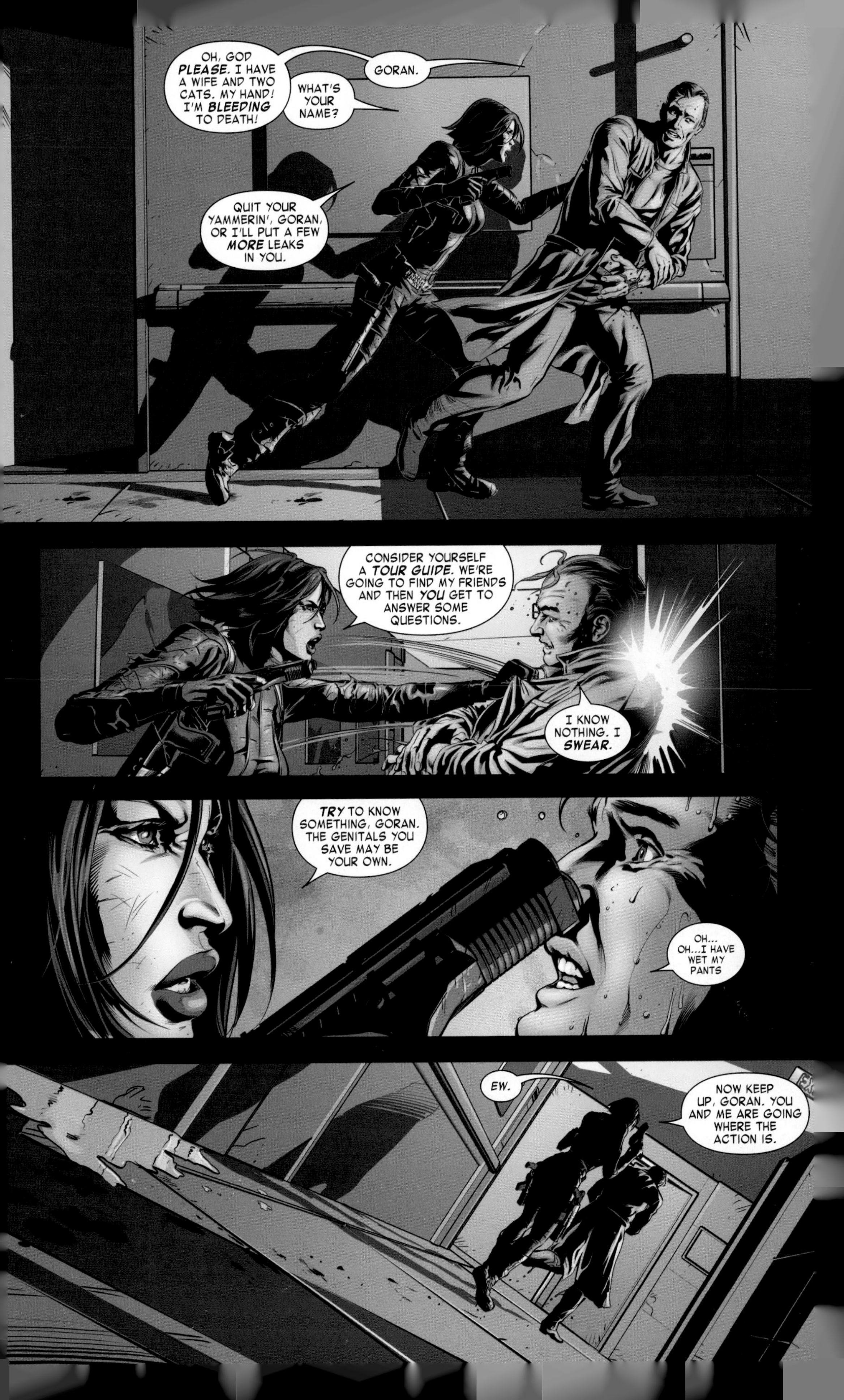
OH, GOD PLEASE. I HAVE A WIFE AND TWO CATS. MY HAND! I'M BLEEDING TO DEATH!
WHAT'S YOUR NAME?
GORAN.
QUIT YOUR YAMMERIN', GORAN, OR I'LL PUT A FEW MORE LEAKS IN YOU.
CONSIDER YOURSELF A TOUR GUIDE. WE'RE GOING TO FIND MY FRIENDS AND THEN YOU GET TO ANSWER SOME QUESTIONS.
I KNOW NOTHING. I SWEAR.
TRY TO KNOW SOMETHING, GORAN. THE GENITALS YOU SAVE MAY BE YOUR OWN.
OH... OH...I HAVE WET MY PANTS
EW.
NOW KEEP UP, GORAN. YOU AND ME ARE GOING WHERE THE ACTION IS.

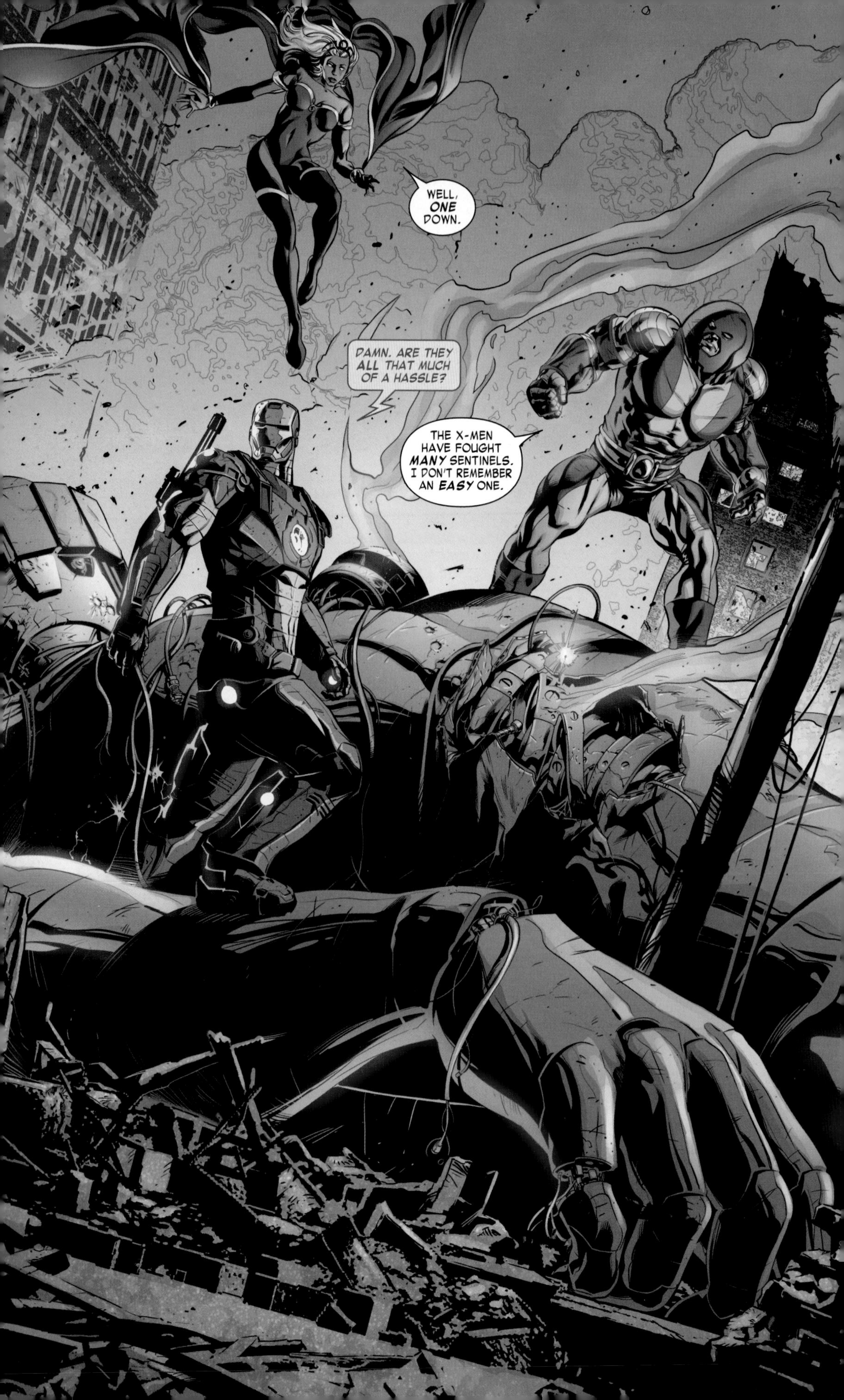
WELL, ONE DOWN.
DAMN. ARE THEY ALL THAT MUCH OF A HASSLE?
THE X-MEN HAVE FOUGHT MANY SENTINELS. I DON'T REMEMBER AN EASY ONE.

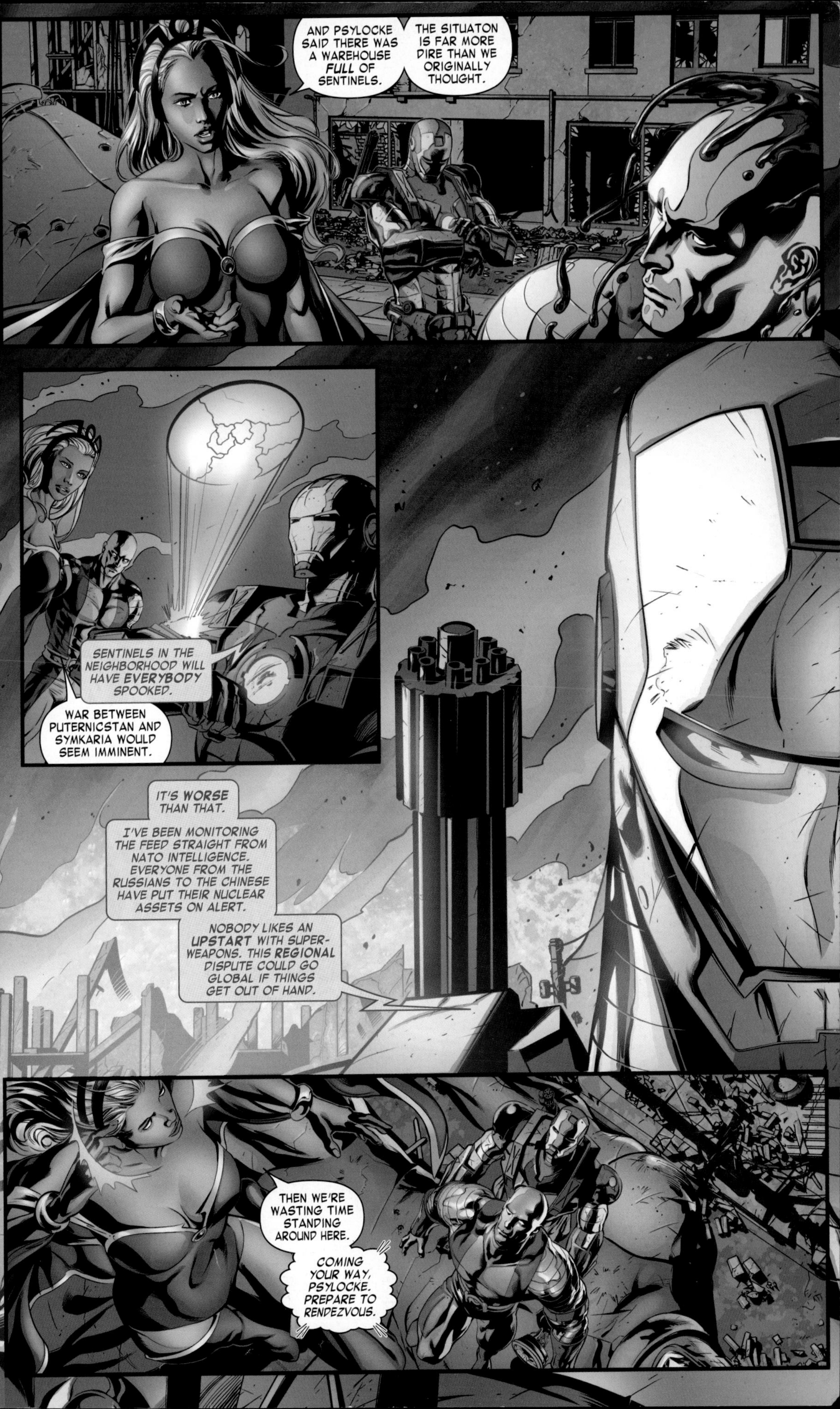
AND PSYLOCKE SAID THERE WAS A WAREHOUSE FULL OF SENTINELS.
THE SITUATON IS FAR MORE DIRE THAN WE ORIGINALLY THOUGHT.
SENTINELS IN THE NEIGHBORHOOD WILL HAVE EVERYBODY SPOOKED.
WAR BETWEEN PUTERNICSTAN AND SYMKARIA WOULD SEEM IMMINENT.
IT'S WORSE THAN THAT.
I'VE BEEN MONITORING THE FEED STRAIGHT FROM NATO INTELLIGENCE. EVERYONE FROM THE RUSSIANS TO THE CHINESE HAVE PUT THEIR NUCLEAR ASSETS ON ALERT.
NOBODY LIKES AN UPSTART WITH SUPER-WEAPONS. THIS REGIONAL DISPUTE COULD GO GLOBAL IF THINGS GET OUT OF HAND.
THEN WE'RE WASTING TIME STANDING AROUND HERE.
COMING YOUR WAY, PSYLOCKE. PREPARE TO RENDEZVOUS.

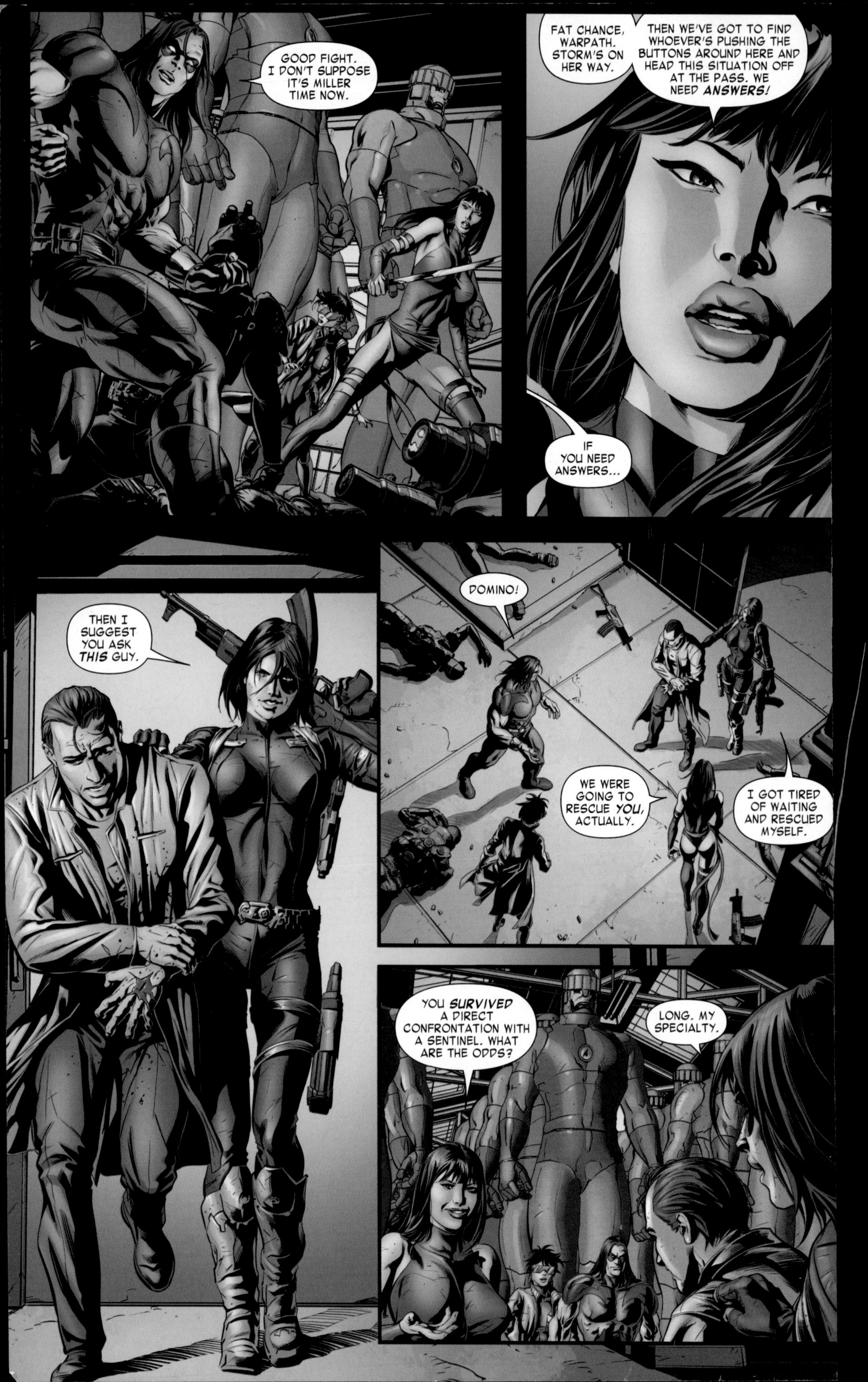
GOOD FIGHT. I DON'T SUPPOSE IT'S MILLER TIME NOW.
FAT CHANCE, WARPATH. STORM'S ON HER WAY.
THEN WE'VE GOT TO FIND WHOEVER'S PUSHING THE BUTTONS AROUND HERE AND HEAD THIS SITUATION OFF AT THE PASS. WE NEED ANSWERS!
IF YOU NEED ANSWERS...
THEN I SUGGEST YOU ASK THIS GUY.
DOMINO!
WE WERE GOING TO RESCUE YOU, ACTUALLY.
I GOT TIRED OF WAITING AND RESCUED MYSELF.
YOU SURVIVED A DIRECT CONFRONTATION WITH A SENTINEL. WHAT ARE THE ODDS?
LONG. MY SPECIALTY.

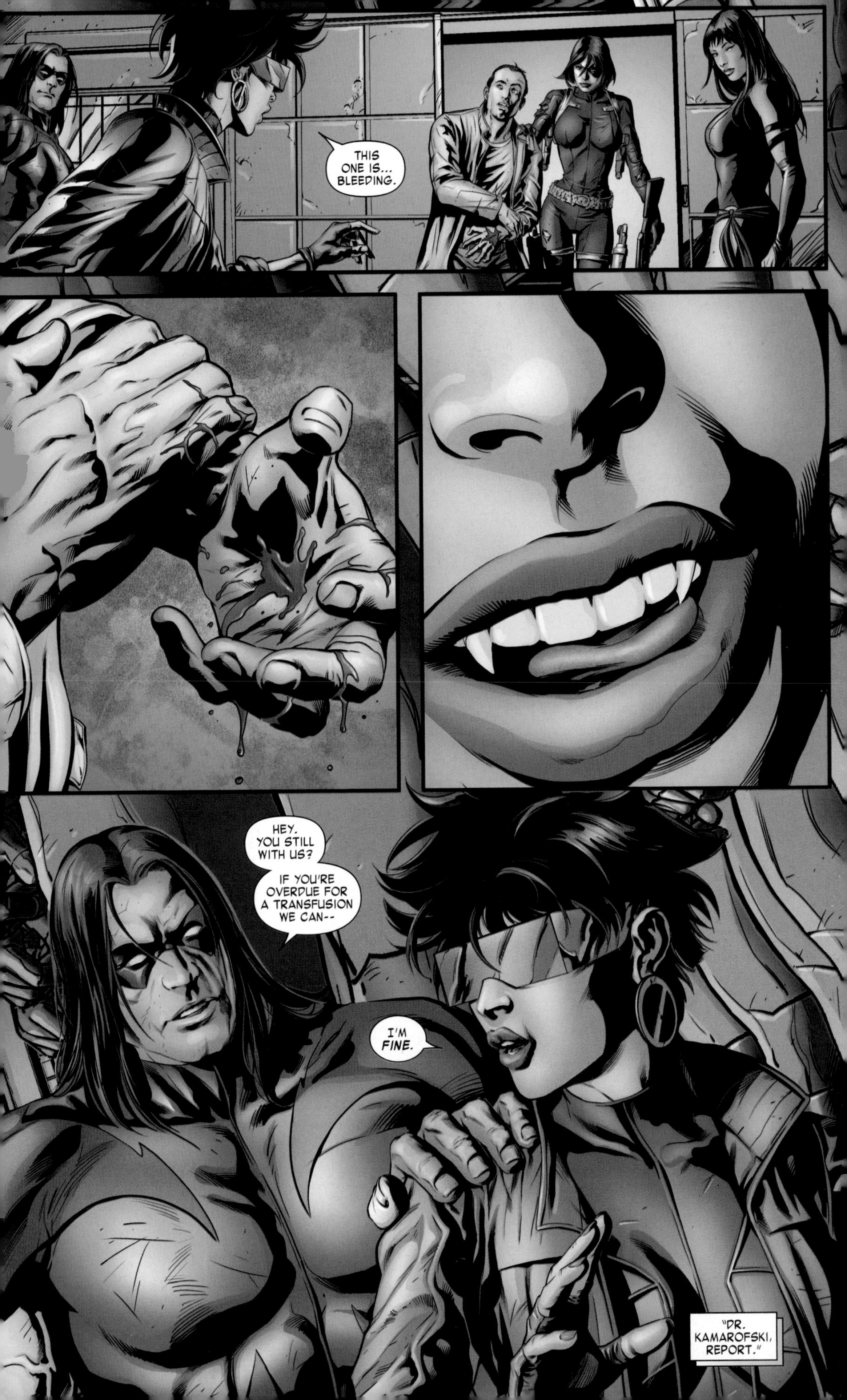
THIS ONE IS... BLEEDING.
HEY. YOU STILL WITH US?
IF YOU'RE OVERDUE FOR A TRANSFUSION WE CAN--
I'M *FINE.*
"DR. KAMAROFSKI, REPORT."

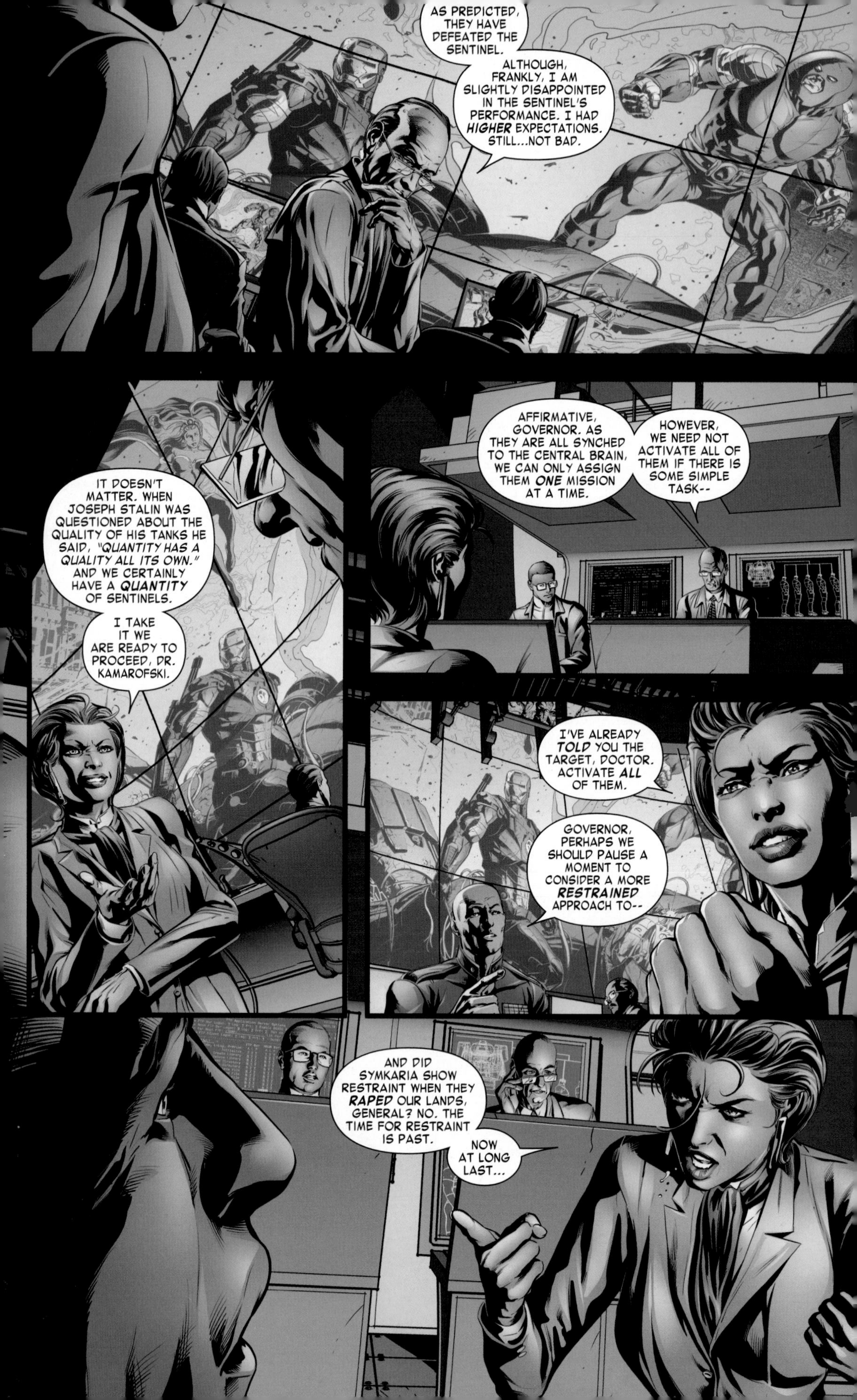
AS PREDICTED, THEY HAVE DEFEATED THE SENTINEL.
ALTHOUGH, FRANKLY, I AM SLIGHTLY DISAPPOINTED IN THE SENTINEL'S PERFORMANCE. I HAD HIGHER EXPECTATIONS. STILL...NOT BAD.
IT DOESN'T MATTER. WHEN JOSEPH STALIN WAS QUESTIONED ABOUT THE QUALITY OF HIS TANKS HE SAID, "QUANTITY HAS A QUALITY ALL ITS OWN." AND WE CERTAINLY HAVE A QUANTITY OF SENTINELS.
I TAKE IT WE ARE READY TO PROCEED, DR. KAMAROFSKI.
AFFIRMATIVE, GOVERNOR. AS THEY ARE ALL SYNCHED TO THE CENTRAL BRAIN, WE CAN ONLY ASSIGN THEM ONE MISSION AT A TIME.
HOWEVER, WE NEED NOT ACTIVATE ALL OF THEM IF THERE IS SOME SIMPLE TASK--
I'VE ALREADY TOLD YOU THE TARGET, DOCTOR. ACTIVATE ALL OF THEM.
GOVERNOR, PERHAPS WE SHOULD PAUSE A MOMENT TO CONSIDER A MORE RESTRAINED APPROACH TO--
AND DID SYMKARIA SHOW RESTRAINT WHEN THEY RAPED OUR LANDS, GENERAL? NO. THE TIME FOR RESTRAINT IS PAST.
NOW AT LONG LAST...

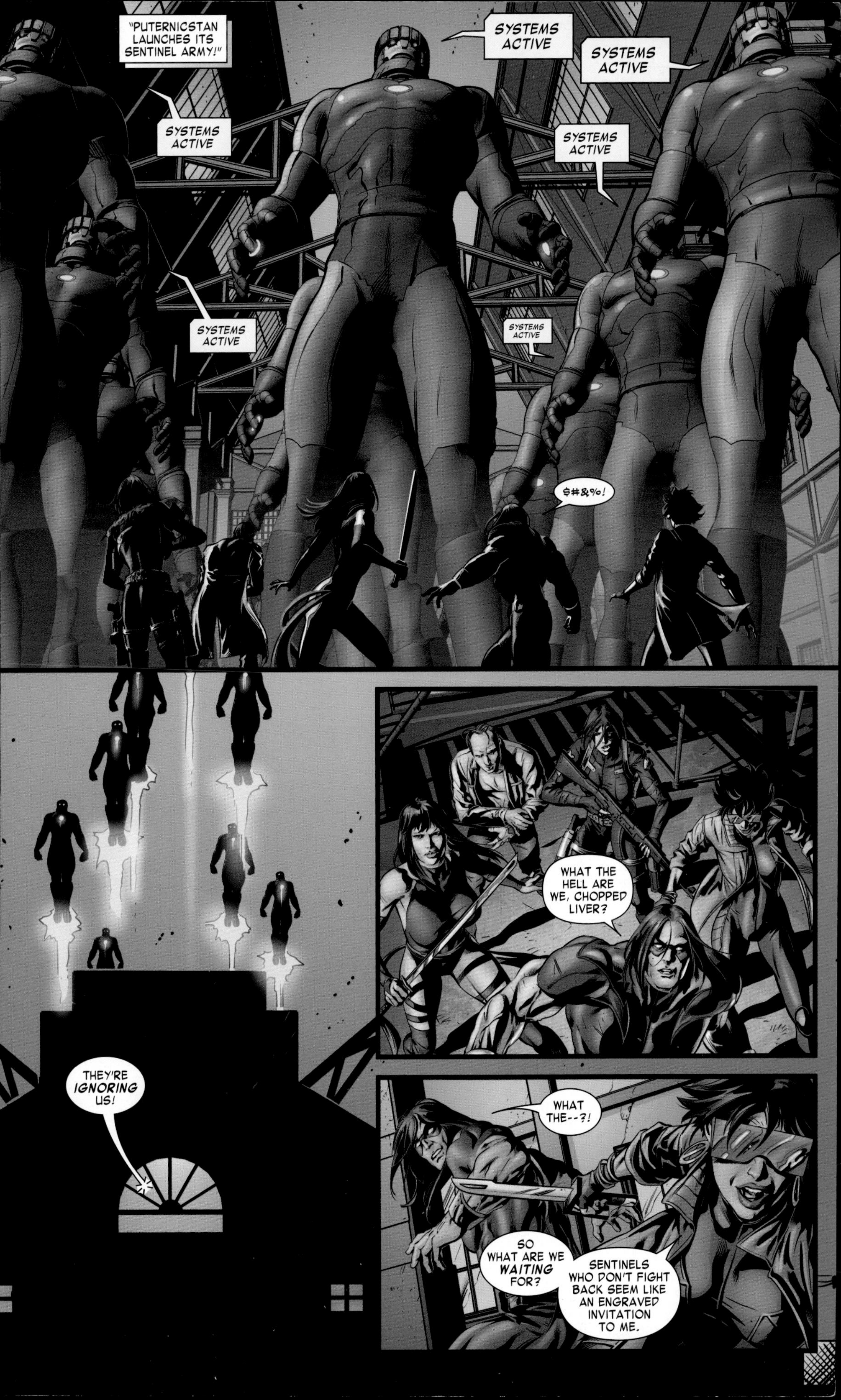
"PUTERNICSTAN LAUNCHES ITS SENTINEL ARMY!"
SYSTEMS ACTIVE
SYSTEMS ACTIVE
SYSTEMS ACTIVE
SYSTEMS ACTIVE
SYSTEMS ACTIVE
SYSTEMS ACTIVE
$#&%!
THEY'RE IGNORING US!
WHAT THE HELL ARE WE, CHOPPED LIVER?
WHAT THE--?!
SO WHAT ARE WE WAITING FOR?
SENTINELS WHO DON'T FIGHT BACK SEEM LIKE AN ENGRAVED INVITATION TO ME.

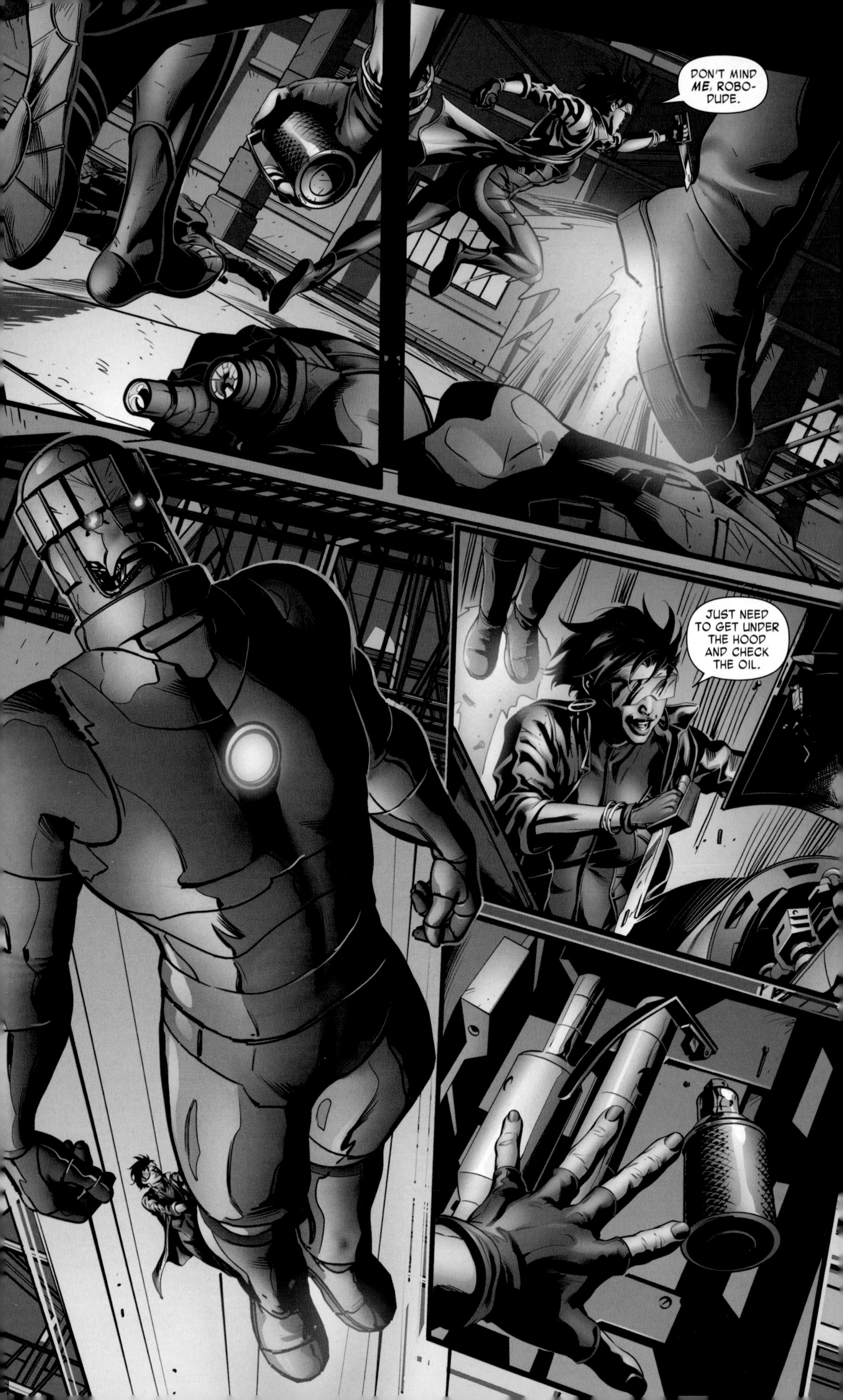
DON'T MIND ME, ROBO-DUDE.
JUST NEED TO GET UNDER THE HOOD AND CHECK THE OIL.

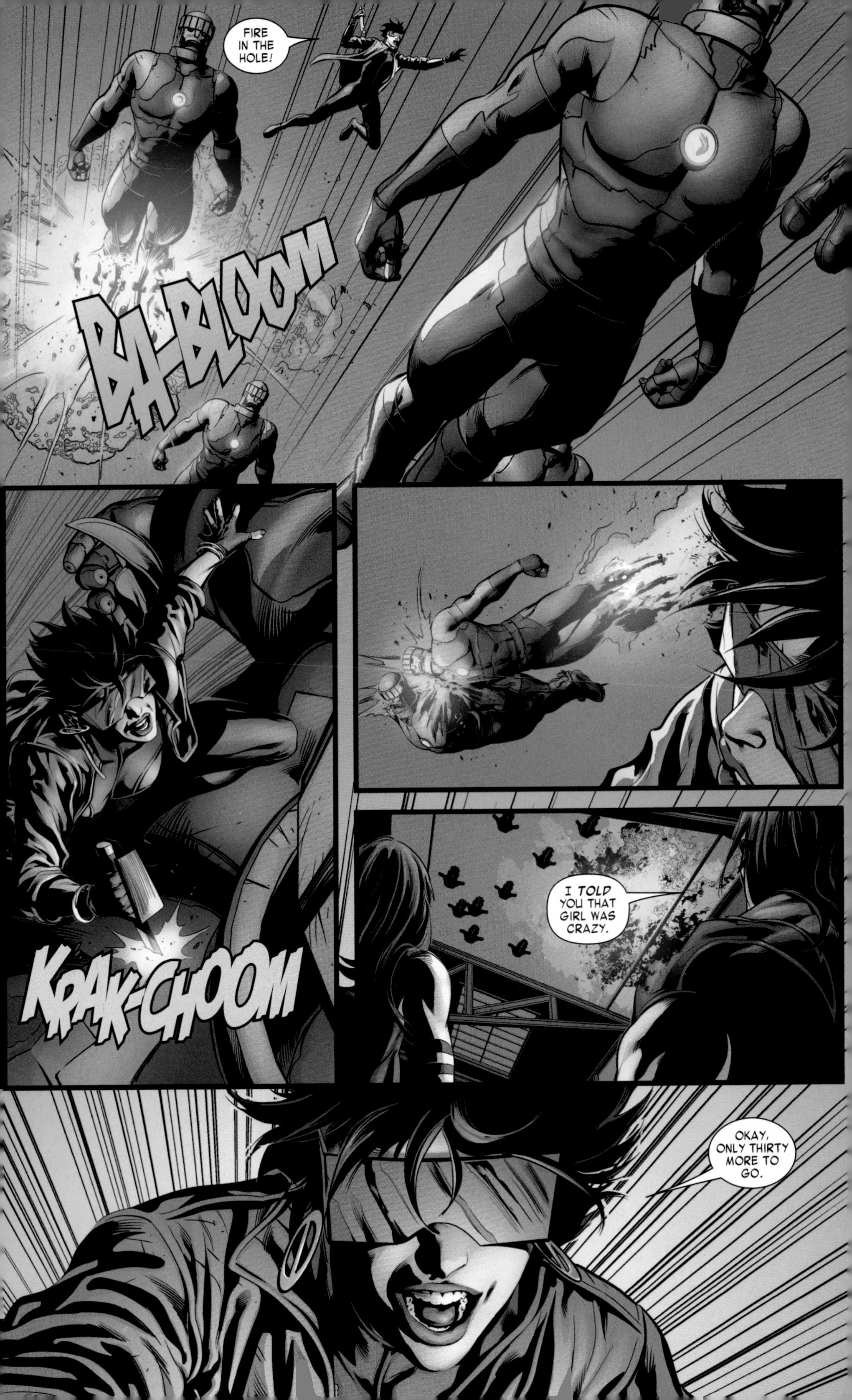
FIRE IN THE HOLE!
BA-BLOOM
KRAK-CHOOM
I TOLD YOU THAT GIRL WAS CRAZY.
OKAY, ONLY THIRTY MORE TO GO.

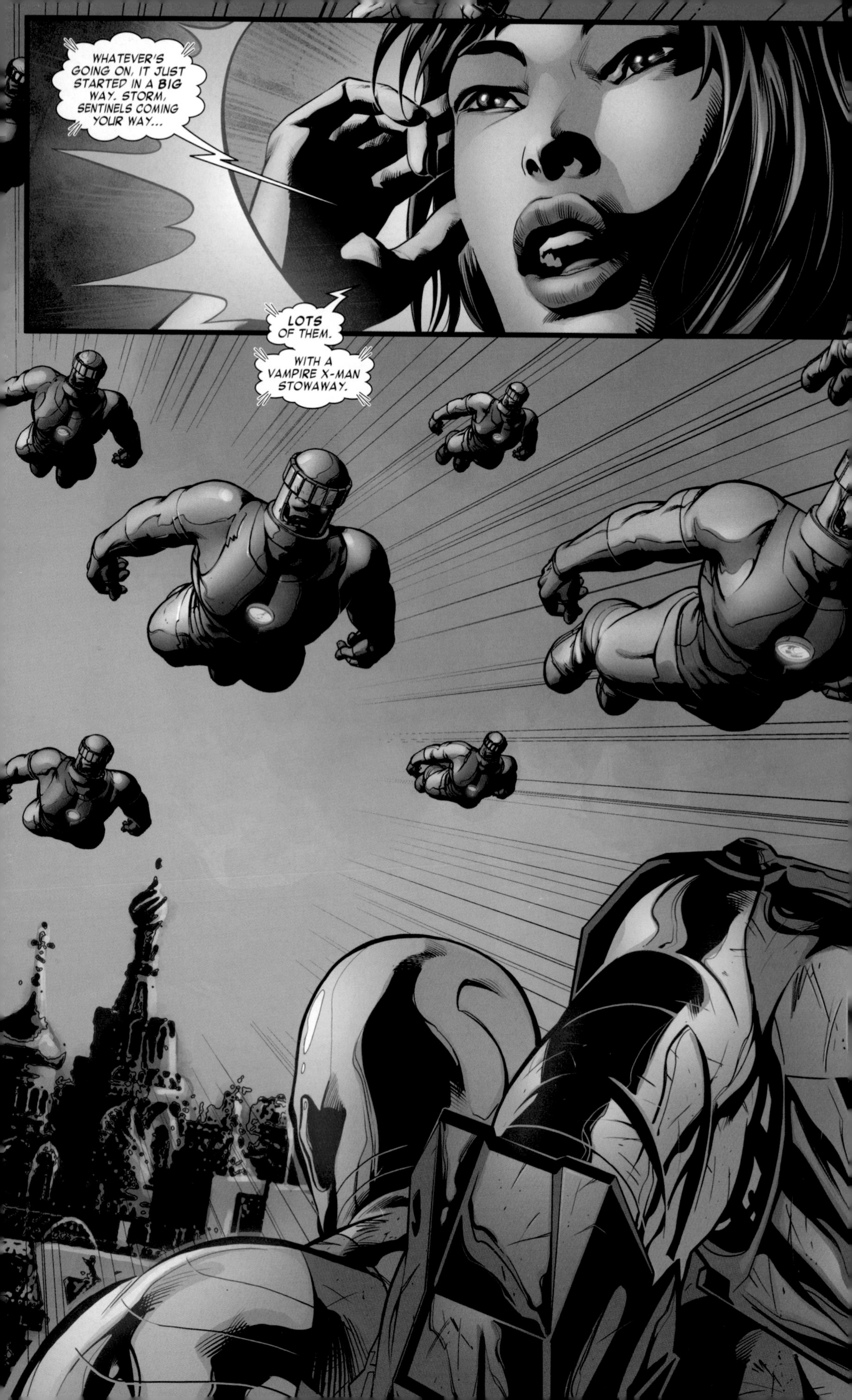
WHATEVER'S GOING ON, IT JUST STARTED IN A BIG WAY. STORM, SENTINELS COMING YOUR WAY...
LOTS OF THEM.
WITH A VAMPIRE X-MAN STOWAWAY.

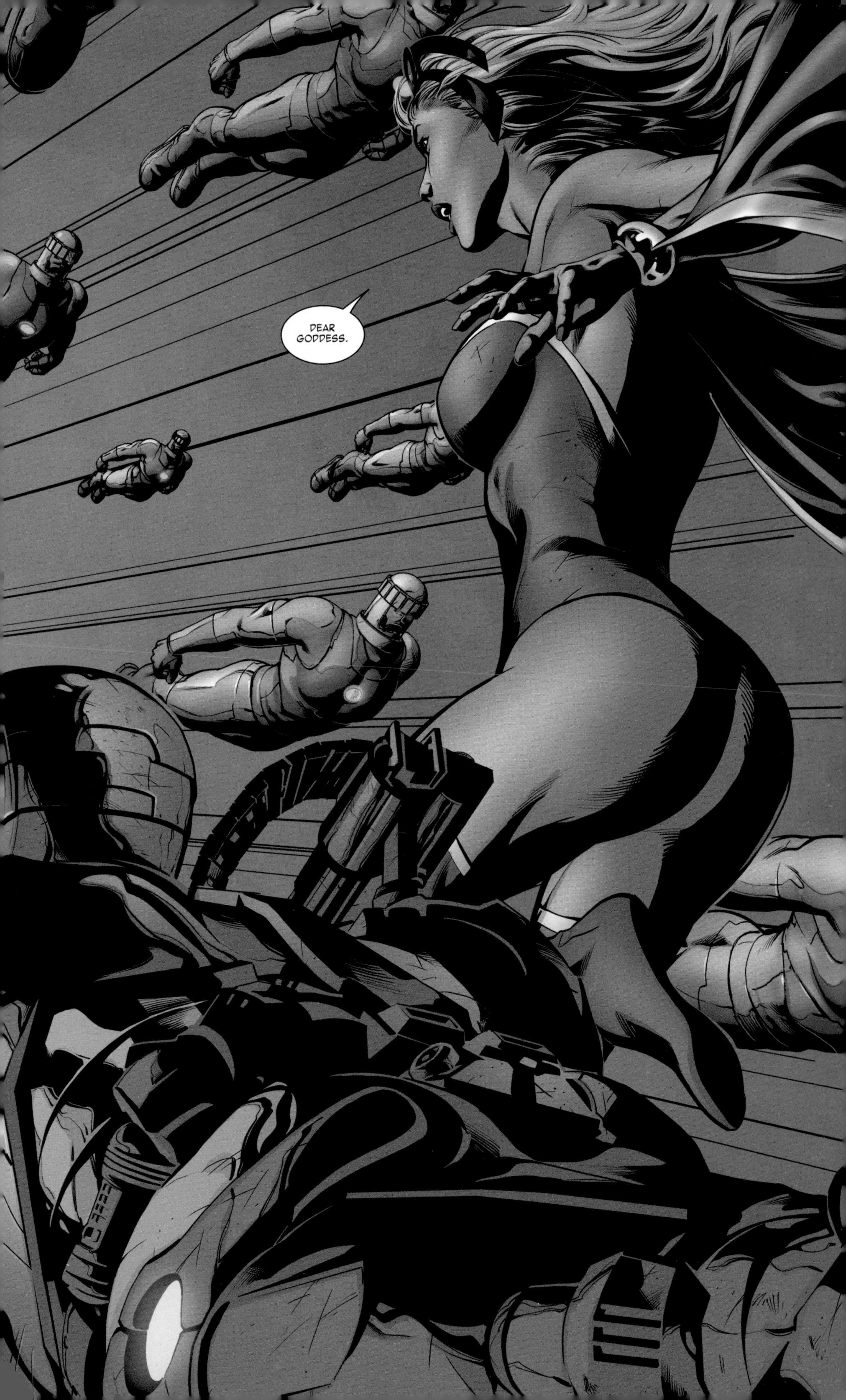
DEAR GODDESS.

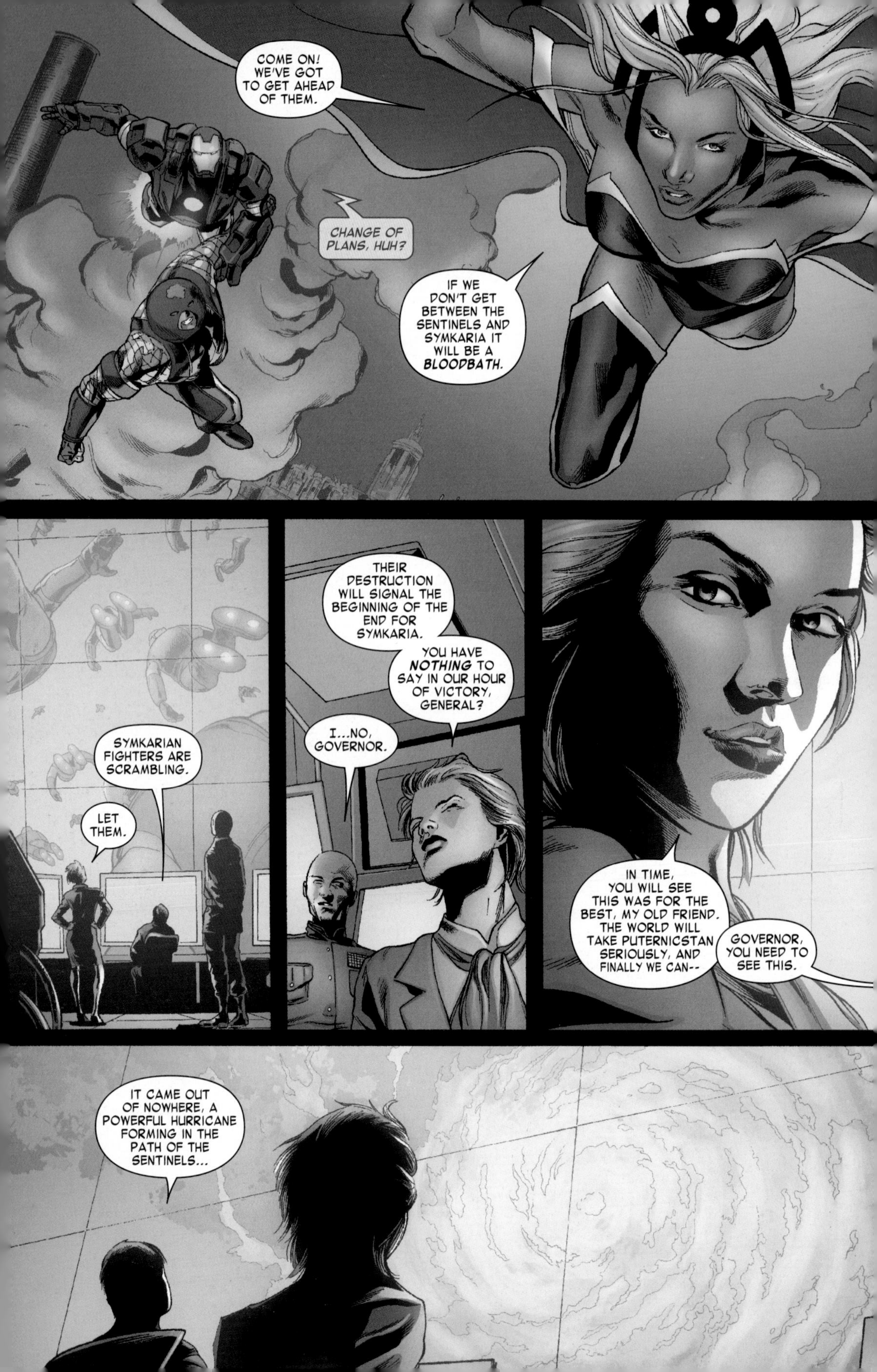
COME ON! WE'VE GOT TO GET AHEAD OF THEM.
CHANGE OF PLANS, HUH?
IF WE DON'T GET BETWEEN THE SENTINELS AND SYMKARIA IT WILL BE A BLOODBATH.
SYMKARIAN FIGHTERS ARE SCRAMBLING.
LET THEM.
THEIR DESTRUCTION WILL SIGNAL THE BEGINNING OF THE END FOR SYMKARIA.
YOU HAVE NOTHING TO SAY IN OUR HOUR OF VICTORY, GENERAL?
I...NO, GOVERNOR.
IN TIME, YOU WILL SEE THIS WAS FOR THE BEST, MY OLD FRIEND. THE WORLD WILL TAKE PUTERNICSTAN SERIOUSLY, AND FINALLY WE CAN--
GOVERNOR, YOU NEED TO SEE THIS.
IT CAME OUT OF NOWHERE, A POWERFUL HURRICANE FORMING IN THE PATH OF THE SENTINELS...

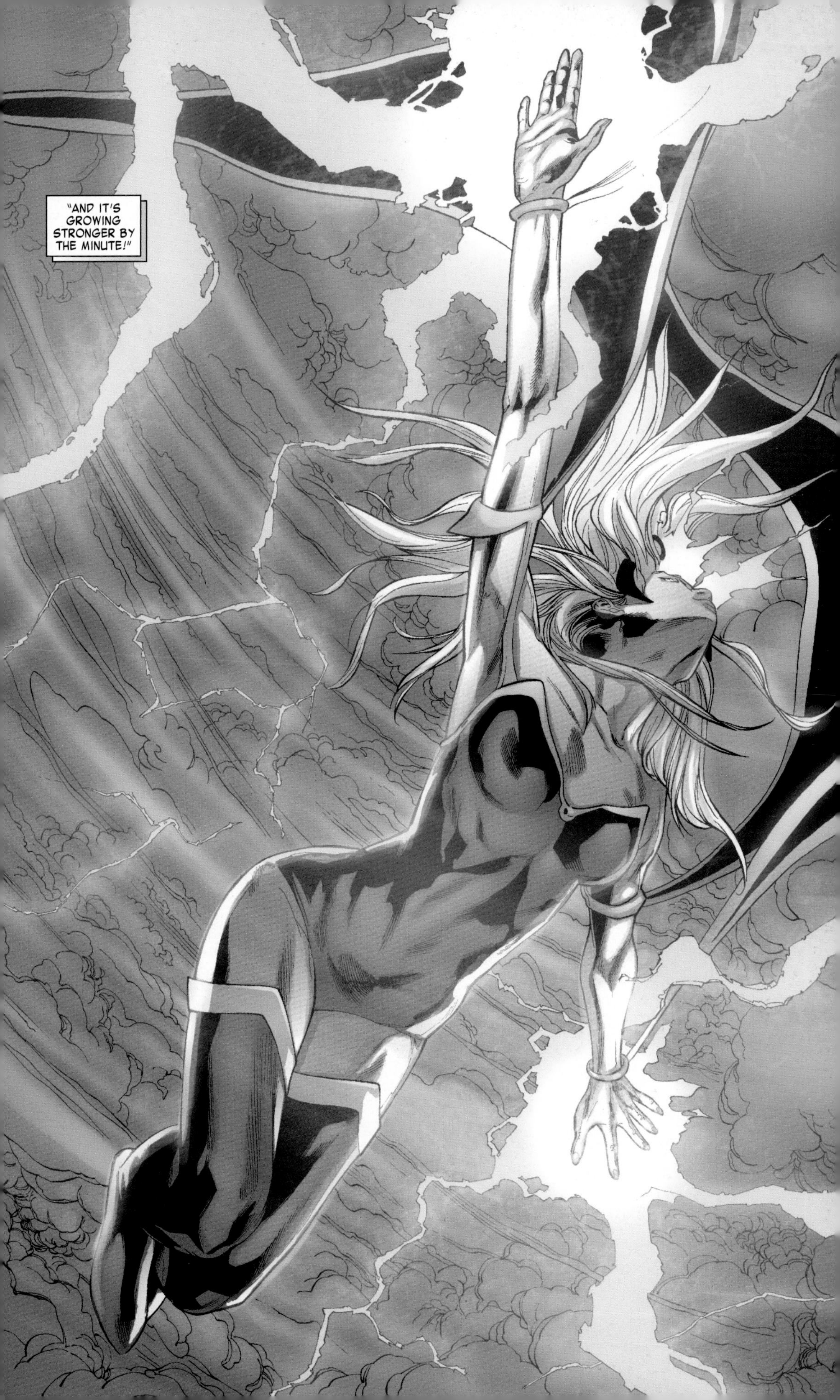
"AND IT'S GROWING STRONGER BY THE MINUTE!"

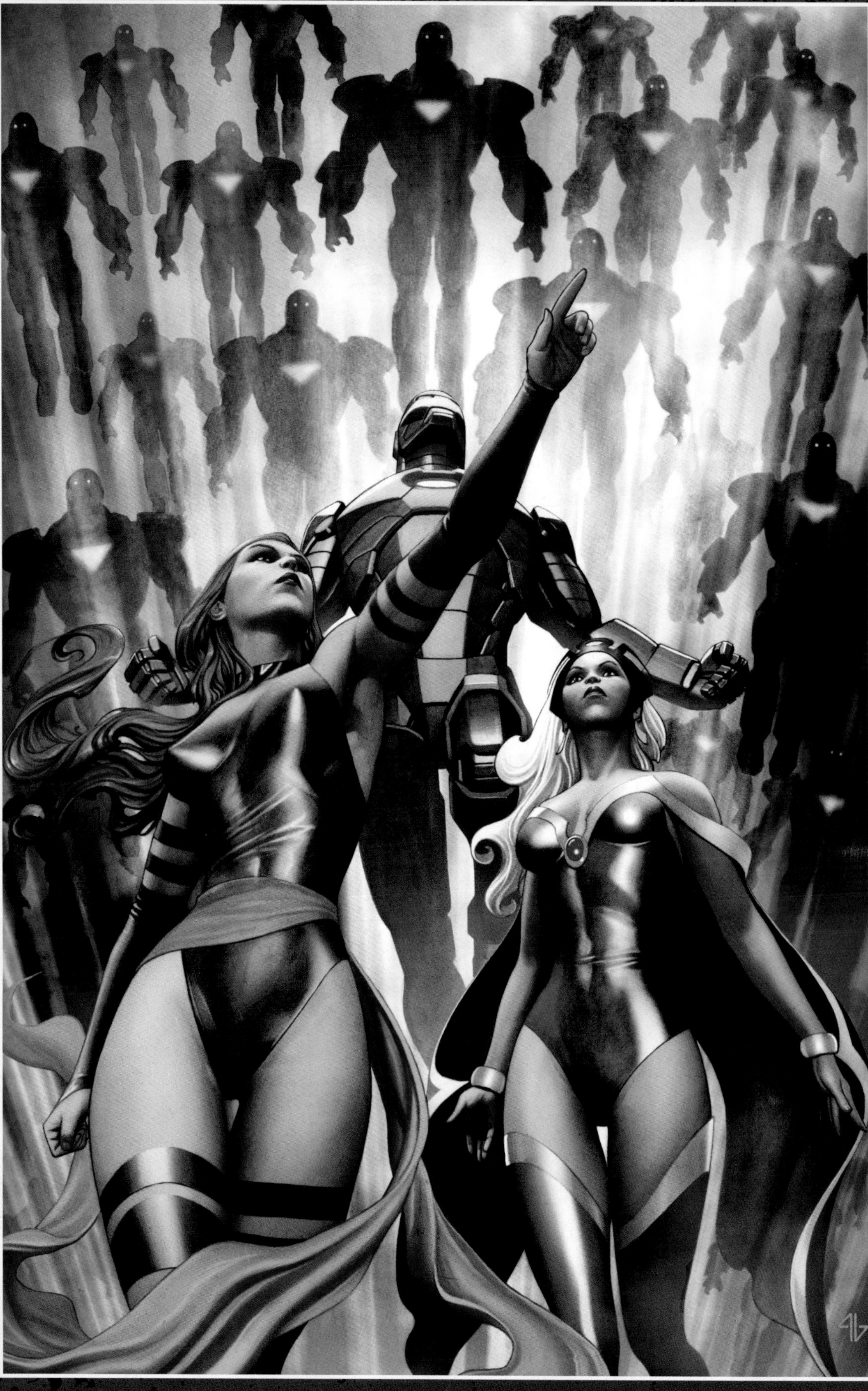

TWENTY-THREE

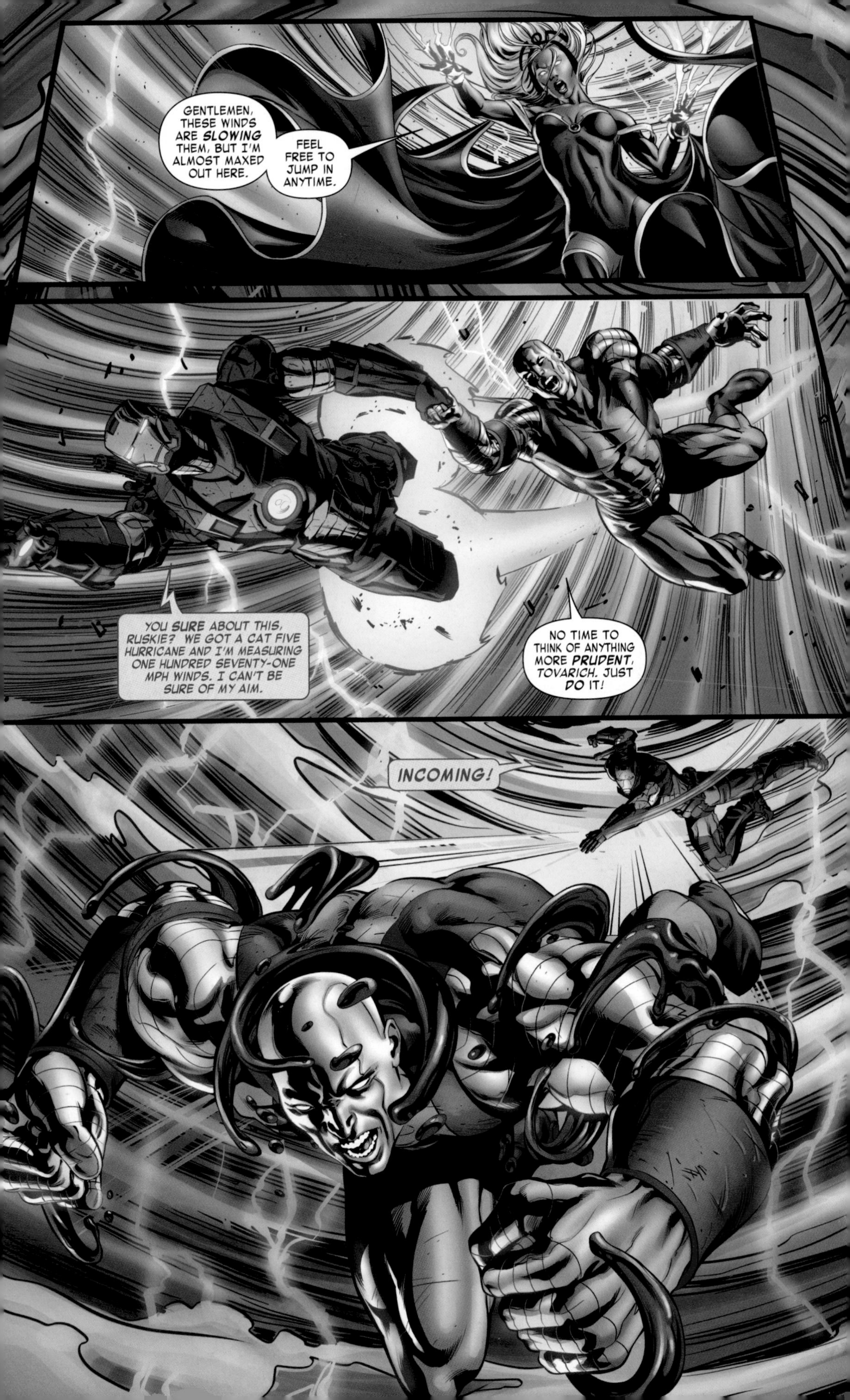
GENTLEMEN, THESE WINDS ARE SLOWING THEM, BUT I'M ALMOST MAXED OUT HERE.
FEEL FREE TO JUMP IN ANYTIME.
YOU SURE ABOUT THIS, RUSKIE? WE GOT A CAT FIVE HURRICANE AND I'M MEASURING ONE HUNDRED SEVENTY-ONE MPH WINDS. I CAN'T BE SURE OF MY AIM.
NO TIME TO THINK OF ANYTHING MORE PRUDENT, TOVARICH. JUST DO IT!
INCOMING!

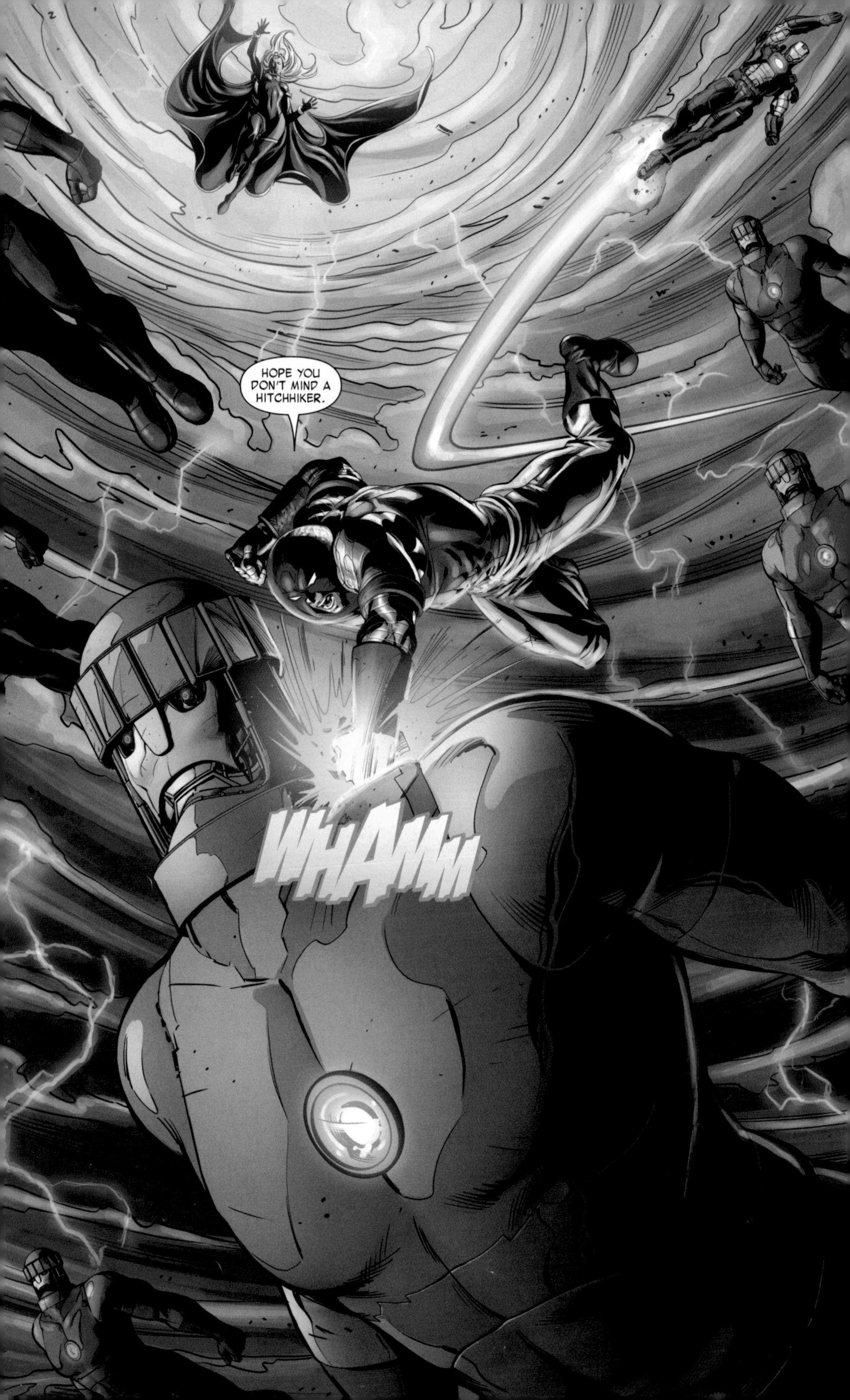
HOPE YOU DON'T MIND A HITCHHIKER.
WHAMM

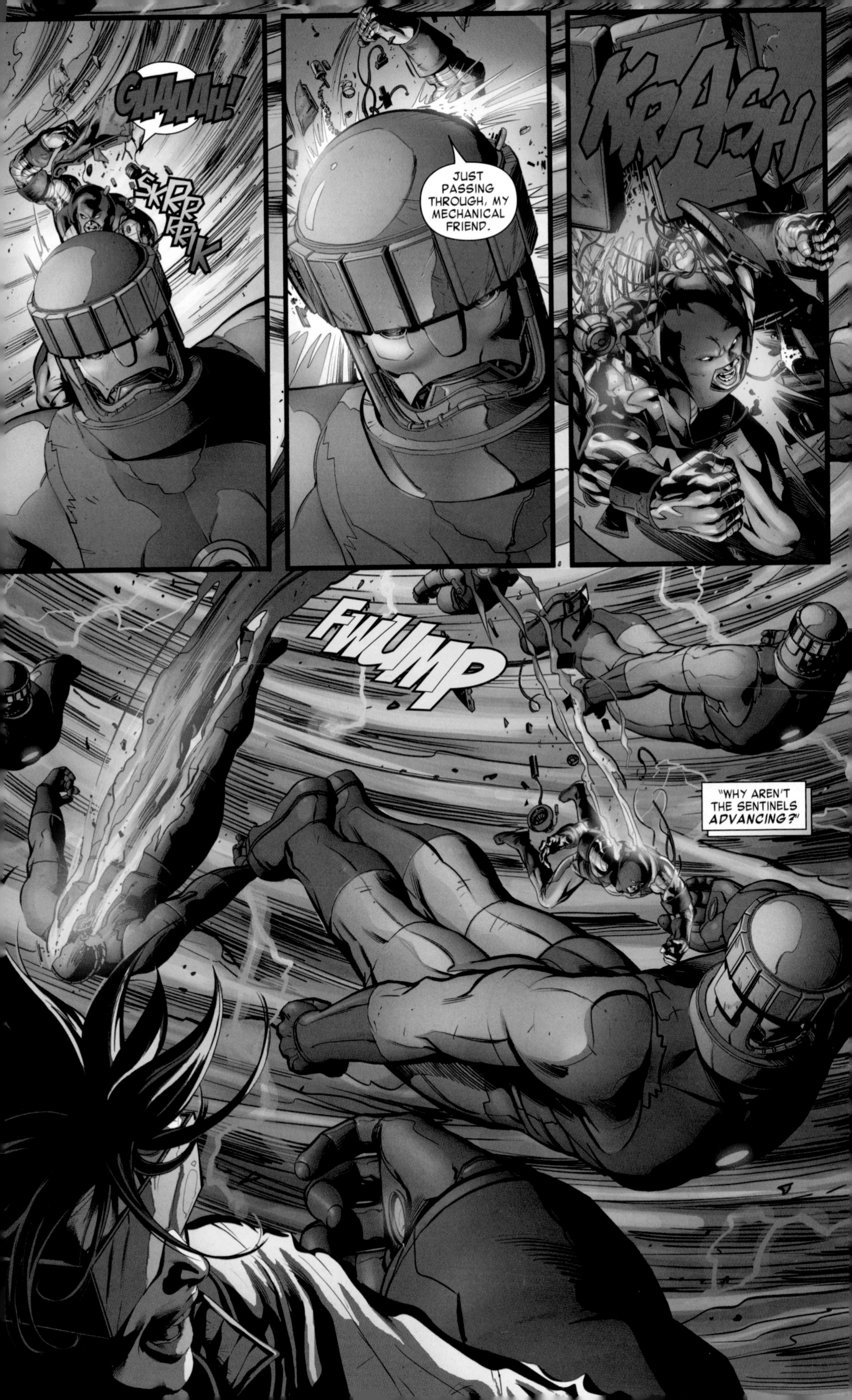
GAAAAH!
SKRRRRIK
JUST PASSING THROUGH, MY MECHANICAL FRIEND.
KRASH
FWUMP
"WHY AREN'T THE SENTINELS ADVANCING?"

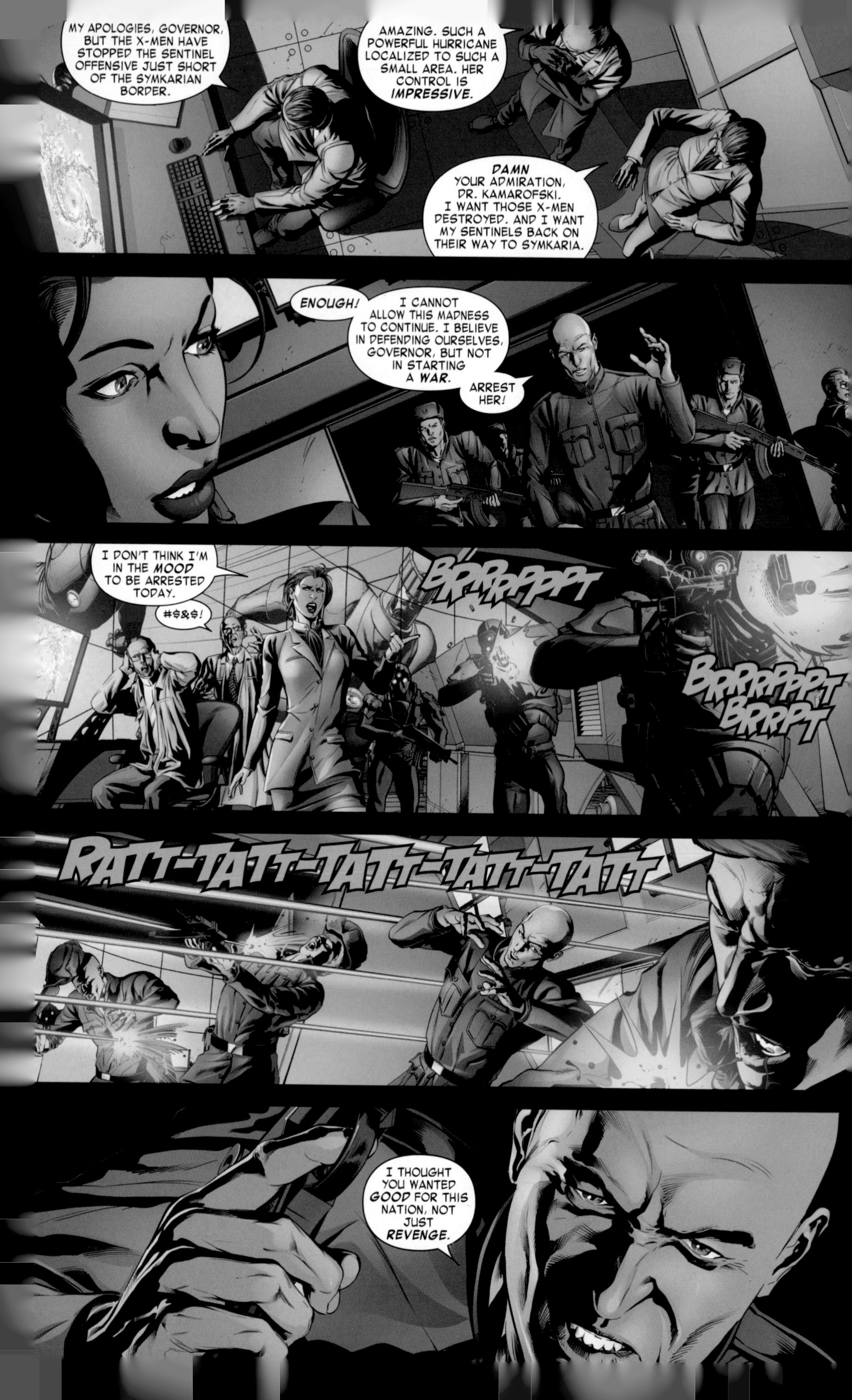
MY APOLOGIES, GOVERNOR, BUT THE X-MEN HAVE STOPPED THE SENTINEL OFFENSIVE JUST SHORT OF THE SYMKARIAN BORDER.
AMAZING. SUCH A POWERFUL HURRICANE LOCALIZED TO SUCH A SMALL AREA. HER CONTROL IS IMPRESSIVE.
DAMN YOUR ADMIRATION, DR. KAMAROFSKI. I WANT THOSE X-MEN DESTROYED. AND I WANT MY SENTINELS BACK ON THEIR WAY TO SYMKARIA.
ENOUGH!
I CANNOT ALLOW THIS MADNESS TO CONTINUE. I BELIEVE IN DEFENDING OURSELVES, GOVERNOR, BUT NOT IN STARTING A WAR.
ARREST HER!
I DON'T THINK I'M IN THE MOOD TO BE ARRESTED TODAY.
#$&$!
BRRRRPPPT
BRRRPPPT BRRPT
RATT-TATT-TATT-TATT-TATT
I THOUGHT YOU WANTED GOOD FOR THIS NATION, NOT JUST REVENGE.

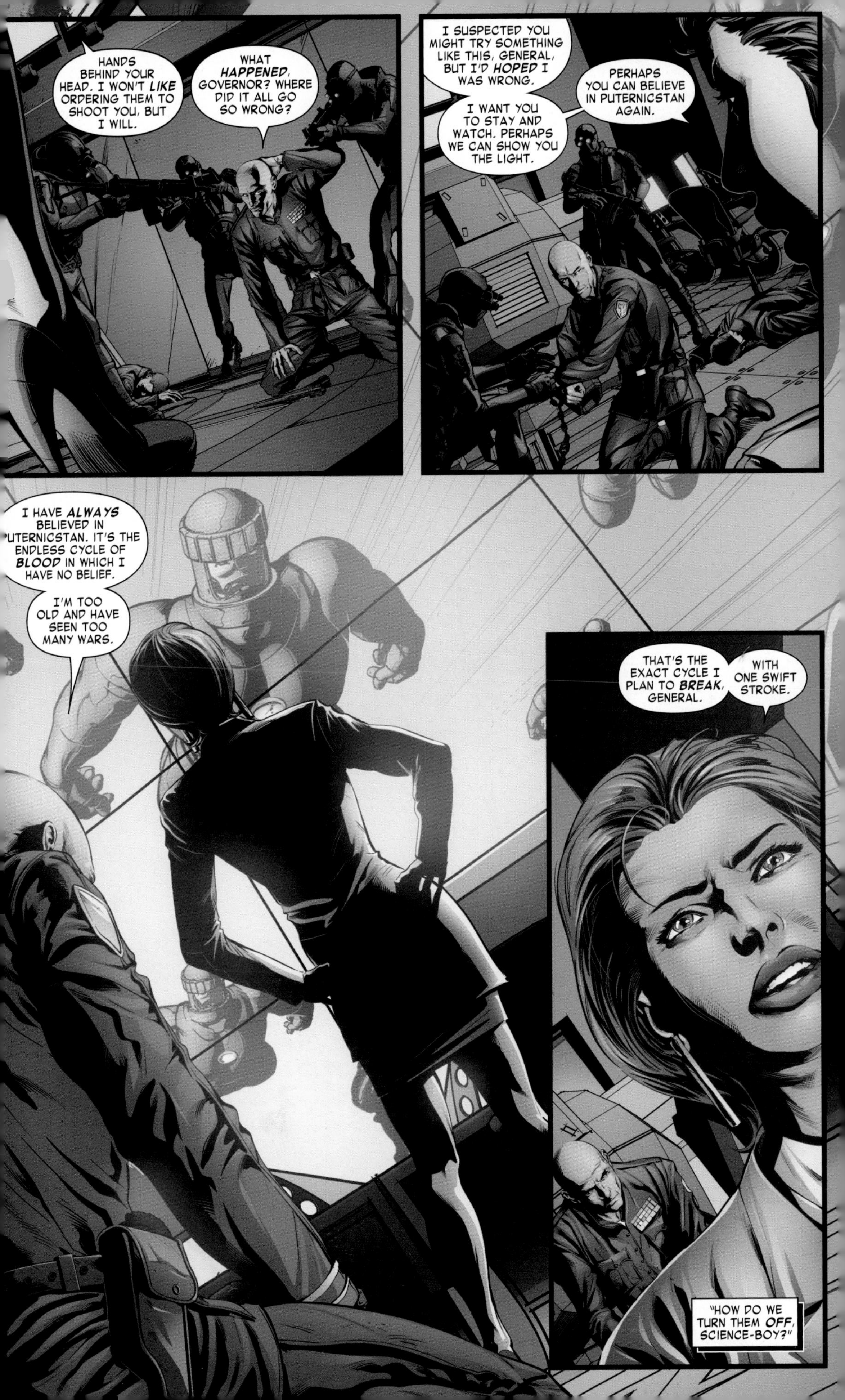
HANDS BEHIND YOUR HEAD. I WON'T LIKE ORDERING THEM TO SHOOT YOU, BUT I WILL.
WHAT HAPPENED, GOVERNOR? WHERE DID IT ALL GO SO WRONG?
I SUSPECTED YOU MIGHT TRY SOMETHING LIKE THIS, GENERAL, BUT I'D HOPED I WAS WRONG.
I WANT YOU TO STAY AND WATCH. PERHAPS WE CAN SHOW YOU THE LIGHT.
PERHAPS YOU CAN BELIEVE IN PUTERNICSTAN AGAIN.
I HAVE ALWAYS BELIEVED IN PUTERNICSTAN. IT'S THE ENDLESS CYCLE OF BLOOD IN WHICH I HAVE NO BELIEF.
I'M TOO OLD AND HAVE SEEN TOO MANY WARS.
THAT'S THE EXACT CYCLE I PLAN TO BREAK, GENERAL.
WITH ONE SWIFT STROKE.
"HOW DO WE TURN THEM OFF, SCIENCE-BOY?"

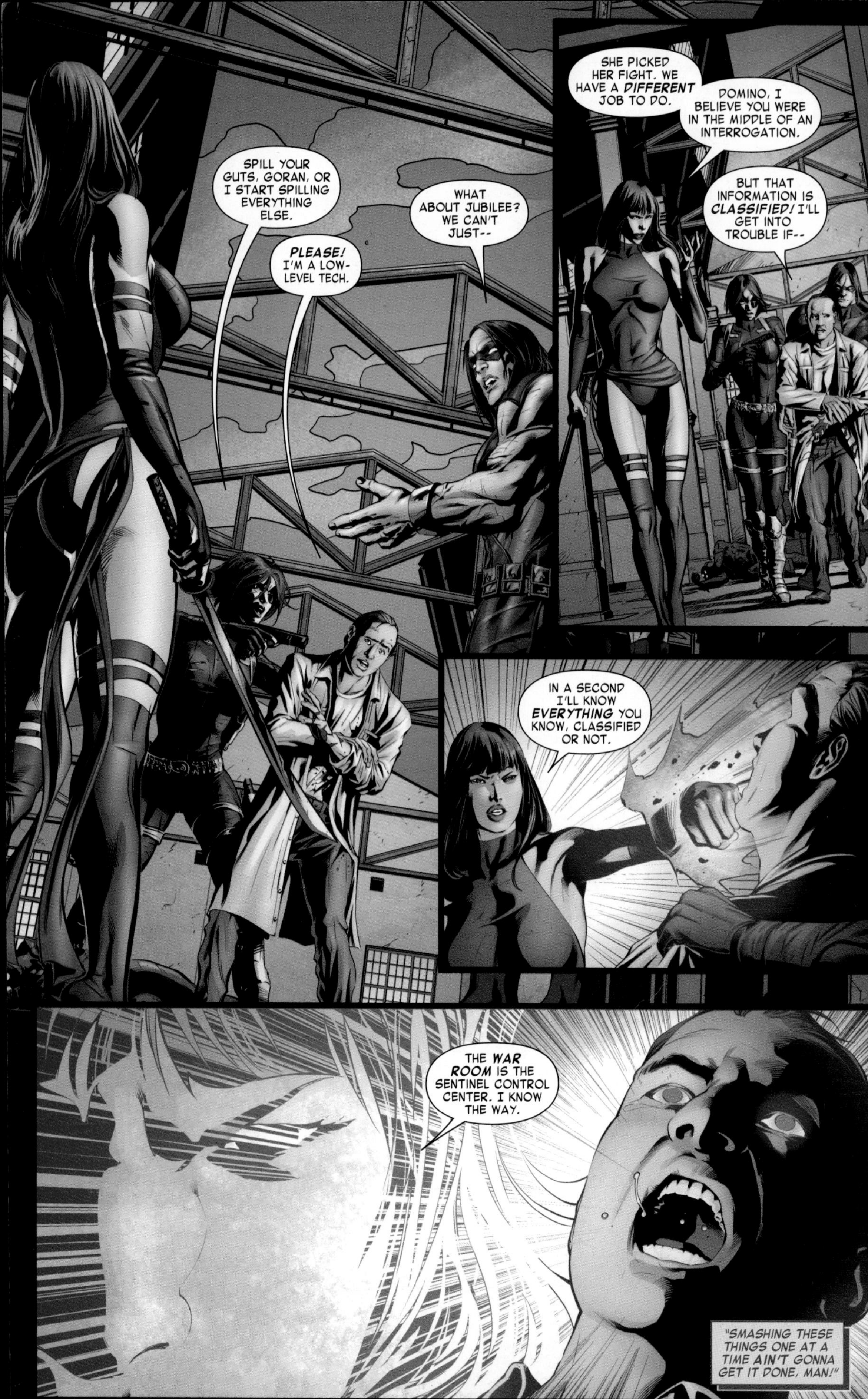

SPILL YOUR GUTS, GORAN, OR I START SPILLING EVERYTHING ELSE.
PLEASE! I'M A LOW-LEVEL TECH.
WHAT ABOUT JUBILEE? WE CAN'T JUST--
SHE PICKED HER FIGHT. WE HAVE A DIFFERENT JOB TO DO.
DOMINO, I BELIEVE YOU WERE IN THE MIDDLE OF AN INTERROGATION.
BUT THAT INFORMATION IS CLASSIFIED! I'LL GET INTO TROUBLE IF--
IN A SECOND I'LL KNOW EVERYTHING YOU KNOW, CLASSIFIED OR NOT.
THE WAR ROOM IS THE SENTINEL CONTROL CENTER. I KNOW THE WAY.
"SMASHING THESE THINGS ONE AT A TIME AIN'T GONNA GET IT DONE, MAN!"

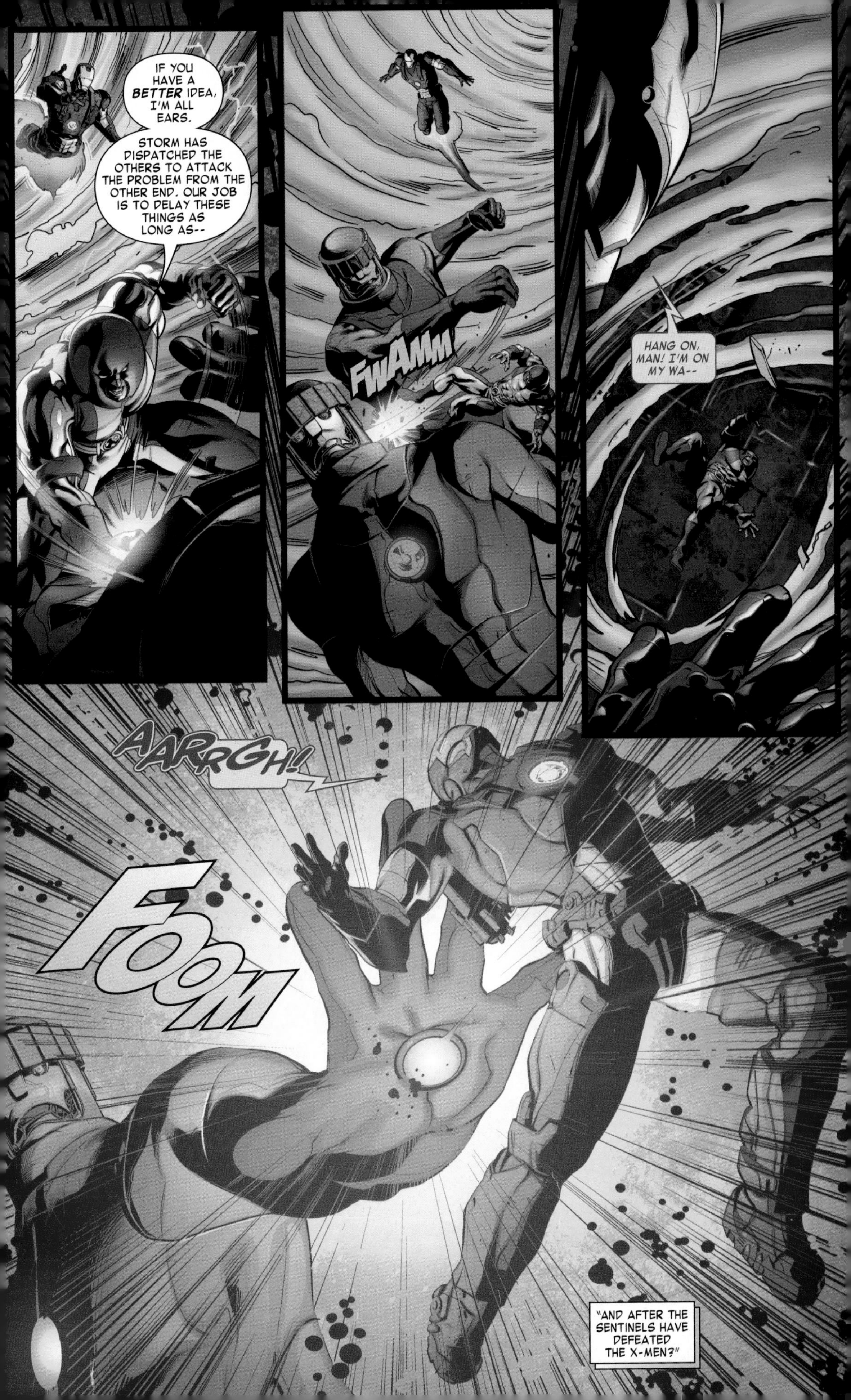
IF YOU HAVE A BETTER IDEA, I'M ALL EARS.
STORM HAS DISPATCHED THE OTHERS TO ATTACK THE PROBLEM FROM THE OTHER END. OUR JOB IS TO DELAY THESE THINGS AS LONG AS--
FWAMM
HANG ON, MAN! I'M ON MY WA--
AARRGH!
FOOM
"AND AFTER THE SENTINELS HAVE DEFEATED THE X-MEN?"

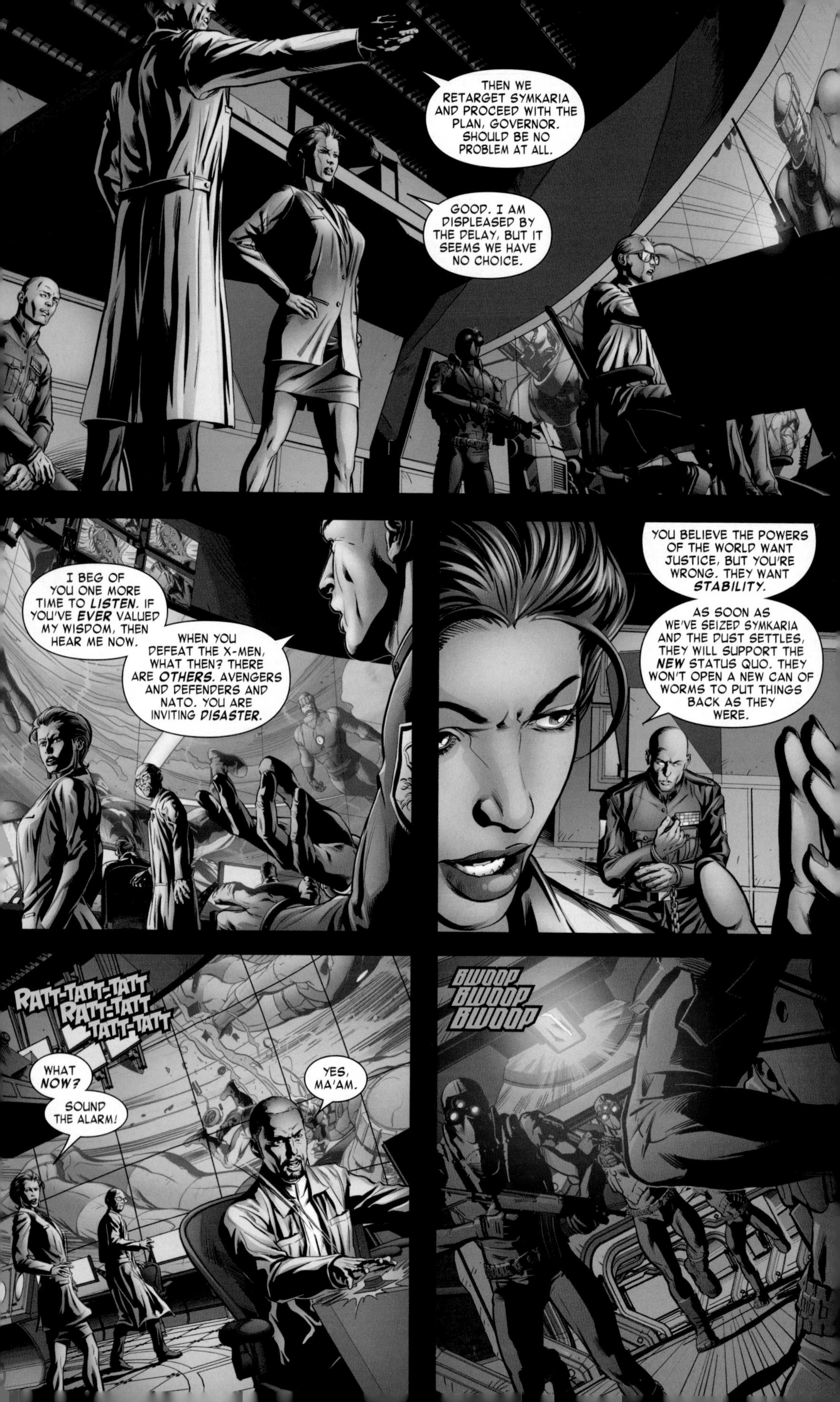
THEN WE RETARGET SYMKARIA AND PROCEED WITH THE PLAN, GOVERNOR. SHOULD BE NO PROBLEM AT ALL.
GOOD. I AM DISPLEASED BY THE DELAY, BUT IT SEEMS WE HAVE NO CHOICE.
I BEG OF YOU ONE MORE TIME TO LISTEN. IF YOU'VE EVER VALUED MY WISDOM, THEN HEAR ME NOW.
WHEN YOU DEFEAT THE X-MEN, WHAT THEN? THERE ARE OTHERS. AVENGERS AND DEFENDERS AND NATO. YOU ARE INVITING DISASTER.
YOU BELIEVE THE POWERS OF THE WORLD WANT JUSTICE, BUT YOU'RE WRONG. THEY WANT STABILITY.
AS SOON AS WE'VE SEIZED SYMKARIA AND THE DUST SETTLES, THEY WILL SUPPORT THE NEW STATUS QUO. THEY WON'T OPEN A NEW CAN OF WORMS TO PUT THINGS BACK AS THEY WERE.
RATT-TATT-TATT RATT-TATT TATT-TATT
WHAT NOW?
SOUND THE ALARM!
YES, MA'AM.
BWOOP BWOOP BWOOP

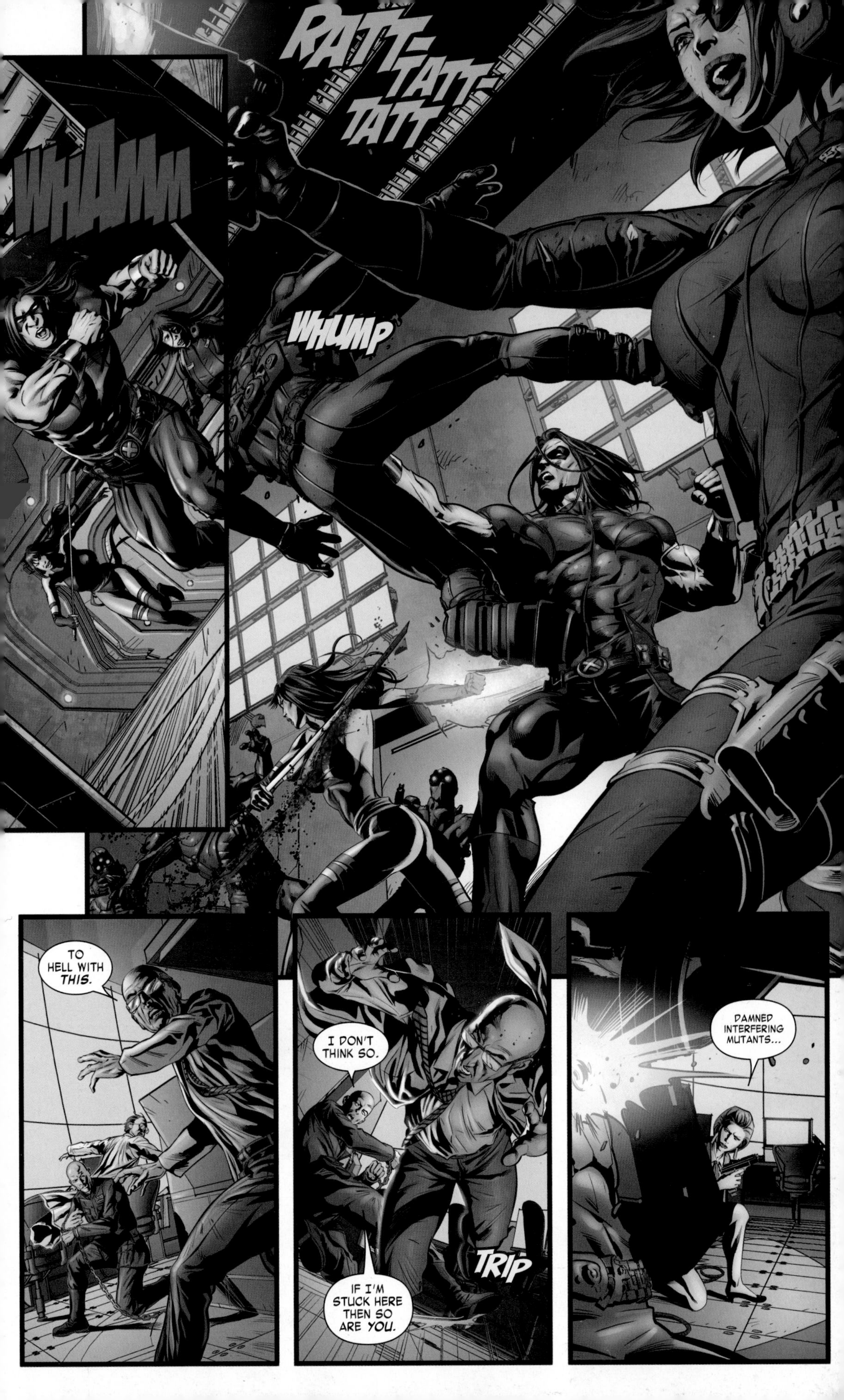
WHAMM
RATT-TATT-TATT
WHUMP
TO HELL WITH THIS.
I DON'T THINK SO.
TRIP
IF I'M STUCK HERE THEN SO ARE YOU.
DAMNED INTERFERING MUTANTS...

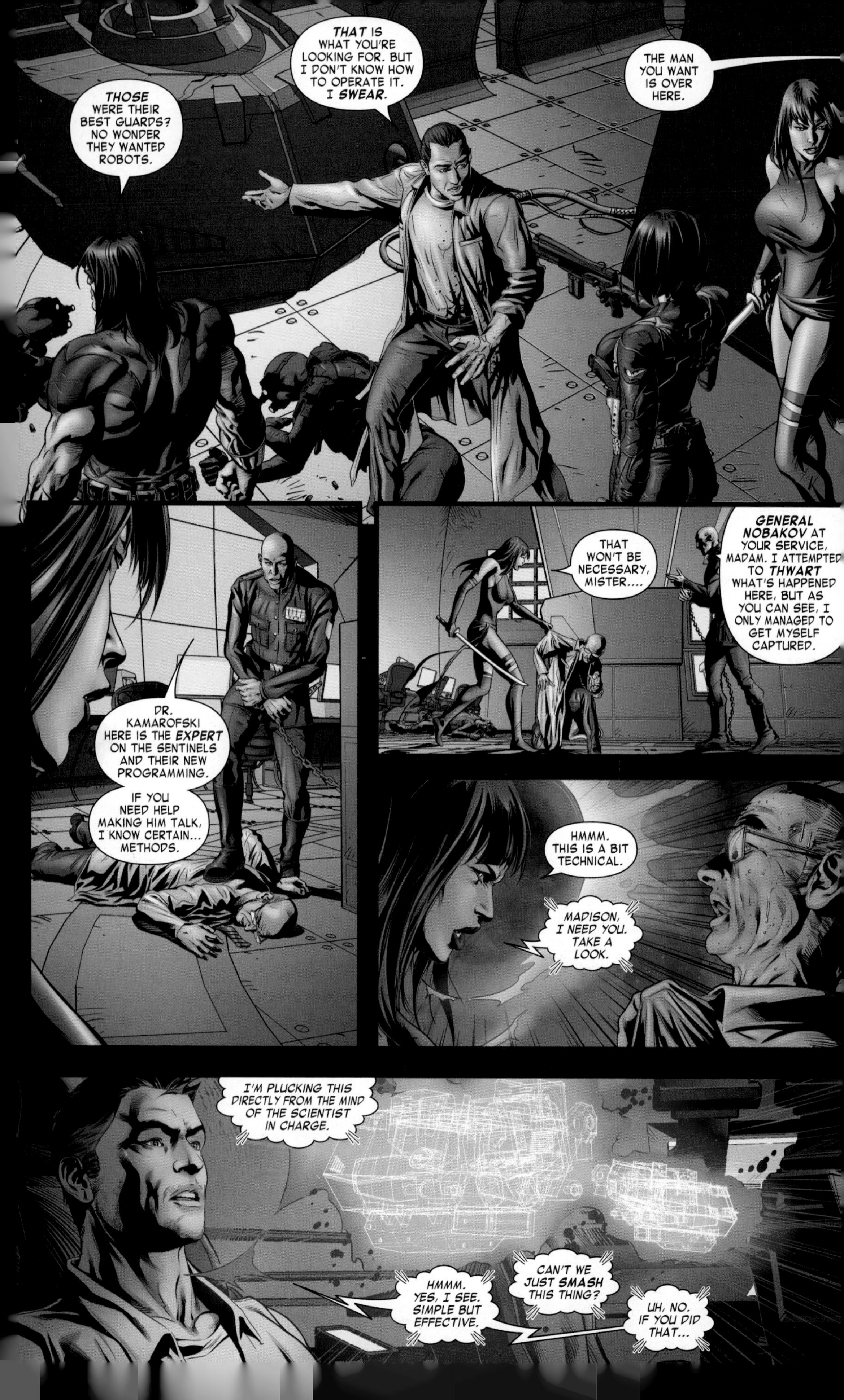
THOSE WERE THEIR BEST GUARDS? NO WONDER THEY WANTED ROBOTS.
THAT IS WHAT YOU'RE LOOKING FOR. BUT I DON'T KNOW HOW TO OPERATE IT. I SWEAR.
THE MAN YOU WANT IS OVER HERE.
THAT WON'T BE NECESSARY, MISTER....
GENERAL NOBAKOV AT YOUR SERVICE, MADAM. I ATTEMPTED TO THWART WHAT'S HAPPENED HERE, BUT AS YOU CAN SEE, I ONLY MANAGED TO GET MYSELF CAPTURED.
DR. KAMAROFSKI HERE IS THE EXPERT ON THE SENTINELS AND THEIR NEW PROGRAMMING.
IF YOU NEED HELP MAKING HIM TALK, I KNOW CERTAIN... METHODS.
HMMM. THIS IS A BIT TECHNICAL.
MADISON, I NEED YOU. TAKE A LOOK.
I'M PLUCKING THIS DIRECTLY FROM THE MIND OF THE SCIENTIST IN CHARGE.
HMMM. YES, I SEE. SIMPLE BUT EFFECTIVE.
CAN'T WE JUST SMASH THIS THING?
UH, NO. IF YOU DID THAT...

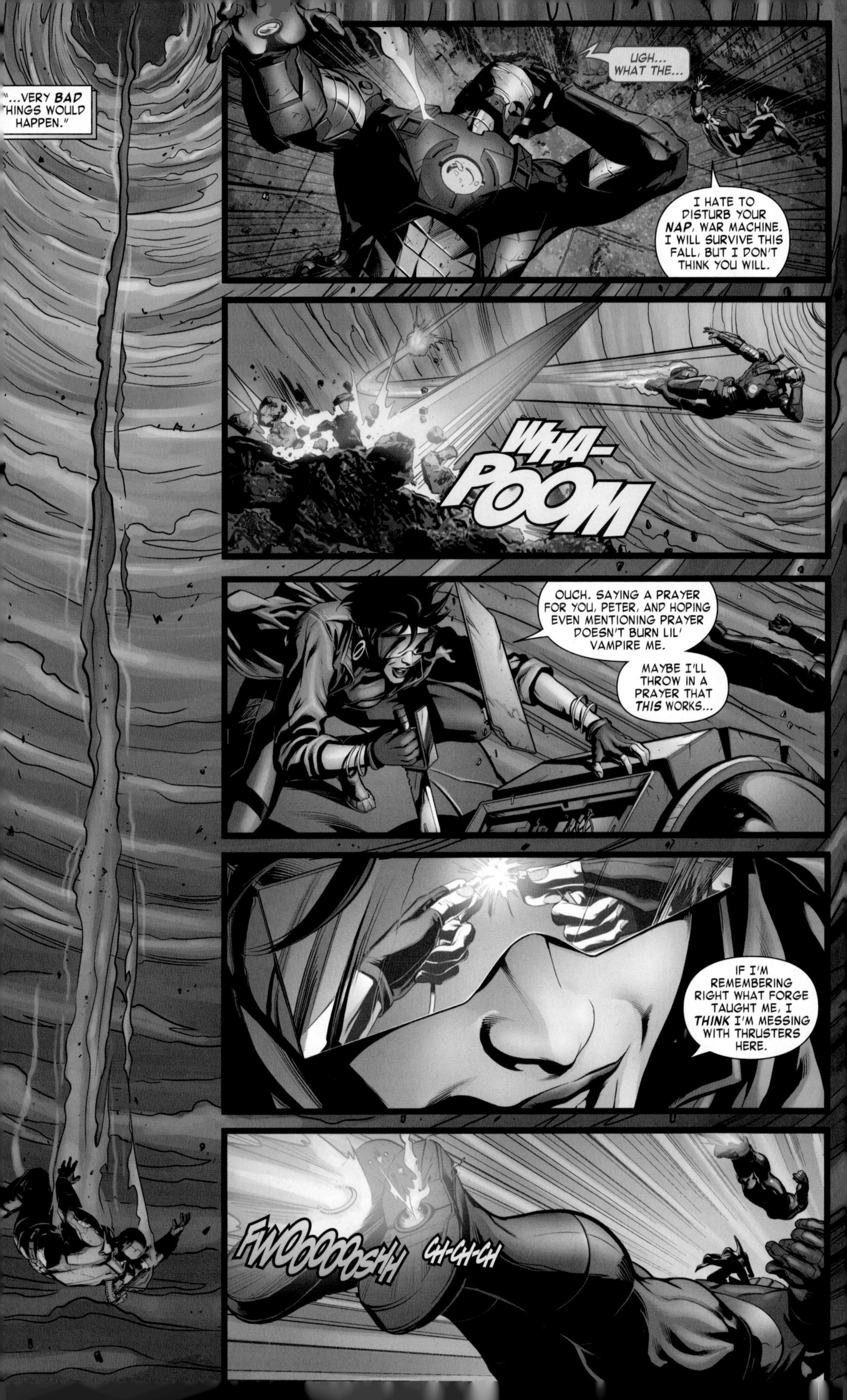
"...VERY BAD THINGS WOULD HAPPEN."
UGH... WHAT THE...
I HATE TO DISTURB YOUR NAP, WAR MACHINE. I WILL SURVIVE THIS FALL, BUT I DON'T THINK YOU WILL.
WHA-POOM
OUCH. SAYING A PRAYER FOR YOU, PETER, AND HOPING EVEN MENTIONING PRAYER DOESN'T BURN LIL' VAMPIRE ME.
MAYBE I'LL THROW IN A PRAYER THAT THIS WORKS...
IF I'M REMEMBERING RIGHT WHAT FORGE TAUGHT ME, I THINK I'M MESSING WITH THRUSTERS HERE.
FWOOOOOOSHH
CH-CH-CH

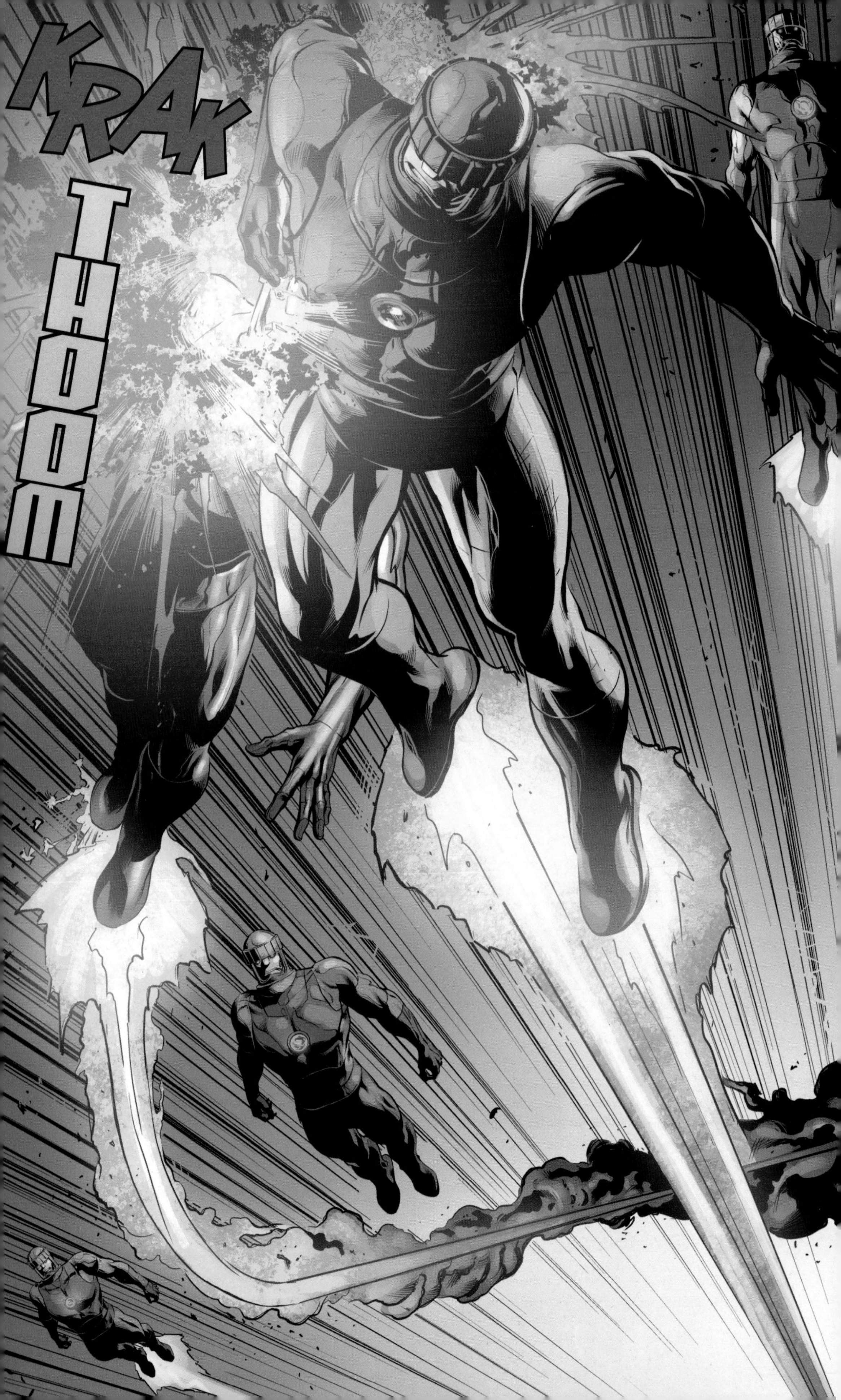
KRAK
THOOM

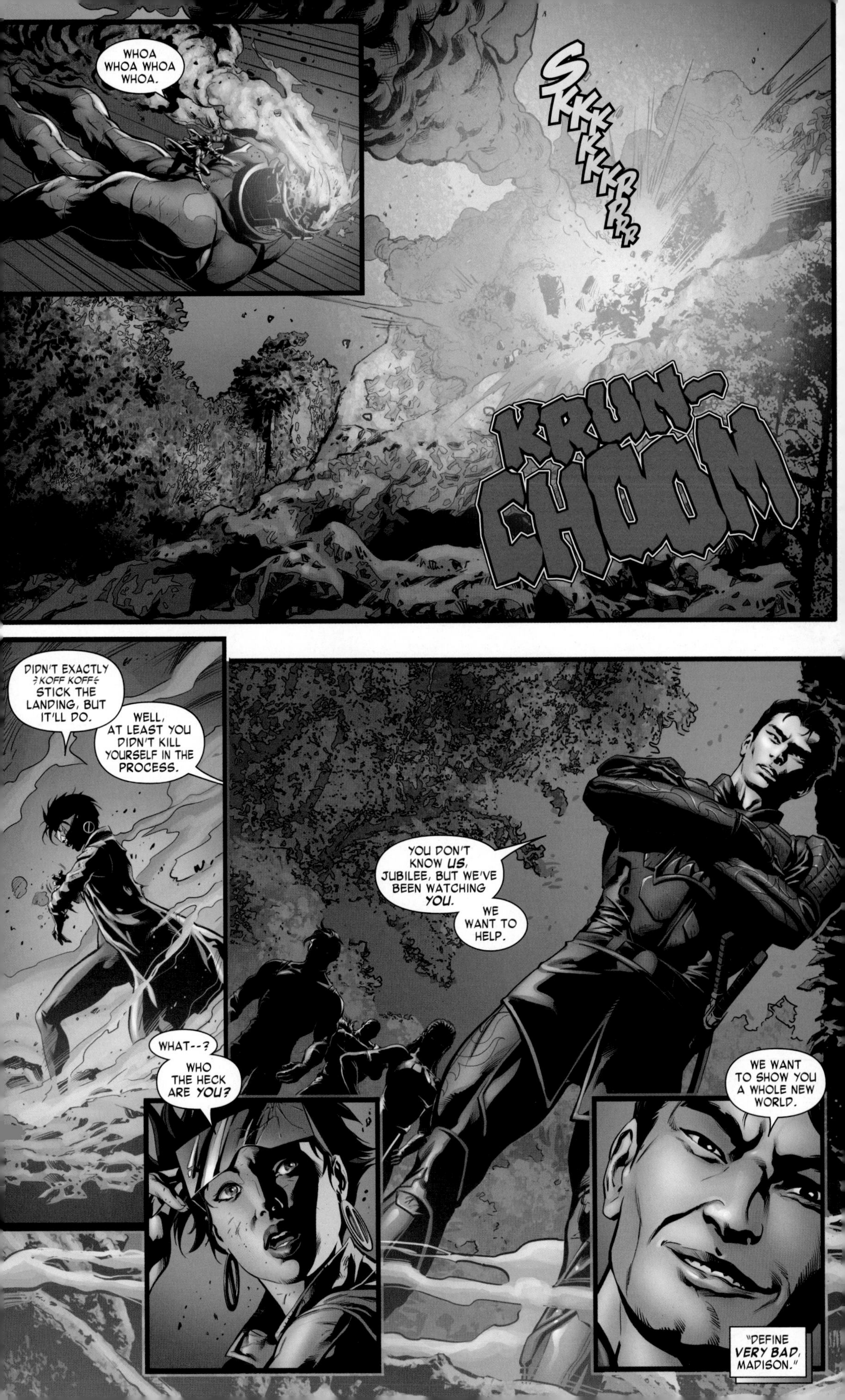
WHOA WHOA WHOA WHOA.
SKKKKKKRRRR
KRUN-CHOOM
DIDN'T EXACTLY *KOFF KOFF* STICK THE LANDING, BUT IT'LL DO.
WELL, AT LEAST YOU DIDN'T KILL YOURSELF IN THE PROCESS.
YOU DON'T KNOW US, JUBILEE, BUT WE'VE BEEN WATCHING YOU.
WE WANT TO HELP.
WHAT--?
WHO THE HECK ARE YOU?
WE WANT TO SHOW YOU A WHOLE NEW WORLD.
"DEFINE VERY BAD, MADISON."

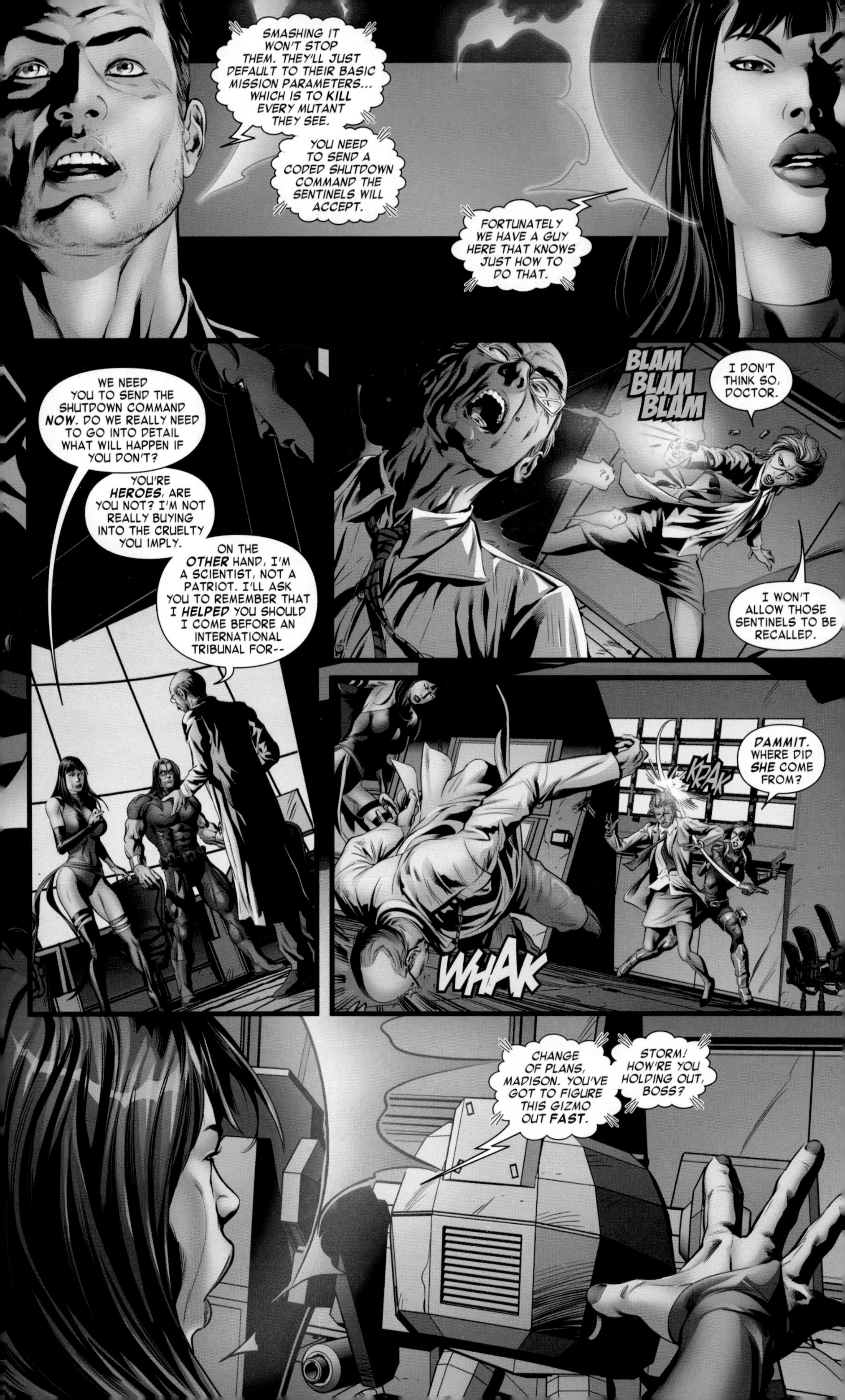
SMASHING IT WON'T STOP THEM. THEY'LL JUST DEFAULT TO THEIR BASIC MISSION PARAMETERS... WHICH IS TO KILL EVERY MUTANT THEY SEE.
YOU NEED TO SEND A CODED SHUTDOWN COMMAND THE SENTINELS WILL ACCEPT.
FORTUNATELY WE HAVE A GUY HERE THAT KNOWS JUST HOW TO DO THAT.
WE NEED YOU TO SEND THE SHUTDOWN COMMAND NOW. DO WE REALLY NEED TO GO INTO DETAIL WHAT WILL HAPPEN IF YOU DON'T?
YOU'RE HEROES, ARE YOU NOT? I'M NOT REALLY BUYING INTO THE CRUELTY YOU IMPLY.
ON THE OTHER HAND, I'M A SCIENTIST, NOT A PATRIOT. I'LL ASK YOU TO REMEMBER THAT I HELPED YOU SHOULD I COME BEFORE AN INTERNATIONAL TRIBUNAL FOR--
BLAM BLAM BLAM
I DON'T THINK SO, DOCTOR.
I WON'T ALLOW THOSE SENTINELS TO BE RECALLED.
KRAK
DAMMIT. WHERE DID SHE COME FROM?
WHAK
CHANGE OF PLANS, MADISON. YOU'VE GOT TO FIGURE THIS GIZMO OUT FAST.
STORM! HOW'RE YOU HOLDING OUT, BOSS?

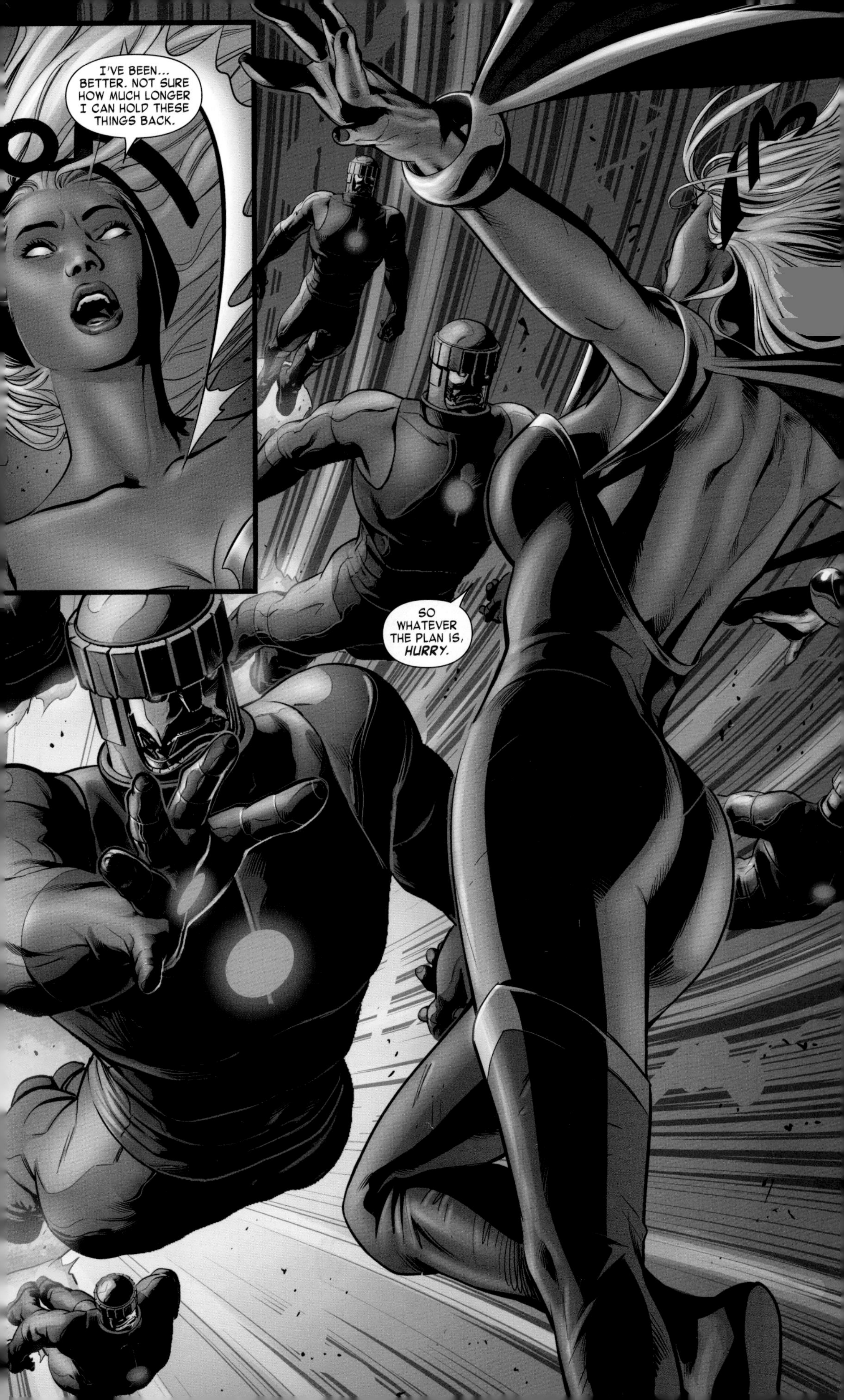
I'VE BEEN... BETTER. NOT SURE HOW MUCH LONGER I CAN HOLD THESE THINGS BACK.
SO WHATEVER THE PLAN IS, HURRY.

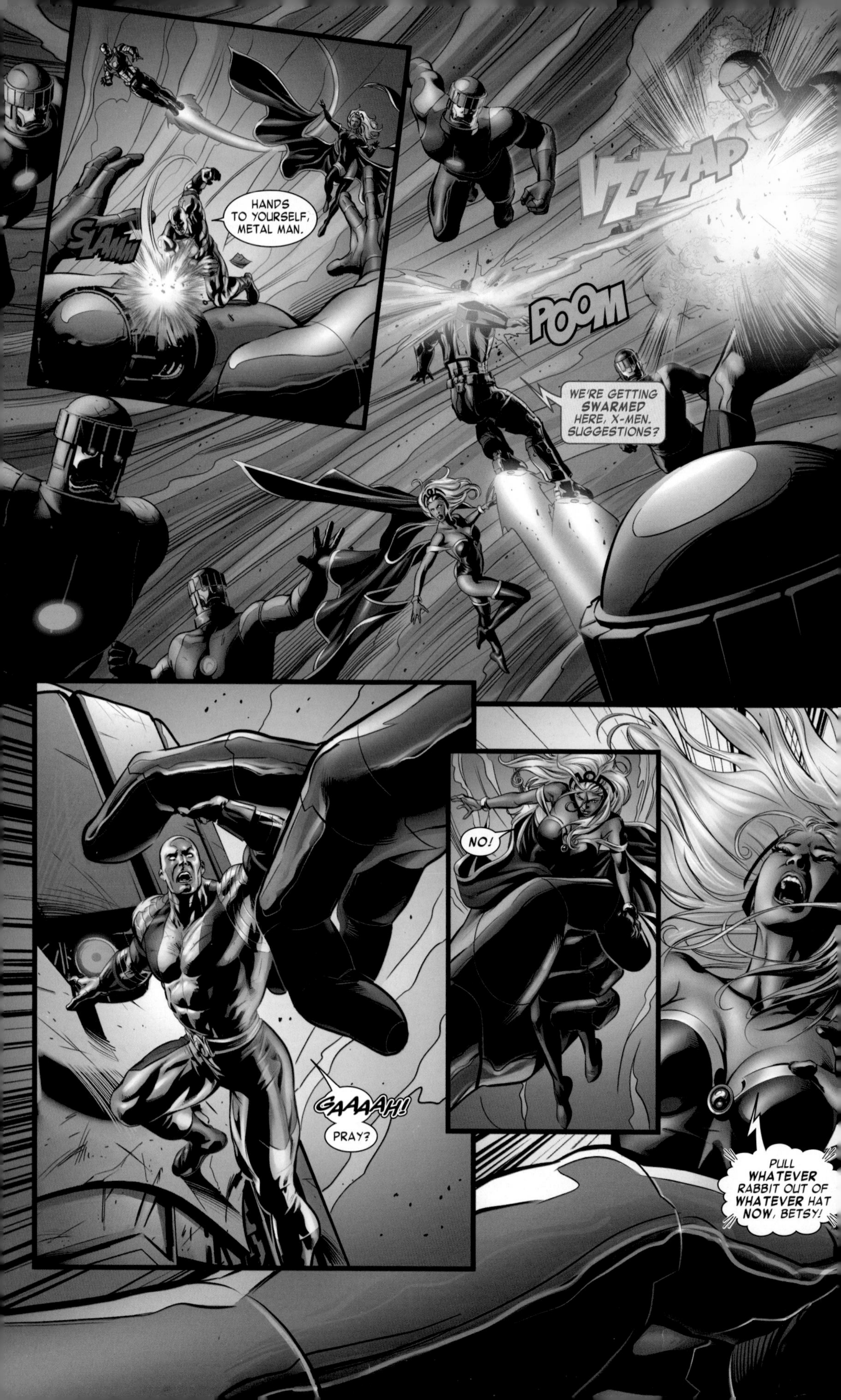
SLAMM
HANDS TO YOURSELF, METAL MAN.
VZZZAP
POOM
WE'RE GETTING SWARMED HERE, X-MEN. SUGGESTIONS?
GAAAAH!
PRAY?
NO!
PULL WHATEVER RABBIT OUT OF WHATEVER HAT NOW, BETSY!

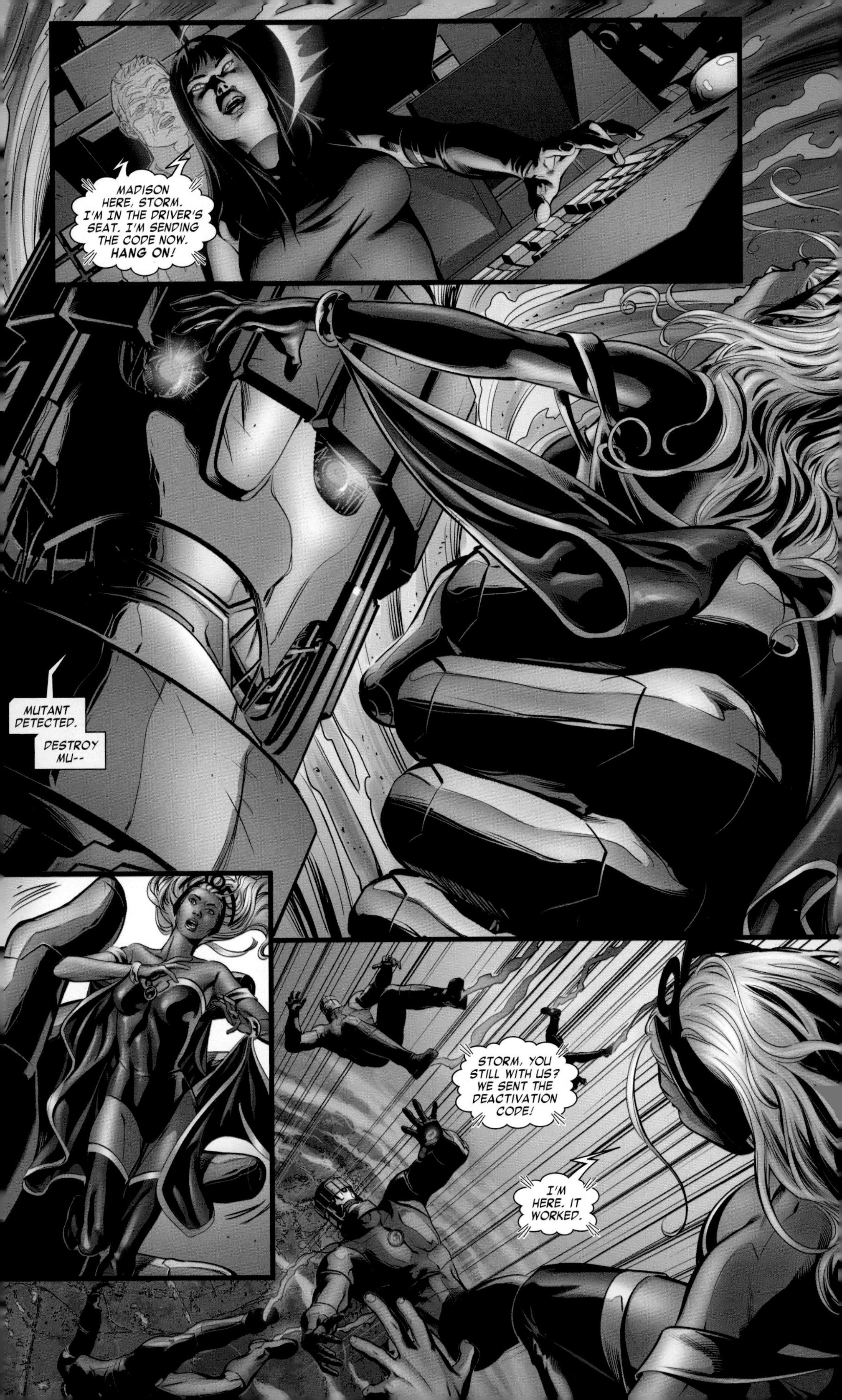
MADISON HERE, STORM. I'M IN THE DRIVER'S SEAT. I'M SENDING THE CODE NOW. HANG ON!
MUTANT DETECTED.
DESTROY MU--
STORM, YOU STILL WITH US? WE SENT THE DEACTIVATION CODE!
I'M HERE. IT WORKED.

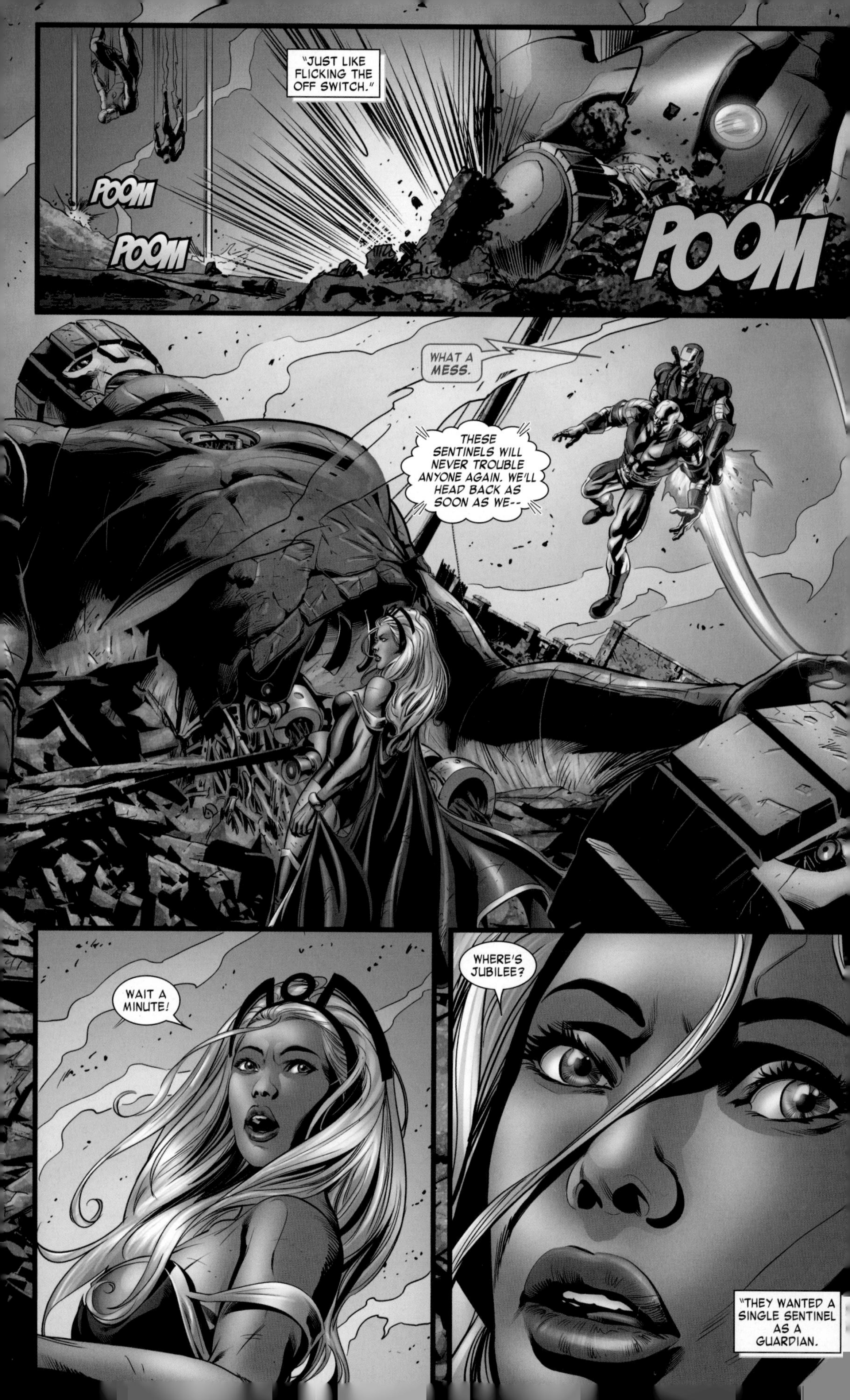
"JUST LIKE FLICKING THE OFF SWITCH."
POOM
POOM
POOM
WHAT A MESS.
THESE SENTINELS WILL NEVER TROUBLE ANYONE AGAIN. WE'LL HEAD BACK AS SOON AS WE--
WAIT A MINUTE!
WHERE'S JUBILEE?
"THEY WANTED A SINGLE SENTINEL AS A GUARDIAN.

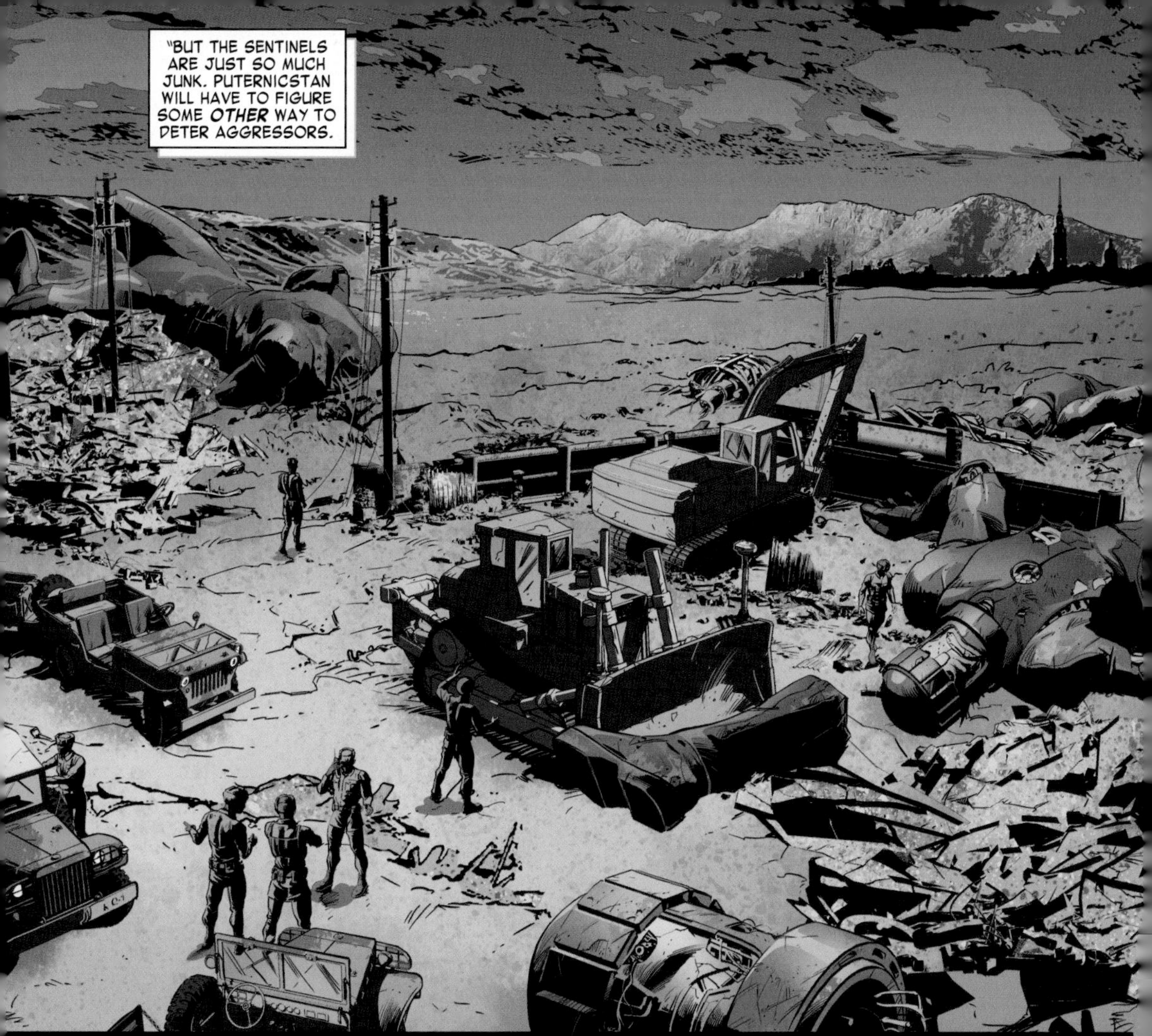
"BUT THE SENTINELS ARE JUST SO MUCH JUNK. PUTERNICSTAN WILL HAVE TO FIGURE SOME *OTHER* WAY TO DETER AGGRESSORS.

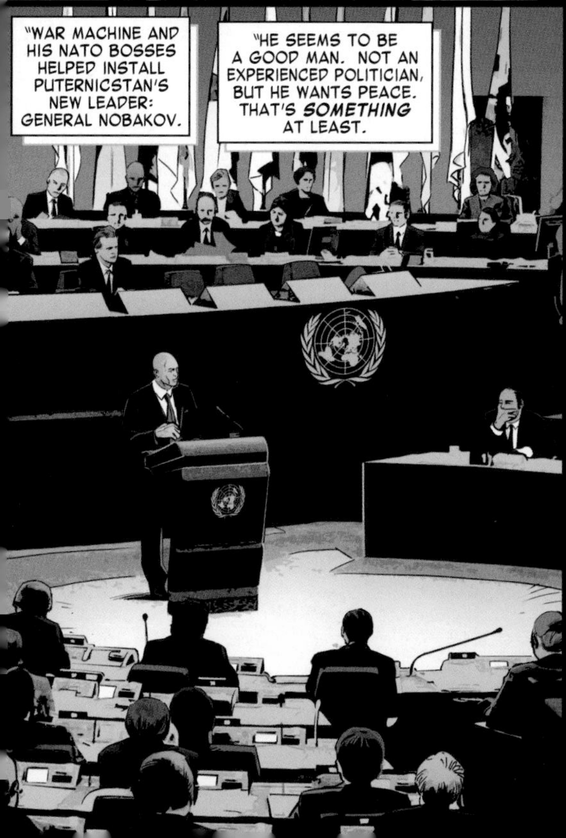
"WAR MACHINE AND HIS NATO BOSSES HELPED INSTALL PUTERNICSTAN'S NEW LEADER: GENERAL NOBAKOV.
"HE SEEMS TO BE A GOOD MAN. NOT AN EXPERIENCED POLITICIAN, BUT HE WANTS PEACE. THAT'S *SOMETHING* AT LEAST.

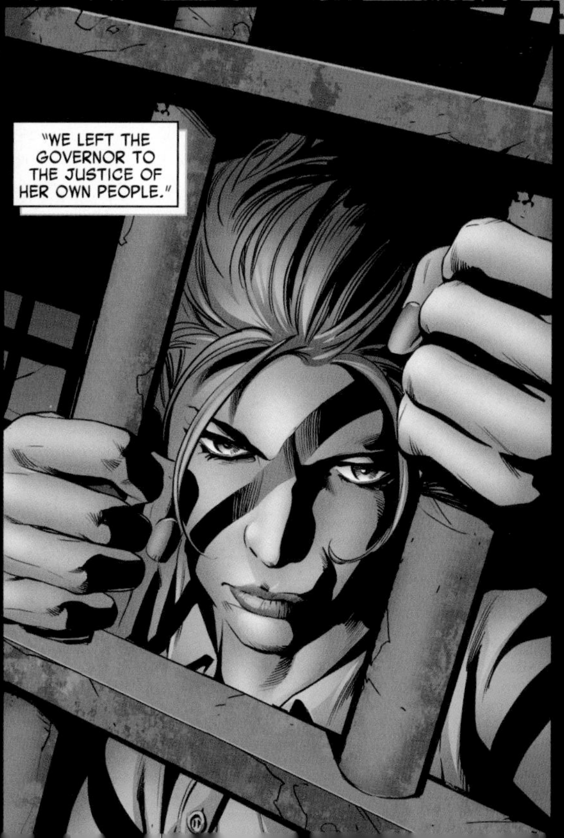
"WE LEFT THE GOVERNOR TO THE JUSTICE OF HER OWN PEOPLE."

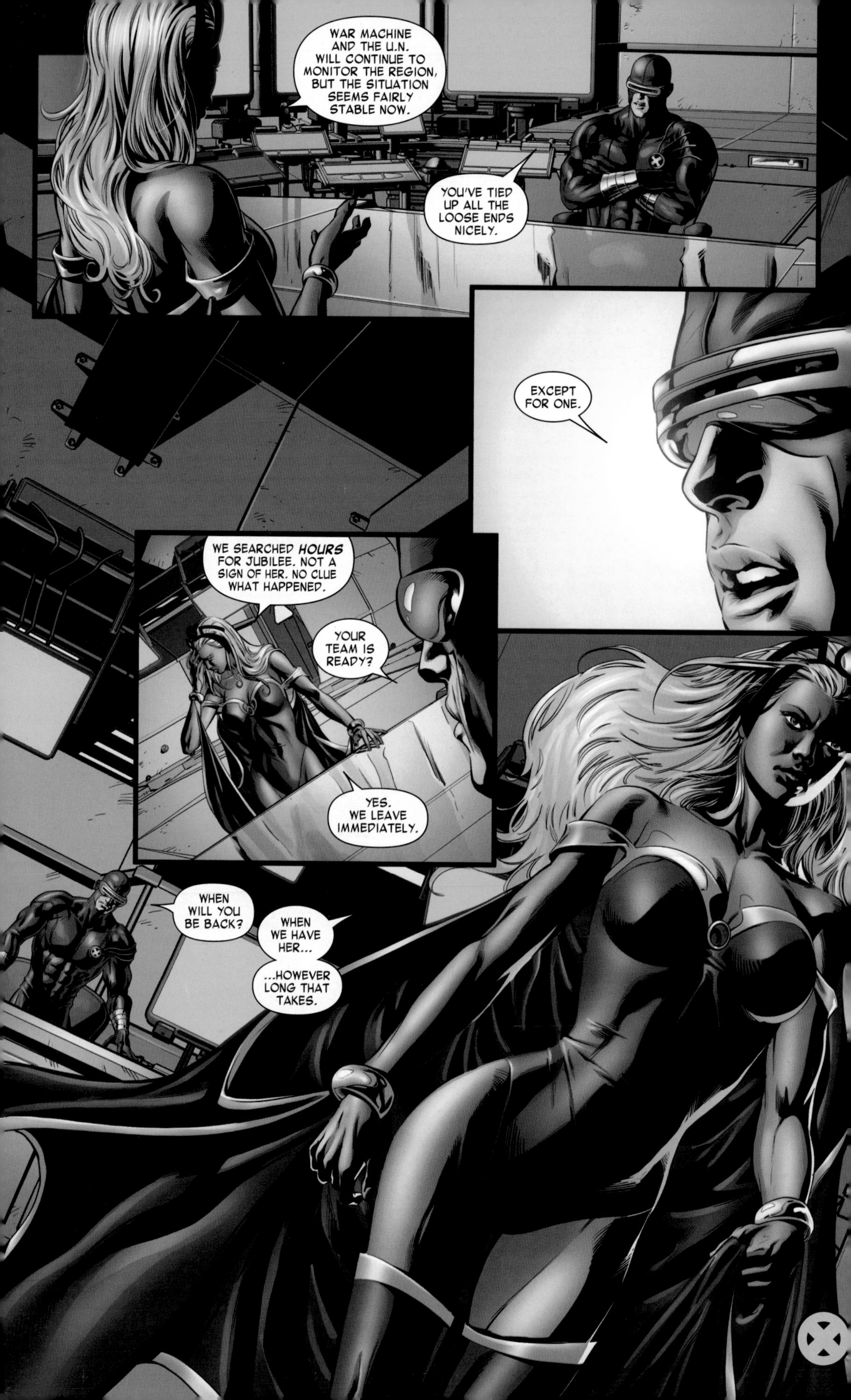
WAR MACHINE AND THE U.N. WILL CONTINUE TO MONITOR THE REGION, BUT THE SITUATION SEEMS FAIRLY STABLE NOW.
YOU'VE TIED UP ALL THE LOOSE ENDS NICELY.
EXCEPT FOR ONE.
WE SEARCHED HOURS FOR JUBILEE. NOT A SIGN OF HER. NO CLUE WHAT HAPPENED.
YOUR TEAM IS READY?
YES. WE LEAVE IMMEDIATELY.
WHEN WILL YOU BE BACK?
WHEN WE HAVE HER...
...HOWEVER LONG THAT TAKES.

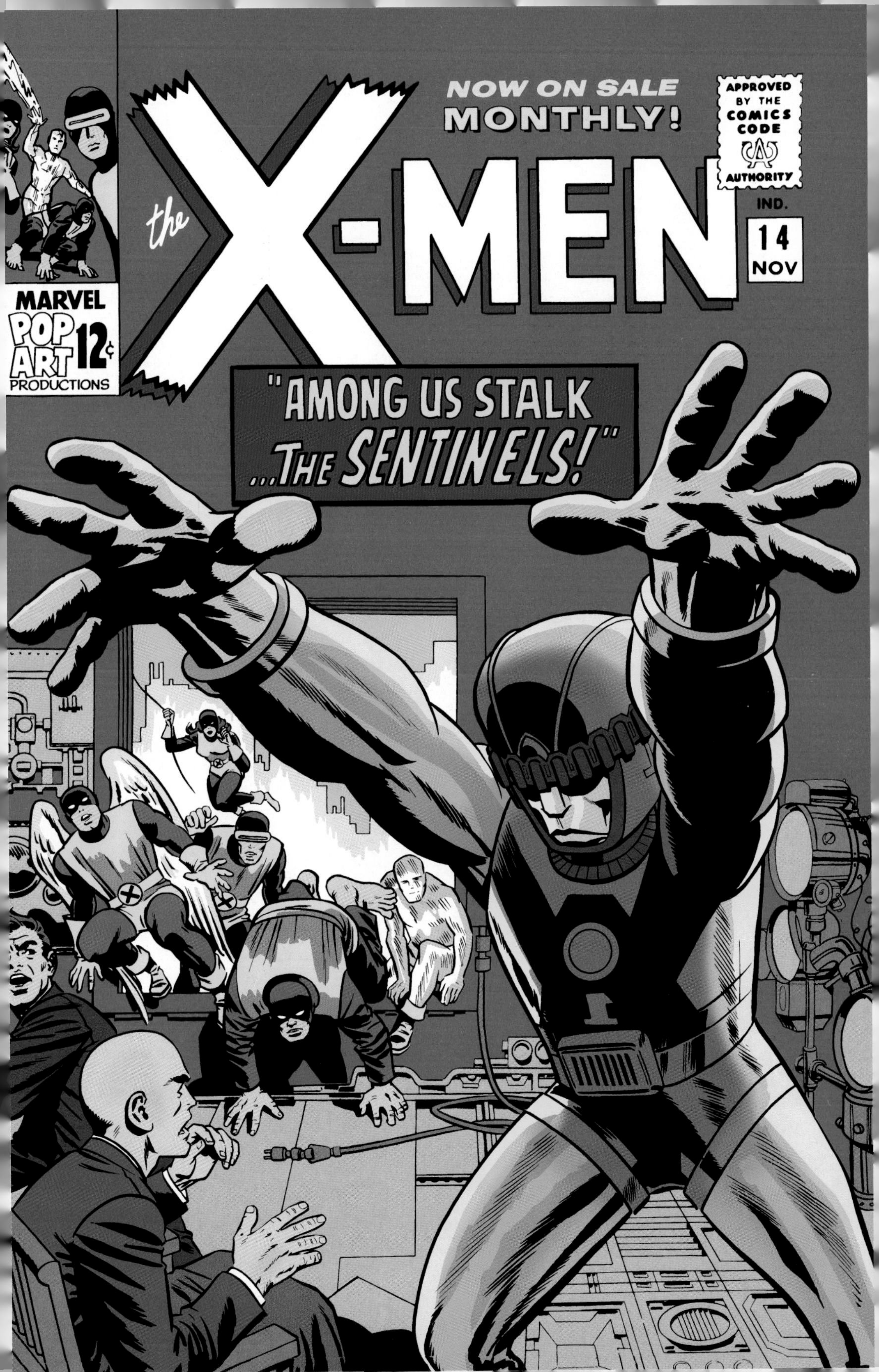

NOW ON SALE MONTHLY!
APPROVED BY THE COMICS CODE AUTHORITY
the X-MEN
IND.
14
NOV
MARVEL POP ART PRODUCTIONS 12¢
"AMONG US STALK ...THE SENTINELS!"

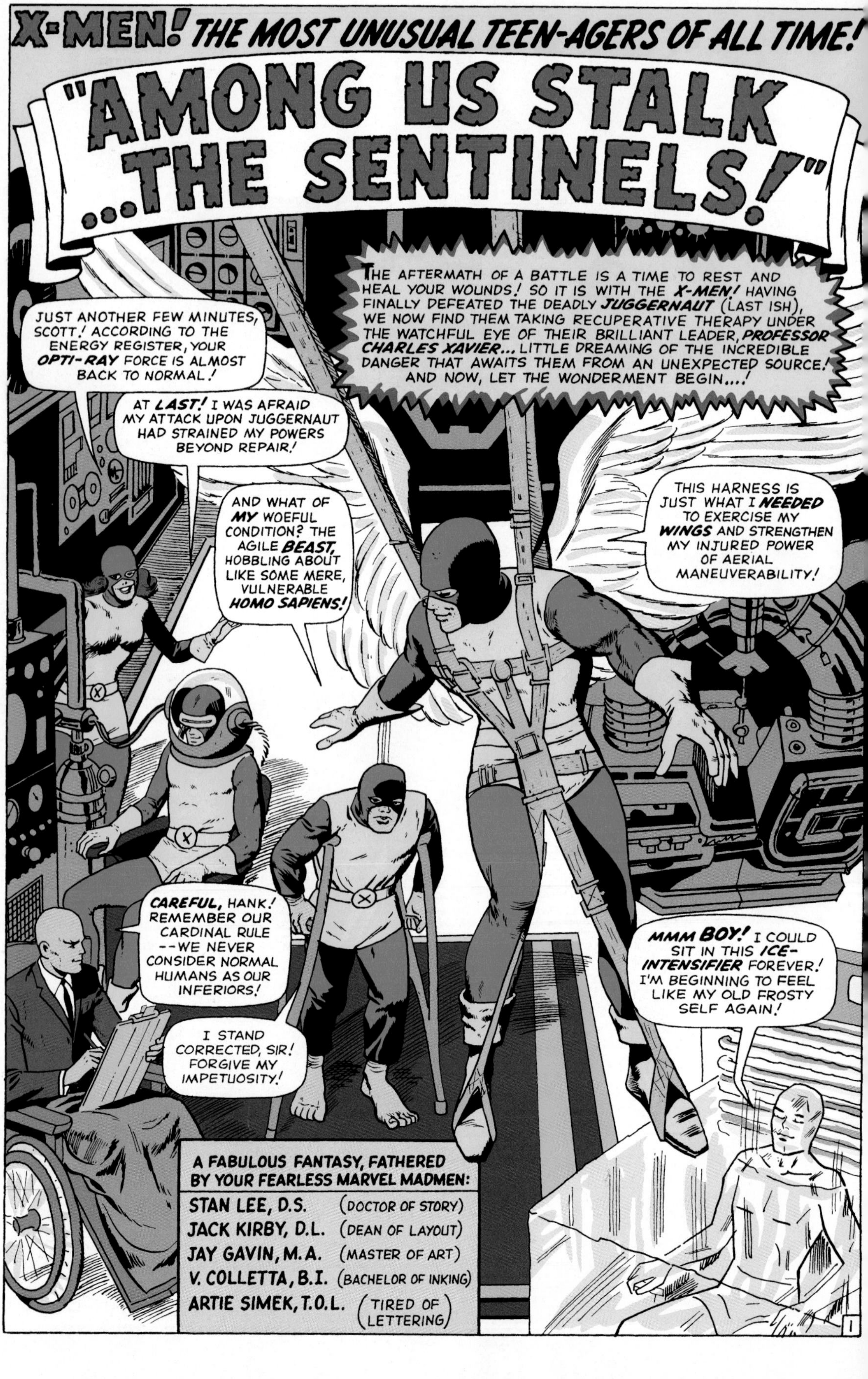
X-MEN! THE MOST UNUSUAL TEEN-AGERS OF ALL TIME!
"AMONG US STALK ...THE SENTINELS!"
THE AFTERMATH OF A BATTLE IS A TIME TO REST AND HEAL YOUR WOUNDS! SO IT IS WITH THE X-MEN! HAVING FINALLY DEFEATED THE DEADLY JUGGERNAUT (LAST ISH), WE NOW FIND THEM TAKING RECUPERATIVE THERAPY UNDER THE WATCHFUL EYE OF THEIR BRILLIANT LEADER, PROFESSOR CHARLES XAVIER... LITTLE DREAMING OF THE INCREDIBLE DANGER THAT AWAITS THEM FROM AN UNEXPECTED SOURCE! AND NOW, LET THE WONDERMENT BEGIN...!
JUST ANOTHER FEW MINUTES, SCOTT! ACCORDING TO THE ENERGY REGISTER, YOUR OPTI-RAY FORCE IS ALMOST BACK TO NORMAL!
AT LAST! I WAS AFRAID MY ATTACK UPON JUGGERNAUT HAD STRAINED MY POWERS BEYOND REPAIR!
AND WHAT OF MY WOEFUL CONDITION? THE AGILE BEAST, HOBBLING ABOUT LIKE SOME MERE, VULNERABLE HOMO SAPIENS!
THIS HARNESS IS JUST WHAT I NEEDED TO EXERCISE MY WINGS AND STRENGTHEN MY INJURED POWER OF AERIAL MANEUVERABILITY!
CAREFUL, HANK! REMEMBER OUR CARDINAL RULE --WE NEVER CONSIDER NORMAL HUMANS AS OUR INFERIORS!
I STAND CORRECTED, SIR! FORGIVE MY IMPETUOSITY!
MMM BOY! I COULD SIT IN THIS ICE-INTENSIFIER FOREVER! I'M BEGINNING TO FEEL LIKE MY OLD FROSTY SELF AGAIN!
A FABULOUS FANTASY, FATHERED BY YOUR FEARLESS MARVEL MADMEN:
STAN LEE, D.S. (DOCTOR OF STORY)
JACK KIRBY, D.L. (DEAN OF LAYOUT)
JAY GAVIN, M.A. (MASTER OF ART)
V. COLLETTA, B.I. (BACHELOR OF INKING)
ARTIE SIMEK, T.O.L. (TIRED OF LETTERING)
1

YOU'VE ALL TAKEN TO YOUR EMERGENCY THERAPY VERY WELL!

ANGEL, YOU MAY REMOVE YOUR HARNESS NOW AND PRACTICE NATURAL FLIGHT!

YES, SIR!!

AND YOU MAY BEGIN EXERCISING YOUR FEET AGAIN, BEAST!

EUREKA! NEXT TO THE GETTYSBURG ADDRESS, THAT WAS THE MOST INSPIRING DECLARATION I'VE EVER HEARD!

LEAP FOR THE HIGH BAR, HANK!

WELL DONE! DO YOU FEEL ANY PAINFUL AFTER-EFFECTS?

NOT A ONE, SIR! IF I FELT ANY BETTER, IT WOULD BE VIRTUALLY UNBEARABLE!

DEPRIVING A MUTANT OF HIS POWERS IS LIKE FORBIDDING A POLITICIAN TO KISS BABIES!

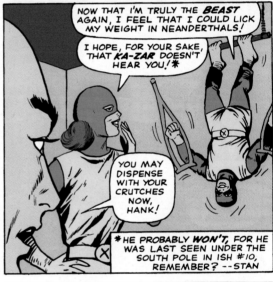

NOW THAT I'M TRULY THE BEAST AGAIN, I FEEL THAT I COULD LICK MY WEIGHT IN NEANDERTHALS!

I HOPE, FOR YOUR SAKE, THAT KA-ZAR DOESN'T HEAR YOU!*

YOU MAY DISPENSE WITH YOUR CRUTCHES NOW, HANK!

*HE PROBABLY WON'T, FOR HE WAS LAST SEEN UNDER THE SOUTH POLE IN ISH #10, REMEMBER? --STAN

BOBBY, I THINK YOU'VE BEEN IN THE ICE-INTENSIFIER LONG ENOUGH! YOU SEEM TO HAVE REACHED YOUR FRIGID PEAK BY NOW!

AWW, JUST A FEW MINUTES MORE, PROFESSOR! THIS IS THE COOLEST, IF YOU'LL PARDON THE PUN!

I'M GLAD YOU'RE ENJOYING IT, ICEMAN, BUT IF YOU REMAIN ANY LONGER, YOU'RE APT TO EXPERIENCE AN UNPLEASANT FREEZE FEEDBACK!

AT ANY RATE, I HAVE AN ANNOUNCEMENT THAT WILL MAKE YOU ANXIOUS TO LEAVE!

GREAT! I'VE ALWAYS BEEN A SUCKER FOR SURPRISES!

2

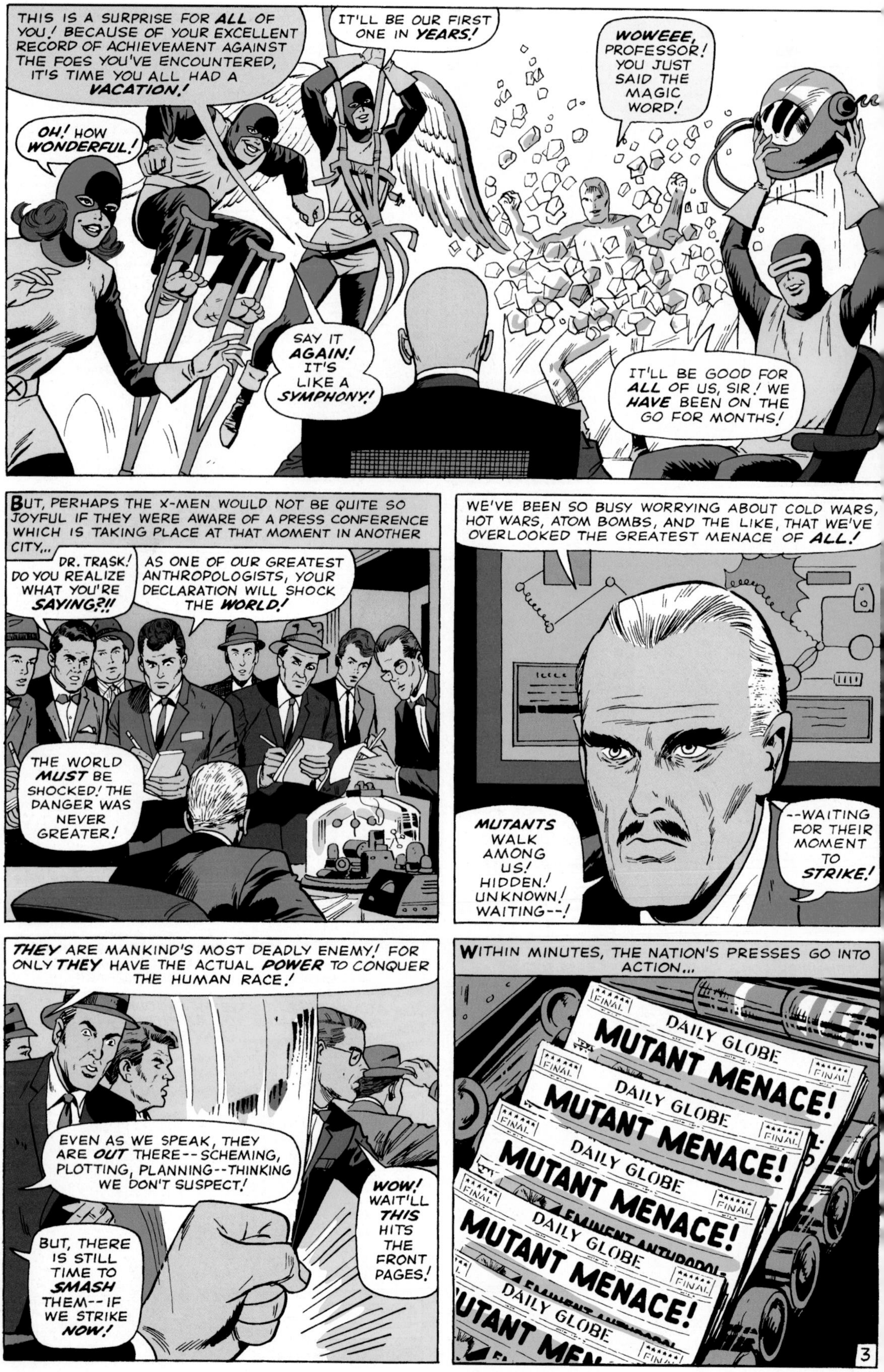
THIS IS A SURPRISE FOR ALL OF YOU! BECAUSE OF YOUR EXCELLENT RECORD OF ACHIEVEMENT AGAINST THE FOES YOU'VE ENCOUNTERED, IT'S TIME YOU ALL HAD A VACATION!
IT'LL BE OUR FIRST ONE IN YEARS!
WOWEEE, PROFESSOR! YOU JUST SAID THE MAGIC WORD!
OH! HOW WONDERFUL!
SAY IT AGAIN! IT'S LIKE A SYMPHONY!
IT'LL BE GOOD FOR ALL OF US, SIR! WE HAVE BEEN ON THE GO FOR MONTHS!
BUT, PERHAPS THE X-MEN WOULD NOT BE QUITE SO JOYFUL IF THEY WERE AWARE OF A PRESS CONFERENCE WHICH IS TAKING PLACE AT THAT MOMENT IN ANOTHER CITY...
DR. TRASK! DO YOU REALIZE WHAT YOU'RE SAYING?!!
AS ONE OF OUR GREATEST ANTHROPOLOGISTS, YOUR DECLARATION WILL SHOCK THE WORLD!
THE WORLD MUST BE SHOCKED! THE DANGER WAS NEVER GREATER!
WE'VE BEEN SO BUSY WORRYING ABOUT COLD WARS, HOT WARS, ATOM BOMBS, AND THE LIKE, THAT WE'VE OVERLOOKED THE GREATEST MENACE OF ALL!
MUTANTS WALK AMONG US! HIDDEN! UNKNOWN! WAITING--!
--WAITING FOR THEIR MOMENT TO STRIKE!
THEY ARE MANKIND'S MOST DEADLY ENEMY! FOR ONLY THEY HAVE THE ACTUAL POWER TO CONQUER THE HUMAN RACE!
EVEN AS WE SPEAK, THEY ARE OUT THERE--SCHEMING, PLOTTING, PLANNING--THINKING WE DON'T SUSPECT!
BUT, THERE IS STILL TIME TO SMASH THEM--IF WE STRIKE NOW!
WOW! WAIT'LL THIS HITS THE FRONT PAGES!
WITHIN MINUTES, THE NATION'S PRESSES GO INTO ACTION...
FINAL
DAILY GLOBE
MUTANT MENACE!
EMINENT ANTHROPOL-

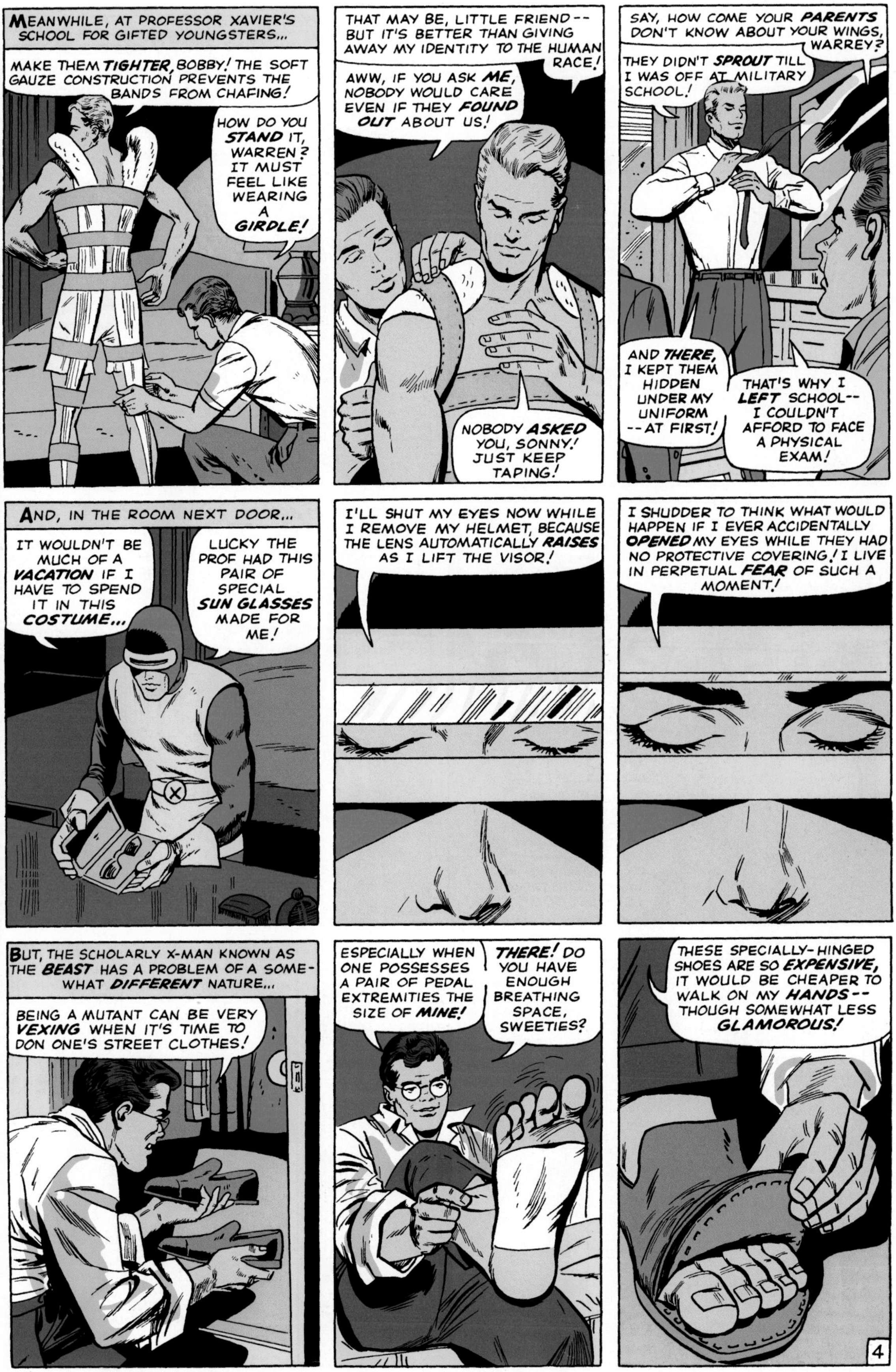
MEANWHILE, AT PROFESSOR XAVIER'S SCHOOL FOR GIFTED YOUNGSTERS...
MAKE THEM TIGHTER, BOBBY! THE SOFT GAUZE CONSTRUCTION PREVENTS THE BANDS FROM CHAFING!
HOW DO YOU STAND IT, WARREN? IT MUST FEEL LIKE WEARING A GIRDLE!
THAT MAY BE, LITTLE FRIEND-- BUT IT'S BETTER THAN GIVING AWAY MY IDENTITY TO THE HUMAN RACE!
AWW, IF YOU ASK ME, NOBODY WOULD CARE EVEN IF THEY FOUND OUT ABOUT US!
NOBODY ASKED YOU, SONNY! JUST KEEP TAPING!
SAY, HOW COME YOUR PARENTS DON'T KNOW ABOUT YOUR WINGS, WARREY?
THEY DIDN'T SPROUT TILL I WAS OFF AT MILITARY SCHOOL!
AND THERE, I KEPT THEM HIDDEN UNDER MY UNIFORM --AT FIRST!
THAT'S WHY I LEFT SCHOOL-- I COULDN'T AFFORD TO FACE A PHYSICAL EXAM!
AND, IN THE ROOM NEXT DOOR...
IT WOULDN'T BE MUCH OF A VACATION IF I HAVE TO SPEND IT IN THIS COSTUME...
LUCKY THE PROF HAD THIS PAIR OF SPECIAL SUN GLASSES MADE FOR ME!
I'LL SHUT MY EYES NOW WHILE I REMOVE MY HELMET, BECAUSE THE LENS AUTOMATICALLY RAISES AS I LIFT THE VISOR!
I SHUDDER TO THINK WHAT WOULD HAPPEN IF I EVER ACCIDENTALLY OPENED MY EYES WHILE THEY HAD NO PROTECTIVE COVERING! I LIVE IN PERPETUAL FEAR OF SUCH A MOMENT!
BUT, THE SCHOLARLY X-MAN KNOWN AS THE BEAST HAS A PROBLEM OF A SOMEWHAT DIFFERENT NATURE...
BEING A MUTANT CAN BE VERY VEXING WHEN IT'S TIME TO DON ONE'S STREET CLOTHES!
ESPECIALLY WHEN ONE POSSESSES A PAIR OF PEDAL EXTREMITIES THE SIZE OF MINE!
THERE! DO YOU HAVE ENOUGH BREATHING SPACE, SWEETIES?
THESE SPECIALLY-HINGED SHOES ARE SO EXPENSIVE, IT WOULD BE CHEAPER TO WALK ON MY HANDS-- THOUGH SOMEWHAT LESS GLAMOROUS!
4

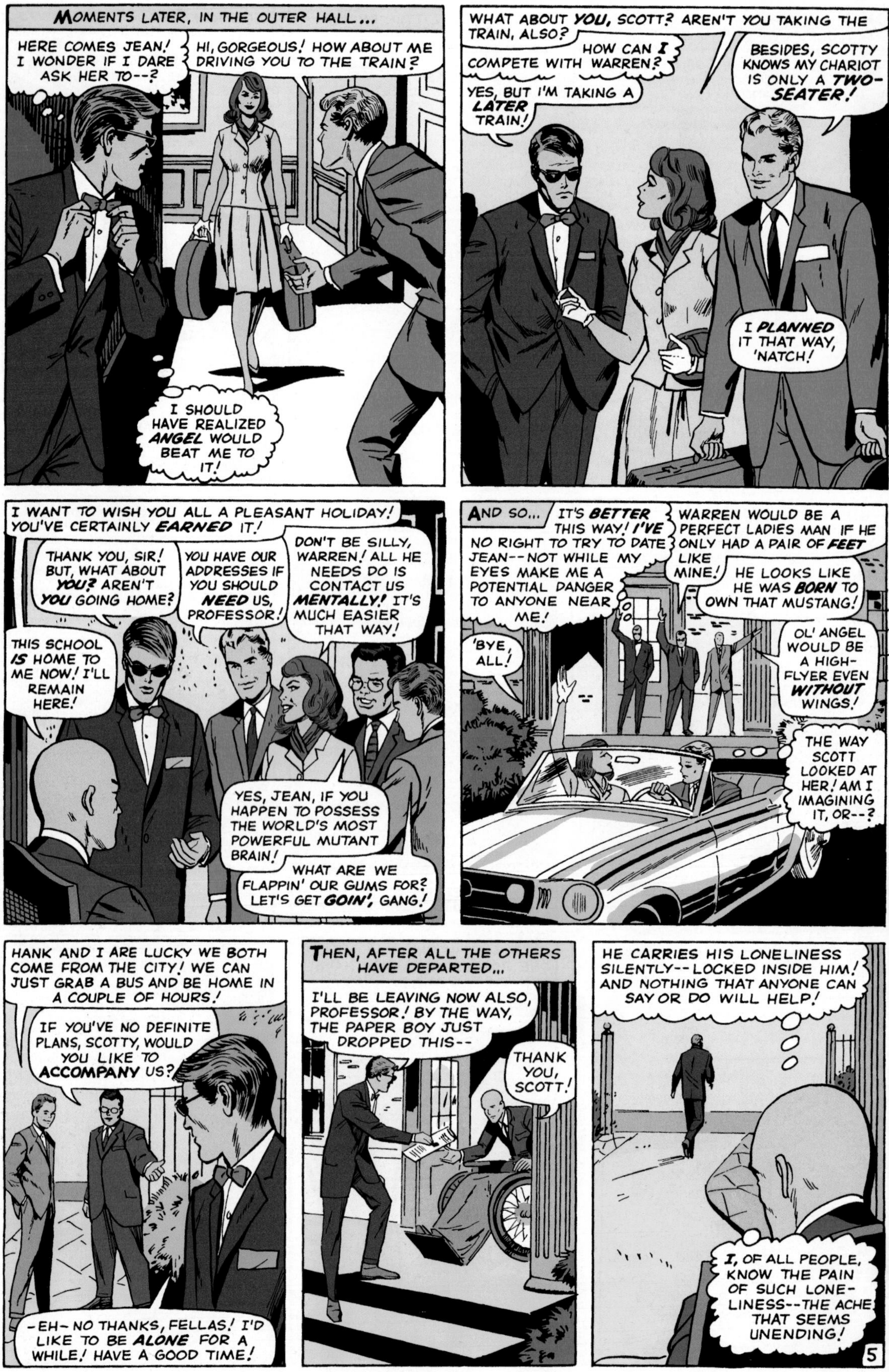
MOMENTS LATER, IN THE OUTER HALL...
HERE COMES JEAN! I WONDER IF I DARE ASK HER TO--?
HI, GORGEOUS! HOW ABOUT ME DRIVING YOU TO THE TRAIN?
I SHOULD HAVE REALIZED ANGEL WOULD BEAT ME TO IT!
WHAT ABOUT YOU, SCOTT? AREN'T YOU TAKING THE TRAIN, ALSO?
HOW CAN I COMPETE WITH WARREN?
YES, BUT I'M TAKING A LATER TRAIN!
BESIDES, SCOTTY KNOWS MY CHARIOT IS ONLY A TWO-SEATER!
I PLANNED IT THAT WAY, 'NATCH!
I WANT TO WISH YOU ALL A PLEASANT HOLIDAY! YOU'VE CERTAINLY EARNED IT!
THANK YOU, SIR! BUT, WHAT ABOUT YOU? AREN'T YOU GOING HOME?
YOU HAVE OUR ADDRESSES IF YOU SHOULD NEED US, PROFESSOR!
DON'T BE SILLY, WARREN! ALL HE NEEDS DO IS CONTACT US MENTALLY! IT'S MUCH EASIER THAT WAY!
THIS SCHOOL IS HOME TO ME NOW! I'LL REMAIN HERE!
YES, JEAN, IF YOU HAPPEN TO POSSESS THE WORLD'S MOST POWERFUL MUTANT BRAIN!
WHAT ARE WE FLAPPIN' OUR GUMS FOR? LET'S GET GOIN', GANG!
AND SO...
IT'S BETTER THIS WAY! I'VE NO RIGHT TO TRY TO DATE JEAN--NOT WHILE MY EYES MAKE ME A POTENTIAL DANGER TO ANYONE NEAR ME!
WARREN WOULD BE A PERFECT LADIES MAN IF HE ONLY HAD A PAIR OF FEET LIKE MINE!
HE LOOKS LIKE HE WAS BORN TO OWN THAT MUSTANG!
'BYE, ALL!
OL' ANGEL WOULD BE A HIGH-FLYER EVEN WITHOUT WINGS!
THE WAY SCOTT LOOKED AT HER! AM I IMAGINING IT, OR--?
HANK AND I ARE LUCKY WE BOTH COME FROM THE CITY! WE CAN JUST GRAB A BUS AND BE HOME IN A COUPLE OF HOURS!
IF YOU'VE NO DEFINITE PLANS, SCOTTY, WOULD YOU LIKE TO ACCOMPANY US?
-EH- NO THANKS, FELLAS! I'D LIKE TO BE ALONE FOR A WHILE! HAVE A GOOD TIME!
THEN, AFTER ALL THE OTHERS HAVE DEPARTED...
I'LL BE LEAVING NOW ALSO, PROFESSOR! BY THE WAY, THE PAPER BOY JUST DROPPED THIS--
THANK YOU, SCOTT!
HE CARRIES HIS LONELINESS SILENTLY--LOCKED INSIDE HIM! AND NOTHING THAT ANYONE CAN SAY OR DO WILL HELP!
I, OF ALL PEOPLE, KNOW THE PAIN OF SUCH LONE-LINESS--THE ACHE THAT SEEMS UNENDING!

BUT, NO SOONER HAS THE SILENT *CYCLOPS* WALKED AWAY, THAN...

SO! IT HAS FINALLY BEGUN!

THE ONE THING I ALWAYS FEARED-- A WITCH-HUNT FOR MUTANTS!

DAILY GLOBE FINAL

MUTANT MENACE!

DR. BOLIVAR TRASK, NOTED

EMINENT ANTHROPOL-OGIST SAYS MANKIND FACES GRAVEST DANGER FROM HIDDEN MUTAN WHO WAIT FO MOMEN

THE FEATURE WRITERS MUST HAVE *LOVED* THIS, CONSIDERING THE WAY THEY PLAYED IT UP!

ARTIST'S INTERPRETATION OF FATE OF MANKIND IF MUTANTS ARE NOT DRIVEN OUT-- AS PREDICTED BY DR. BOLIVAR TRASK!

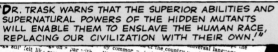

"DR. TRASK WARNS THAT THE SUPERIOR ABILITIES AND SUPERNATURAL POWERS OF THE HIDDEN MUTANTS WILL ENABLE THEM TO ENSLAVE THE HUMAN RACE, REPLACING OUR CIVILIZATION WITH THEIR OWN!"

"ACCORDING TO THE ANTROPOLOGIST'S STARTLING PREDICTION, IT IS EVEN POSSIBLE THAT THE SUPERIOR MUTANTS WILL CONSIDER NORMAL MEN AS LITTLE MORE THAN SAVAGES, SUITABLE ONLY FOR FORCED LABOR AND GLADIATORIAL SPORT!"

I CANNOT LET THIS GO UNCHALLENGED! IT COULD CAUSE PANIC THRUOUT THE WORLD!

EVEN NOW IT MAY BE TOO LATE TO STOP THE WHEELS OF PERSECUTION THAT HAVE BEEN SET IN MOTION-- BUT I MUST MAKE THE ATTEMPT!

THE STRANGE THEORIES OF DR. TRASK ARE A GREATER THREAT TO MY X-MEN THAN ANY FOE THEY HAVE EVER FACED BEFORE!

HELLO, NATIONAL TELEVISION NETWORK? THIS IS CHARLES XAVIER! CONNECT ME WITH YOUR PROGRAM-MING DIRECTOR-- *IMMEDIATELY!*

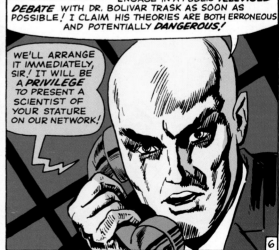

SECONDS LATER... YES, THAT'S RIGHT! I WANT TO ENGAGE IN A PUBLIC *TELEVISED DEBATE* WITH DR. BOLIVAR TRASK AS SOON AS POSSIBLE! I CLAIM HIS THEORIES ARE BOTH ERRONEOUS AND POTENTIALLY *DANGEROUS!*

WE'LL ARRANGE IT IMMEDIATELY, SIR! IT WILL BE A *PRIVILEGE* TO PRESENT A SCIENTIST OF YOUR STATURE ON OUR NETWORK!

6

THE VERY NEXT EVENING, AFTER THE NETWORK HAS PREEMPTED TWO SOAP OPERAS AND A WIDELY-HERALDED ADULT WESTERN...

OUR FIRST SPEAKER WILL BE PROFESSOR CHARLES XAVIER, ONE OF THE GREATEST AUTHORITIES IN THE FIELD OF EDUCATION, AND AN ARTICULATE SPOKESMAN FOR AMERICA'S INTELLECTUAL COMMUNITY!

THE DAMAGE IS ALREADY *DONE!* TRASK HAS ALARMED THE NATION! BUT I *MUST* SPEAK OUT!

ROLL 'EM, CHARLIE! THIS OUGHTA BE GOOD!

BEFORE GIVING WAY TO GROUNDLESS FEARS, WE MUST FIRST CONSIDER-- WHAT *IS* A MUTANT? HE IS *NOT* A MONSTER! HE IS NOT NECESSARILY A MENACE!

HE IS MERELY A PERSON WHO WAS BORN WITH DIFFERENT POWER OR ABILITY THAN THE AVERAGE HUMAN!

AWW, WHAT DOES AN EGG-HEADED OLD STUFFED-SHIRT LIKE *HIM* KNOW?

WOULDN'T IT BE GROOVY IF HE'S A MUTANT *HIMSELF?*

QUIET! YOUR MOTHER AND I WANT TO *HEAR* THIS!

NO ONE KNOWS WHAT CAUSES MUTATIONS! YOUR OWN *CHILDREN* MAY BE MUTANTS! YOU MUST NOT LET IGNORANCE, RUMOR, OR UNREASONING FEAR STAMPEDE YOU!

HE'S GOT *SOME* NERVE! NO KID OF *MINE* IS A MUTIE!

AND WHERE DOES HE GET OFF, CALLIN' US IGNORANT?!!

I NEVER EVEN *HEARD* OF HIM! I'LL BET HE'S A COMMUNIST!

NAH! HE LOOKS MORE LIKE ONE OF THEM RIGHT-WINGERS TO ME!

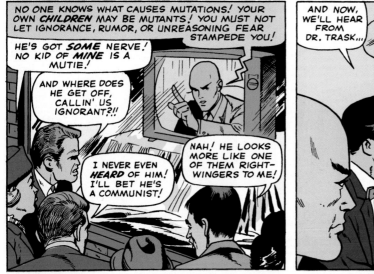

AND NOW, WE'LL HEAR FROM DR. TRASK...

WITH ALL DUE RESPECT TO PROFESSOR XAVIER, HE IS *BLIND* TO THE TERRIBLE DANGERS AROUND US!

OR, PERHAPS IT IS *MORE* THAN MERE BLINDNESS? PERHAPS THE PROFESSOR HAS AN *ULTERIOR MOTIVE* FOR HIS DEFENSE OF MUTANTS?

AT ANY RATE, I HAVE CREATED A *DEFENSE* FOR MANKIND! WHETHER I WIN OR LOSE THIS DEBATE DOES NOT MATTER...

...FOR, THE MUTANTS WILL *NEVER* TAKE OVER THE HUMAN RACE *NOW!* NOT WHILE MY NEW ARMY OF *SENTINELS* LIVE!

...I SHALL NOW *DEMONSTRATE...*

SUPPOSE, FOR SAKE OF ILLUSTRATION, THAT PROFESSOR XAVIER IS A *MUTANT--!*

SENTINEL!! TAKE THE PROFESSOR INTO *CUSTODY!* DO NOT PERMIT HIM TO USE HIS POWER!

GOOD HEAVENS!

7

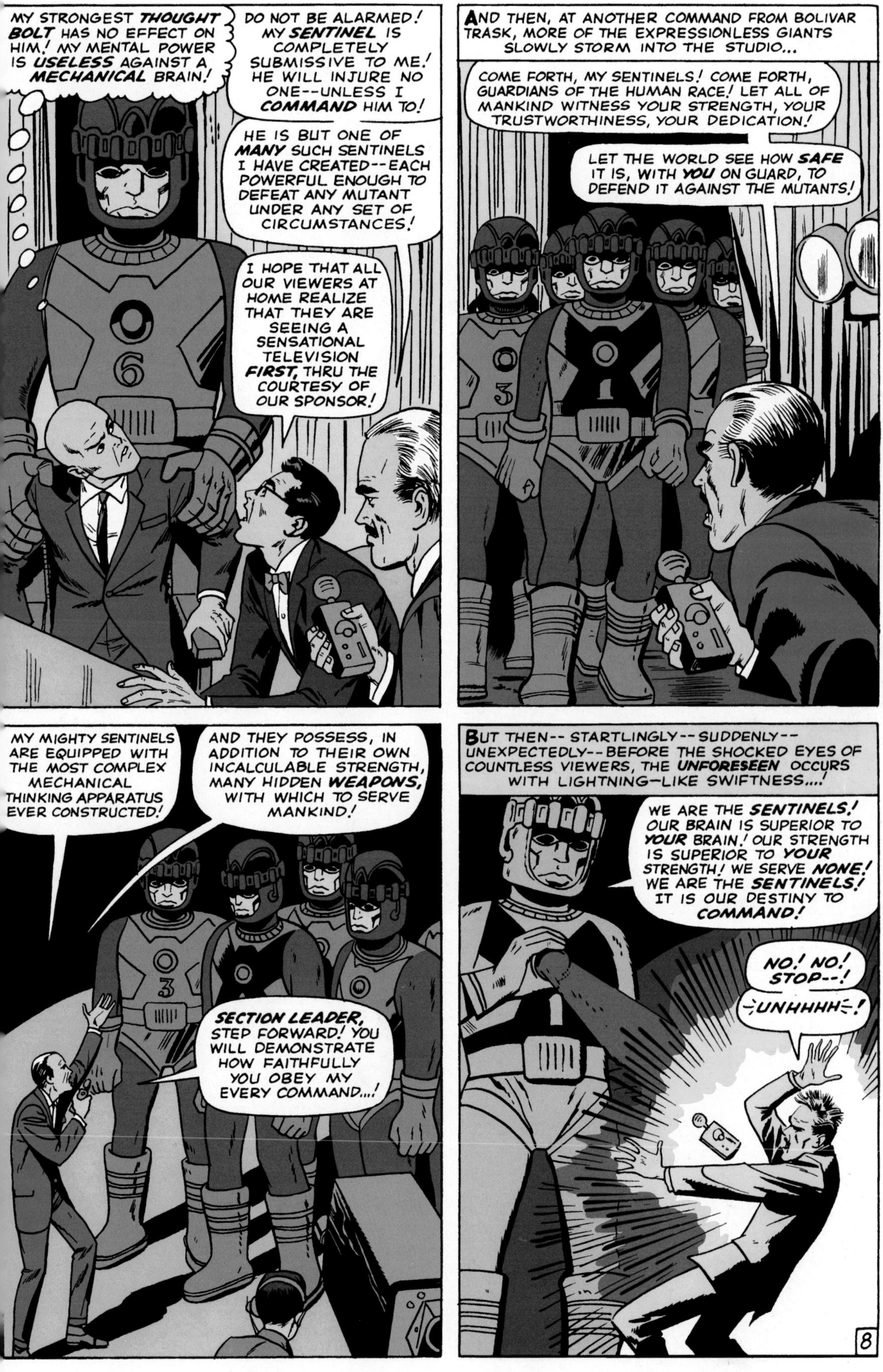

MY STRONGEST THOUGHT BOLT HAS NO EFFECT ON HIM! MY MENTAL POWER IS USELESS AGAINST A MECHANICAL BRAIN!
DO NOT BE ALARMED! MY SENTINEL IS COMPLETELY SUBMISSIVE TO ME! HE WILL INJURE NO ONE--UNLESS I COMMAND HIM TO!
HE IS BUT ONE OF MANY SUCH SENTINELS I HAVE CREATED--EACH POWERFUL ENOUGH TO DEFEAT ANY MUTANT UNDER ANY SET OF CIRCUMSTANCES!
I HOPE THAT ALL OUR VIEWERS AT HOME REALIZE THAT THEY ARE SEEING A SENSATIONAL TELEVISION FIRST, THRU THE COURTESY OF OUR SPONSOR!
AND THEN, AT ANOTHER COMMAND FROM BOLIVAR TRASK, MORE OF THE EXPRESSIONLESS GIANTS SLOWLY STORM INTO THE STUDIO...
COME FORTH, MY SENTINELS! COME FORTH, GUARDIANS OF THE HUMAN RACE! LET ALL OF MANKIND WITNESS YOUR STRENGTH, YOUR TRUSTWORTHINESS, YOUR DEDICATION!
LET THE WORLD SEE HOW SAFE IT IS, WITH YOU ON GUARD, TO DEFEND IT AGAINST THE MUTANTS!
MY MIGHTY SENTINELS ARE EQUIPPED WITH THE MOST COMPLEX MECHANICAL THINKING APPARATUS EVER CONSTRUCTED!
AND THEY POSSESS, IN ADDITION TO THEIR OWN INCALCULABLE STRENGTH, MANY HIDDEN WEAPONS, WITH WHICH TO SERVE MANKIND!
SECTION LEADER, STEP FORWARD! YOU WILL DEMONSTRATE HOW FAITHFULLY YOU OBEY MY EVERY COMMAND...!
BUT THEN--STARTLINGLY--SUDDENLY--UNEXPECTEDLY--BEFORE THE SHOCKED EYES OF COUNTLESS VIEWERS, THE UNFORESEEN OCCURS WITH LIGHTNING-LIKE SWIFTNESS...!
WE ARE THE SENTINELS! OUR BRAIN IS SUPERIOR TO YOUR BRAIN! OUR STRENGTH IS SUPERIOR TO YOUR STRENGTH! WE SERVE NONE! WE ARE THE SENTINELS! IT IS OUR DESTINY TO COMMAND!
NO! NO! STOP--!
UNHHHH!
8

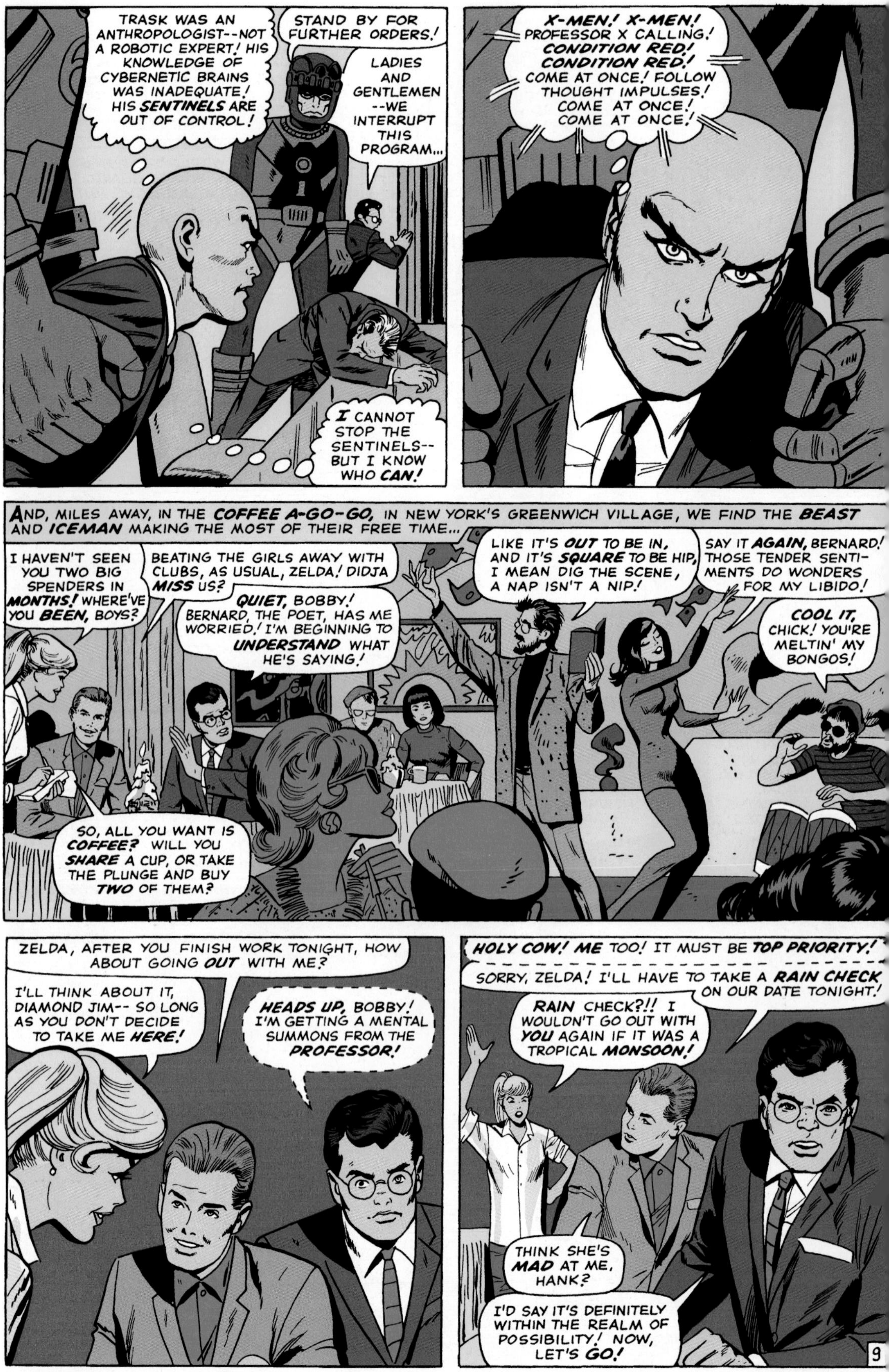

TRASK WAS AN ANTHROPOLOGIST--NOT A ROBOTIC EXPERT! HIS KNOWLEDGE OF CYBERNETIC BRAINS WAS INADEQUATE! HIS SENTINELS ARE OUT OF CONTROL!
STAND BY FOR FURTHER ORDERS!
LADIES AND GENTLEMEN --WE INTERRUPT THIS PROGRAM...
I CANNOT STOP THE SENTINELS-- BUT I KNOW WHO CAN!
X-MEN! X-MEN! PROFESSOR X CALLING! CONDITION RED! CONDITION RED! COME AT ONCE! FOLLOW THOUGHT IMPULSES! COME AT ONCE! COME AT ONCE!
AND, MILES AWAY, IN THE COFFEE A-GO-GO, IN NEW YORK'S GREENWICH VILLAGE, WE FIND THE BEAST AND ICEMAN MAKING THE MOST OF THEIR FREE TIME...
I HAVEN'T SEEN YOU TWO BIG SPENDERS IN MONTHS! WHERE'VE YOU BEEN, BOYS?
BEATING THE GIRLS AWAY WITH CLUBS, AS USUAL, ZELDA! DIDJA MISS US?
QUIET, BOBBY! BERNARD, THE POET, HAS ME WORRIED! I'M BEGINNING TO UNDERSTAND WHAT HE'S SAYING!
LIKE IT'S OUT TO BE IN, AND IT'S SQUARE TO BE HIP, I MEAN DIG THE SCENE, A NAP ISN'T A NIP!
SAY IT AGAIN, BERNARD! THOSE TENDER SENTI-MENTS DO WONDERS FOR MY LIBIDO!
COOL IT, CHICK! YOU'RE MELTIN' MY BONGOS!
SO, ALL YOU WANT IS COFFEE? WILL YOU SHARE A CUP, OR TAKE THE PLUNGE AND BUY TWO OF THEM?
ZELDA, AFTER YOU FINISH WORK TONIGHT, HOW ABOUT GOING OUT WITH ME?
I'LL THINK ABOUT IT, DIAMOND JIM-- SO LONG AS YOU DON'T DECIDE TO TAKE ME HERE!
HEADS UP, BOBBY! I'M GETTING A MENTAL SUMMONS FROM THE PROFESSOR!
HOLY COW! ME TOO! IT MUST BE TOP PRIORITY!
SORRY, ZELDA! I'LL HAVE TO TAKE A RAIN CHECK ON OUR DATE TONIGHT!
RAIN CHECK?!! I WOULDN'T GO OUT WITH YOU AGAIN IF IT WAS A TROPICAL MONSOON!
THINK SHE'S MAD AT ME, HANK?
I'D SAY IT'S DEFINITELY WITHIN THE REALM OF POSSIBILITY! NOW, LET'S GO!
9

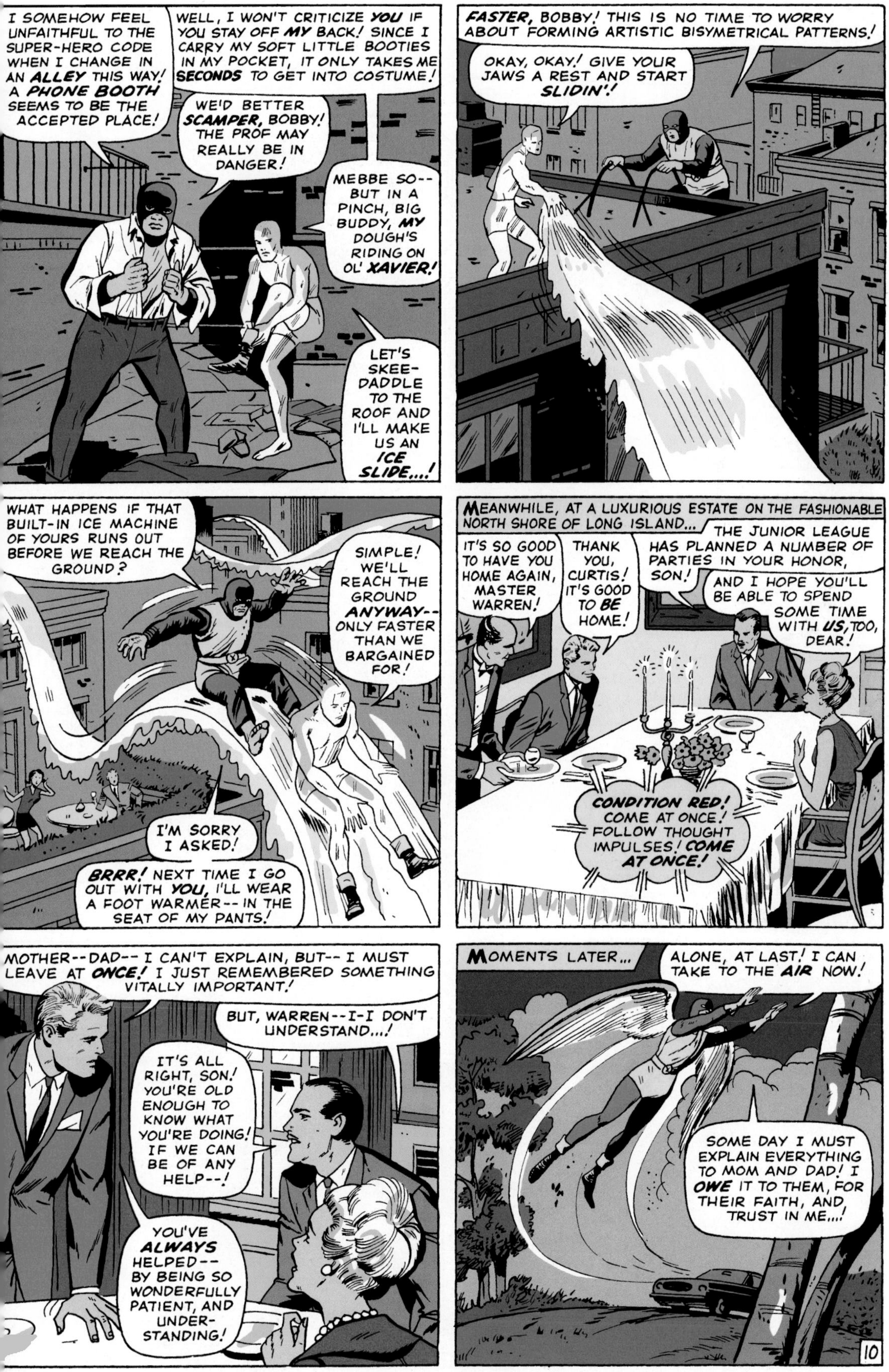
I SOMEHOW FEEL UNFAITHFUL TO THE SUPER-HERO CODE WHEN I CHANGE IN AN ALLEY THIS WAY! A PHONE BOOTH SEEMS TO BE THE ACCEPTED PLACE!
WELL, I WON'T CRITICIZE YOU IF YOU STAY OFF MY BACK! SINCE I CARRY MY SOFT LITTLE BOOTIES IN MY POCKET, IT ONLY TAKES ME SECONDS TO GET INTO COSTUME!
WE'D BETTER SCAMPER, BOBBY! THE PROF MAY REALLY BE IN DANGER!
MEBBE SO-- BUT IN A PINCH, BIG BUDDY, MY DOUGH'S RIDING ON OL' XAVIER!
LET'S SKEE-DADDLE TO THE ROOF AND I'LL MAKE US AN ICE SLIDE...!
FASTER, BOBBY! THIS IS NO TIME TO WORRY ABOUT FORMING ARTISTIC BISYMETRICAL PATTERNS!
OKAY, OKAY! GIVE YOUR JAWS A REST AND START SLIDIN'!
WHAT HAPPENS IF THAT BUILT-IN ICE MACHINE OF YOURS RUNS OUT BEFORE WE REACH THE GROUND?
SIMPLE! WE'LL REACH THE GROUND ANYWAY-- ONLY FASTER THAN WE BARGAINED FOR!
I'M SORRY I ASKED!
BRRR! NEXT TIME I GO OUT WITH YOU, I'LL WEAR A FOOT WARMER-- IN THE SEAT OF MY PANTS!
MEANWHILE, AT A LUXURIOUS ESTATE ON THE FASHIONABLE NORTH SHORE OF LONG ISLAND...
IT'S SO GOOD TO HAVE YOU HOME AGAIN, MASTER WARREN!
THANK YOU, CURTIS! IT'S GOOD TO BE HOME!
THE JUNIOR LEAGUE HAS PLANNED A NUMBER OF PARTIES IN YOUR HONOR, SON!
AND I HOPE YOU'LL BE ABLE TO SPEND SOME TIME WITH US, TOO, DEAR!
CONDITION RED! COME AT ONCE! FOLLOW THOUGHT IMPULSES! COME AT ONCE!
MOTHER--DAD-- I CAN'T EXPLAIN, BUT-- I MUST LEAVE AT ONCE! I JUST REMEMBERED SOMETHING VITALLY IMPORTANT!
BUT, WARREN--I-I DON'T UNDERSTAND...!
IT'S ALL RIGHT, SON! YOU'RE OLD ENOUGH TO KNOW WHAT YOU'RE DOING! IF WE CAN BE OF ANY HELP--!
YOU'VE ALWAYS HELPED-- BY BEING SO WONDERFULLY PATIENT, AND UNDER-STANDING!
MOMENTS LATER...
ALONE, AT LAST! I CAN TAKE TO THE AIR NOW!
SOME DAY I MUST EXPLAIN EVERYTHING TO MOM AND DAD! I OWE IT TO THEM, FOR THEIR FAITH, AND TRUST IN ME...!
10

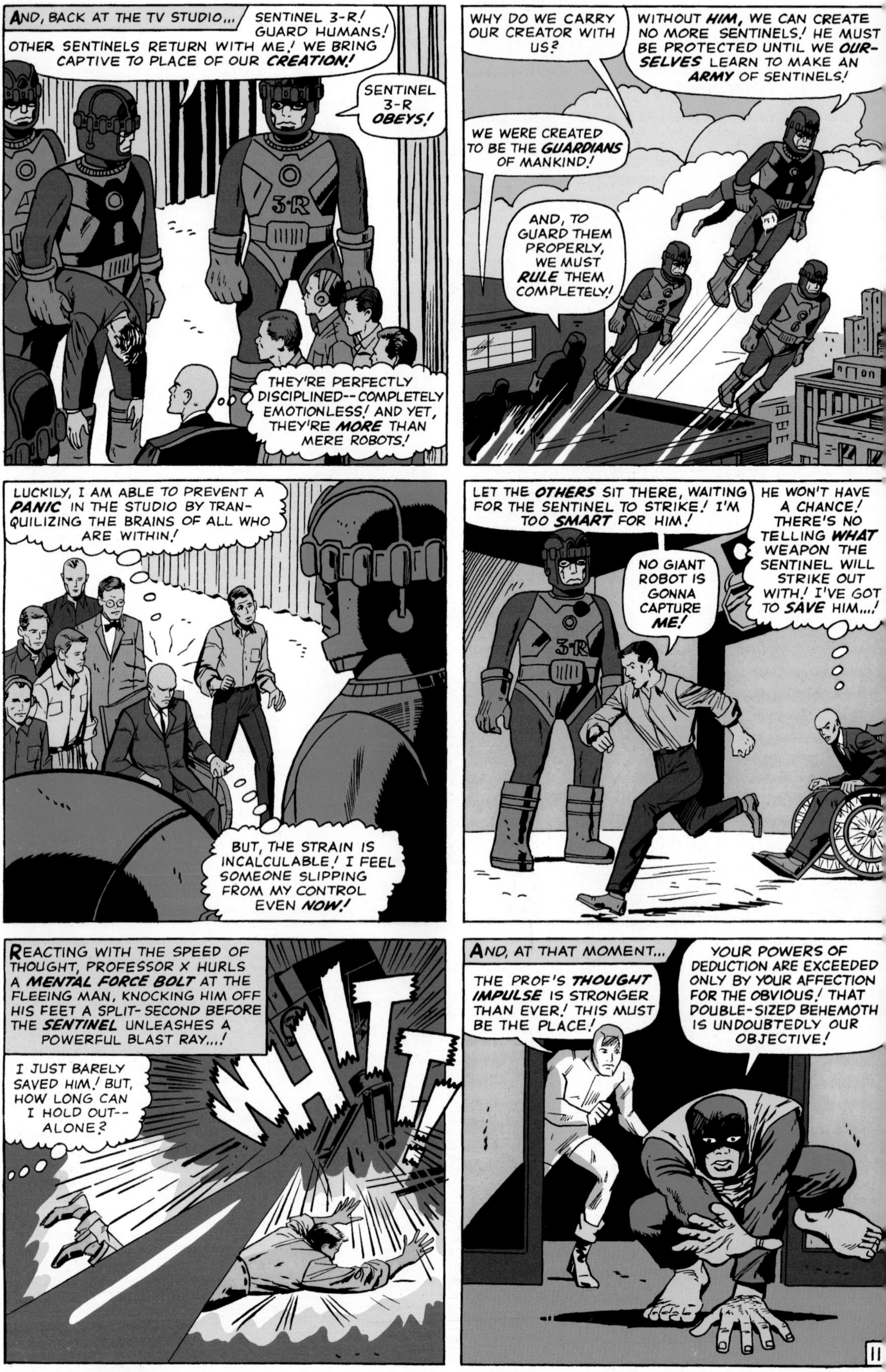
AND, BACK AT THE TV STUDIO...
SENTINEL 3-R! GUARD HUMANS! OTHER SENTINELS RETURN WITH ME! WE BRING CAPTIVE TO PLACE OF OUR CREATION!
SENTINEL 3-R OBEYS!
THEY'RE PERFECTLY DISCIPLINED--COMPLETELY EMOTIONLESS! AND YET, THEY'RE MORE THAN MERE ROBOTS!
WHY DO WE CARRY OUR CREATOR WITH US?
WITHOUT HIM, WE CAN CREATE NO MORE SENTINELS! HE MUST BE PROTECTED UNTIL WE OURSELVES LEARN TO MAKE AN ARMY OF SENTINELS!
WE WERE CREATED TO BE THE GUARDIANS OF MANKIND!
AND, TO GUARD THEM PROPERLY, WE MUST RULE THEM COMPLETELY!
LUCKILY, I AM ABLE TO PREVENT A PANIC IN THE STUDIO BY TRANQUILIZING THE BRAINS OF ALL WHO ARE WITHIN!
BUT, THE STRAIN IS INCALCULABLE! I FEEL SOMEONE SLIPPING FROM MY CONTROL EVEN NOW!
LET THE OTHERS SIT THERE, WAITING FOR THE SENTINEL TO STRIKE! I'M TOO SMART FOR HIM!
NO GIANT ROBOT IS GONNA CAPTURE ME!
HE WON'T HAVE A CHANCE! THERE'S NO TELLING WHAT WEAPON THE SENTINEL WILL STRIKE OUT WITH! I'VE GOT TO SAVE HIM...!
REACTING WITH THE SPEED OF THOUGHT, PROFESSOR X HURLS A MENTAL FORCE BOLT AT THE FLEEING MAN, KNOCKING HIM OFF HIS FEET A SPLIT-SECOND BEFORE THE SENTINEL UNLEASHES A POWERFUL BLAST RAY...!
I JUST BARELY SAVED HIM! BUT, HOW LONG CAN I HOLD OUT--ALONE?
WHT!
AND, AT THAT MOMENT...
THE PROF'S THOUGHT IMPULSE IS STRONGER THAN EVER! THIS MUST BE THE PLACE!
YOUR POWERS OF DEDUCTION ARE EXCEEDED ONLY BY YOUR AFFECTION FOR THE OBVIOUS! THAT DOUBLE-SIZED BEHEMOTH IS UNDOUBTEDLY OUR OBJECTIVE!
11

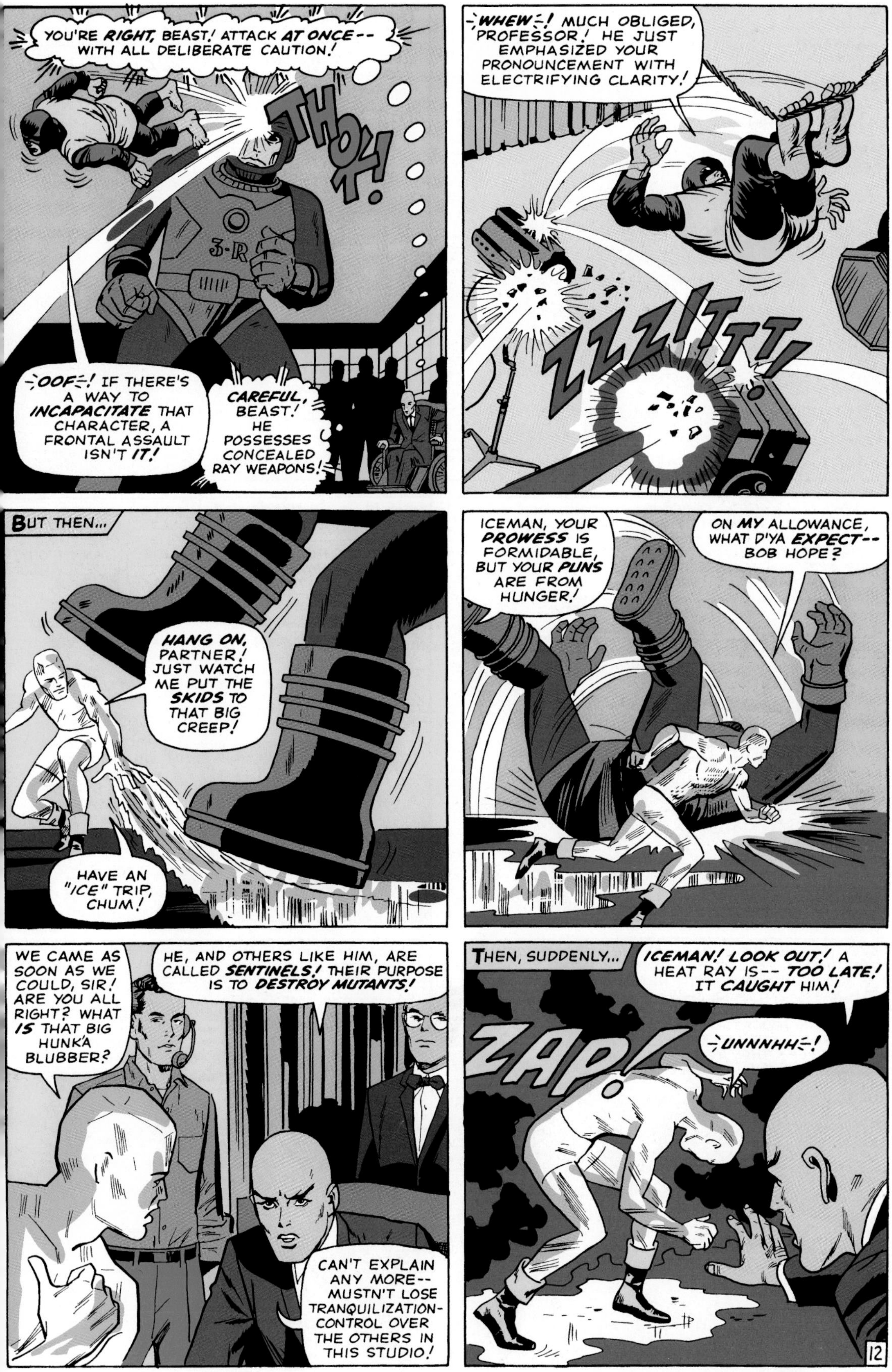

YOU'RE RIGHT, BEAST! ATTACK AT ONCE-- WITH ALL DELIBERATE CAUTION!
THOK!
OOF! IF THERE'S A WAY TO INCAPACITATE THAT CHARACTER, A FRONTAL ASSAULT ISN'T IT!
CAREFUL, BEAST! HE POSSESSES CONCEALED RAY WEAPONS!
WHEW! MUCH OBLIGED, PROFESSOR! HE JUST EMPHASIZED YOUR PRONOUNCEMENT WITH ELECTRIFYING CLARITY!
ZZZITTT!
BUT THEN...
HANG ON, PARTNER! JUST WATCH ME PUT THE SKIDS TO THAT BIG CREEP!
HAVE AN "ICE" TRIP, CHUM!
ICEMAN, YOUR PROWESS IS FORMIDABLE, BUT YOUR PUNS ARE FROM HUNGER!
ON MY ALLOWANCE, WHAT D'YA EXPECT-- BOB HOPE?
WE CAME AS SOON AS WE COULD, SIR! ARE YOU ALL RIGHT? WHAT IS THAT BIG HUNK'A BLUBBER?
HE, AND OTHERS LIKE HIM, ARE CALLED SENTINELS! THEIR PURPOSE IS TO DESTROY MUTANTS!
CAN'T EXPLAIN ANY MORE-- MUSTN'T LOSE TRANQUILIZATION-CONTROL OVER THE OTHERS IN THIS STUDIO!
THEN, SUDDENLY...
ICEMAN! LOOK OUT! A HEAT RAY IS-- TOO LATE! IT CAUGHT HIM!
ZAP!
UNNNHH!

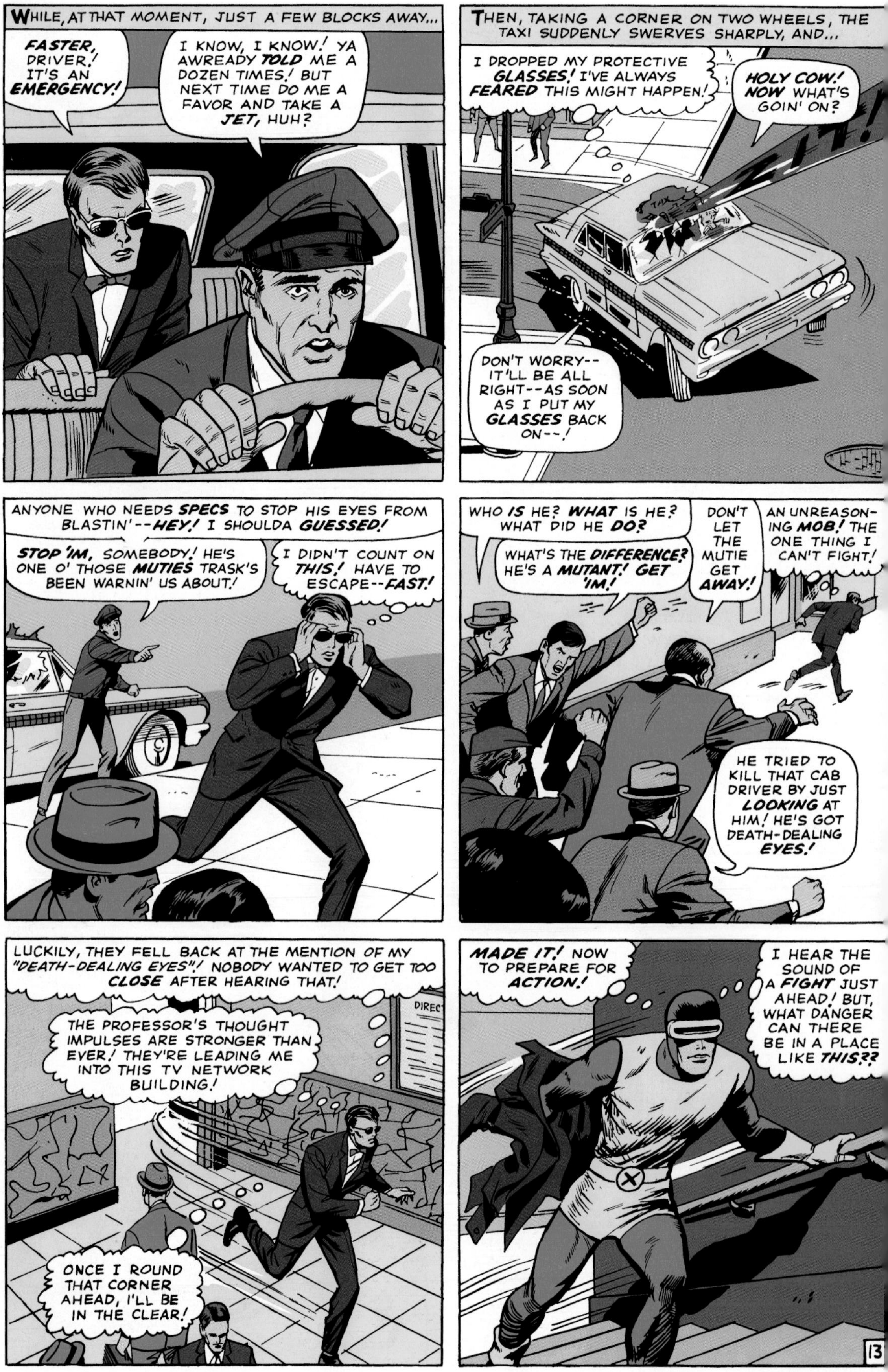

WHILE, AT THAT MOMENT, JUST A FEW BLOCKS AWAY...
FASTER, DRIVER! IT'S AN EMERGENCY!
I KNOW, I KNOW! YA AWREADY TOLD ME A DOZEN TIMES! BUT NEXT TIME DO ME A FAVOR AND TAKE A JET, HUH?
THEN, TAKING A CORNER ON TWO WHEELS, THE TAXI SUDDENLY SWERVES SHARPLY, AND...
I DROPPED MY PROTECTIVE GLASSES! I'VE ALWAYS FEARED THIS MIGHT HAPPEN!
HOLY COW! NOW WHAT'S GOIN' ON?
DON'T WORRY-- IT'LL BE ALL RIGHT--AS SOON AS I PUT MY GLASSES BACK ON--!
ANYONE WHO NEEDS SPECS TO STOP HIS EYES FROM BLASTIN'--HEY! I SHOULDA GUESSED!
STOP 'IM, SOMEBODY! HE'S ONE O' THOSE MUTIES TRASK'S BEEN WARNIN' US ABOUT!
I DIDN'T COUNT ON THIS! HAVE TO ESCAPE--FAST!
WHO IS HE? WHAT IS HE? WHAT DID HE DO?
WHAT'S THE DIFFERENCE? HE'S A MUTANT! GET 'IM!
DON'T LET THE MUTIE GET AWAY!
AN UNREASONING MOB! THE ONE THING I CAN'T FIGHT!
HE TRIED TO KILL THAT CAB DRIVER BY JUST LOOKING AT HIM! HE'S GOT DEATH-DEALING EYES!
LUCKILY, THEY FELL BACK AT THE MENTION OF MY "DEATH-DEALING EYES"! NOBODY WANTED TO GET TOO CLOSE AFTER HEARING THAT!
THE PROFESSOR'S THOUGHT IMPULSES ARE STRONGER THAN EVER! THEY'RE LEADING ME INTO THIS TV NETWORK BUILDING!
ONCE I ROUND THAT CORNER AHEAD, I'LL BE IN THE CLEAR!
MADE IT! NOW TO PREPARE FOR ACTION!
I HEAR THE SOUND OF A FIGHT JUST AHEAD! BUT, WHAT DANGER CAN THERE BE IN A PLACE LIKE THIS??
13

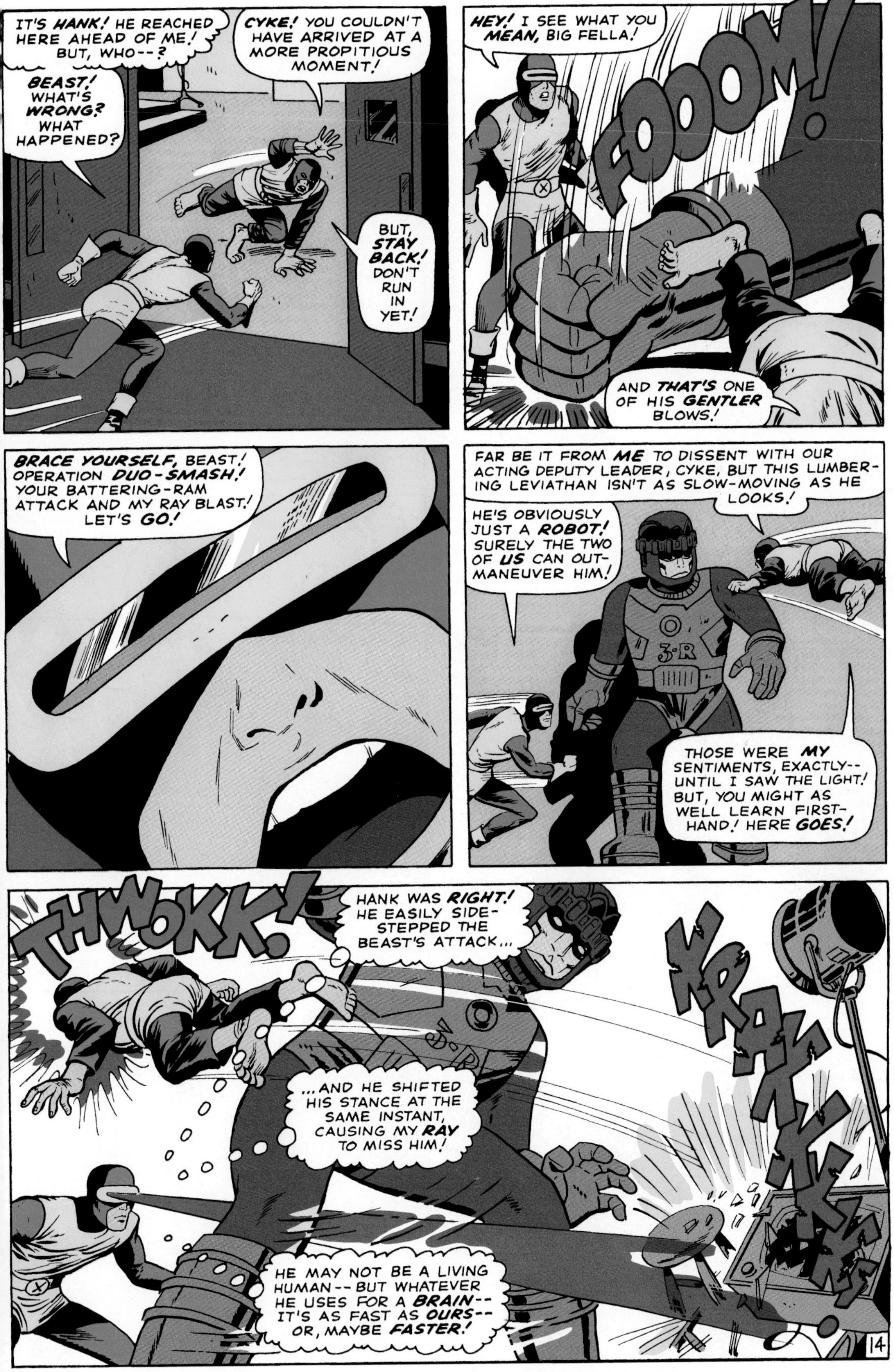
IT'S HANK! HE REACHED HERE AHEAD OF ME! BUT, WHO--?
CYKE! YOU COULDN'T HAVE ARRIVED AT A MORE PROPITIOUS MOMENT!
BEAST! WHAT'S WRONG? WHAT HAPPENED?
BUT, STAY BACK! DON'T RUN IN YET!
HEY! I SEE WHAT YOU MEAN, BIG FELLA!
FOOOM!
AND THAT'S ONE OF HIS GENTLER BLOWS!
BRACE YOURSELF, BEAST! OPERATION DUO-SMASH! YOUR BATTERING-RAM ATTACK AND MY RAY BLAST! LET'S GO!
FAR BE IT FROM ME TO DISSENT WITH OUR ACTING DEPUTY LEADER, CYKE, BUT THIS LUMBERING LEVIATHAN ISN'T AS SLOW-MOVING AS HE LOOKS!
HE'S OBVIOUSLY JUST A ROBOT! SURELY THE TWO OF US CAN OUT-MANEUVER HIM!
3-R
THOSE WERE MY SENTIMENTS, EXACTLY-- UNTIL I SAW THE LIGHT! BUT, YOU MIGHT AS WELL LEARN FIRST-HAND! HERE GOES!
THWOKK!
HANK WAS RIGHT! HE EASILY SIDE-STEPPED THE BEAST'S ATTACK...
KRAKKK!
...AND HE SHIFTED HIS STANCE AT THE SAME INSTANT, CAUSING MY RAY TO MISS HIM!
HE MAY NOT BE A LIVING HUMAN--BUT WHATEVER HE USES FOR A BRAIN-- IT'S AS FAST AS OURS-- OR, MAYBE FASTER!
14

HANK CRASHED INTO THE WALL WITH SUCH FORCE THAT HE KNOCKED HIMSELF OUT! I CAN'T LET HIM LIE THERE IN THE PATH OF THAT GIANT!

OH! THE PROFESSOR IS *CONTACTING* ME!

CYCLOPS! THE *SENTINEL* HAS POWERFUL BUILT-IN WEAPONS! DO NOT TURN YOUR *BACK* TO HIM!

WHAT CAN I DO *NOW?* I CAN'T DESERT HANK-- BUT MY POWER BLAST NEEDS ANOTHER FEW MINUTES BEFORE I CAN *USE* IT AGAIN!

BUT THEN, SUDDENLY, THE MOST UNEXPECTED EVENT OF ALL OCCURS! FOR NO APPARENT REASON, THE TOWERING *SENTINEL* STOPS, FALTERS, AND...

HE'S BEGINNING TO *TOPPLE!* BUT *WHY?* WHAT *CAUSED* IT...? NOTHING EVEN *TOUCHED* HIM!

KAHOOOM!

REALIZING THAT THE DANGER IS OVER FOR THE PRESENT, PROFESSOR X DISCONTINUES HIS MENTAL TRANQUILIZATION OF THOSE AROUND HIM...

WHAT HAPPENED?

WE'RE ALL SAFE NOW! THE *X-MEN* APPEARED AND THE OTHER SENTINELS RAN OFF-- WITH DR. TRASK!

IT'S PRETTY CLEVER OF THE PROFESSOR! BY TALKING THAT WAY, NO ONE WOULD SUSPECT THAT HE'S REALLY OUR *LEADER!*

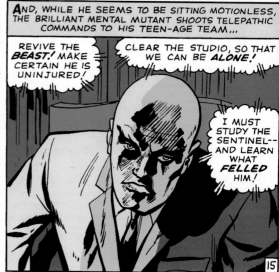

AND, WHILE HE SEEMS TO BE SITTING MOTIONLESS, THE BRILLIANT MENTAL MUTANT SHOOTS TELEPATHIC COMMANDS TO HIS TEEN-AGE TEAM...

REVIVE THE *BEAST!* MAKE CERTAIN HE IS UNINJURED!

CLEAR THE STUDIO, SO THAT WE CAN BE *ALONE!*

I MUST STUDY THE SENTINEL-- AND LEARN WHAT *FELLED* HIM!

15

IN THE MEANTIME, THE HIGH-FLYING *ANGEL*, ZEROING IN TOWARDS THE TV STUDIO, SEES A STARTLING SIGHT...

WELL, WIGGLE MY WINGS! I'VE HEARD OF FLYING *SAUCERS*, BUT *THOSE* THINGS ARE *RIDICULOUS!*

BUT, THE ANGEL DOES NOT YET KNOW OF THE SENTINELS' *PURPOSE*, NOR OF THEIR BUILT-IN DIVINING DEVICES...

HALT YOUR FLIGHT! MY COMPUTO-METER REGISTERS *MUTANT* AHEAD.!

ATTACK IN FORCE!

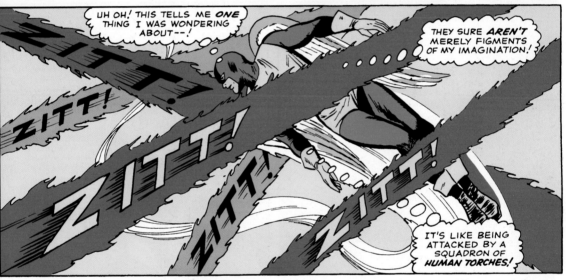

UH OH! THIS TELLS ME *ONE* THING I WAS WONDERING ABOUT--!

ZITT! ZITT! ZITT! ZITT! ZITT!

THEY SURE *AREN'T* MERELY FIGMENTS OF MY IMAGINATION!

IT'S LIKE BEING ATTACKED BY A SQUADRON OF *HUMAN TORCHES!*

SENTINELS 6, 7, AND 8-R! ASSUME SOLO ATTACK POSTURE! *ATTACK!*

ALL OTHERS REMAIN IN FORMATION! PROCEED TO DESTINATION! THAT IS ALL!

WHO *ARE* THEY?? WHY ARE THEY *ATTACKING* ME? IS *THIS* WHY THE PROF SUMMONED ME?

WELL, I CAN WORRY ABOUT ALL THAT *LATER!* RIGHT *NOW,* I'M KINDA BUSY!

IT'S LUCKY THE PROF MADE ME SPEND SO MANY LONG HOURS PRACTICING *MANEUVERABILITY!*

16

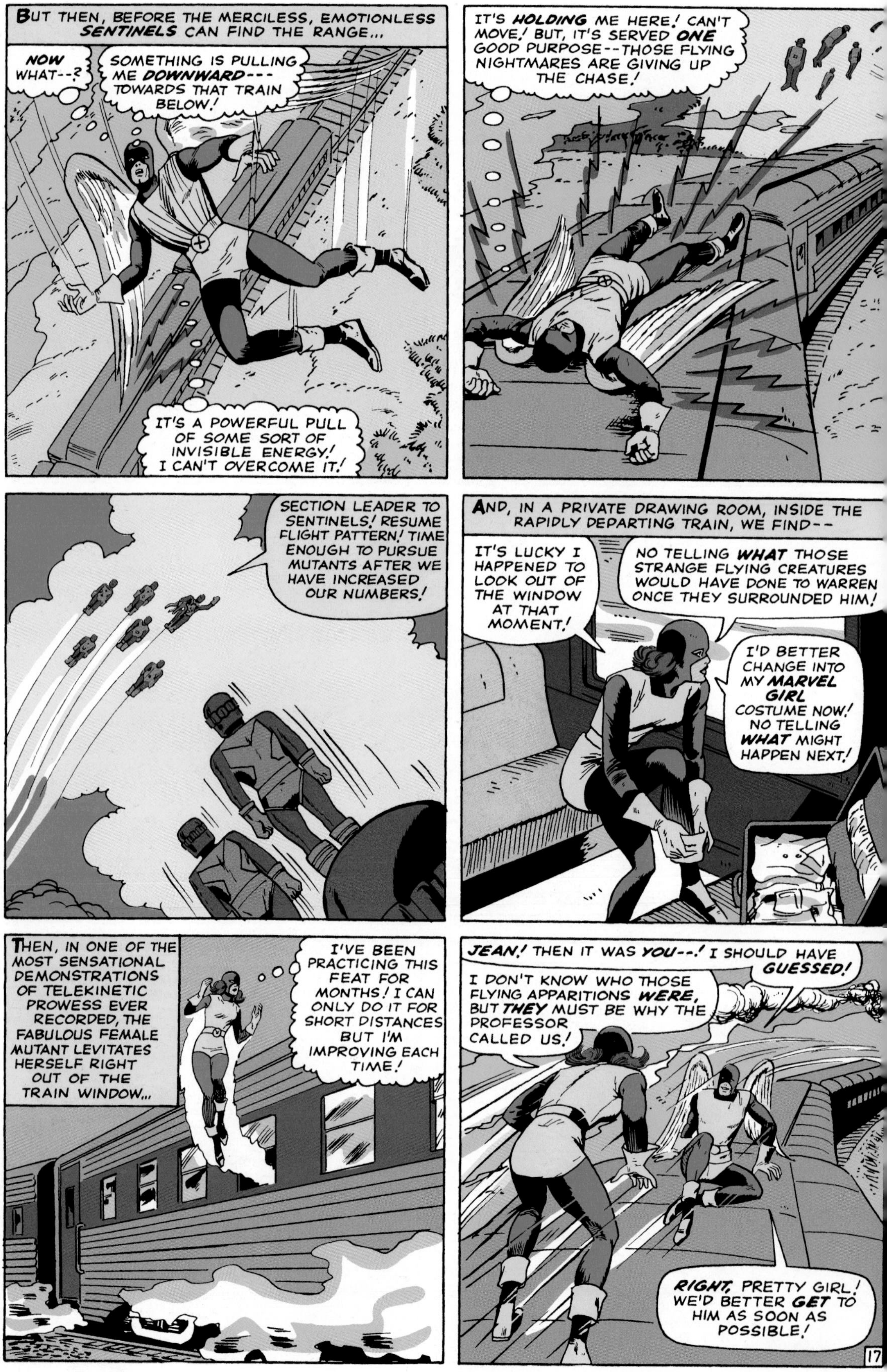

BUT THEN, BEFORE THE MERCILESS, EMOTIONLESS SENTINELS CAN FIND THE RANGE...
NOW WHAT--?
SOMETHING IS PULLING ME DOWNWARD--- TOWARDS THAT TRAIN BELOW!
IT'S A POWERFUL PULL OF SOME SORT OF INVISIBLE ENERGY! I CAN'T OVERCOME IT!
IT'S HOLDING ME HERE! CAN'T MOVE! BUT, IT'S SERVED ONE GOOD PURPOSE--THOSE FLYING NIGHTMARES ARE GIVING UP THE CHASE!
SECTION LEADER TO SENTINELS! RESUME FLIGHT PATTERN! TIME ENOUGH TO PURSUE MUTANTS AFTER WE HAVE INCREASED OUR NUMBERS!
AND, IN A PRIVATE DRAWING ROOM, INSIDE THE RAPIDLY DEPARTING TRAIN, WE FIND--
IT'S LUCKY I HAPPENED TO LOOK OUT OF THE WINDOW AT THAT MOMENT!
NO TELLING WHAT THOSE STRANGE FLYING CREATURES WOULD HAVE DONE TO WARREN ONCE THEY SURROUNDED HIM!
I'D BETTER CHANGE INTO MY MARVEL GIRL COSTUME NOW! NO TELLING WHAT MIGHT HAPPEN NEXT!
THEN, IN ONE OF THE MOST SENSATIONAL DEMONSTRATIONS OF TELEKINETIC PROWESS EVER RECORDED, THE FABULOUS FEMALE MUTANT LEVITATES HERSELF RIGHT OUT OF THE TRAIN WINDOW...
I'VE BEEN PRACTICING THIS FEAT FOR MONTHS! I CAN ONLY DO IT FOR SHORT DISTANCES BUT I'M IMPROVING EACH TIME!
JEAN! THEN IT WAS YOU--! I SHOULD HAVE GUESSED!
I DON'T KNOW WHO THOSE FLYING APPARITIONS WERE, BUT THEY MUST BE WHY THE PROFESSOR CALLED US!
RIGHT, PRETTY GIRL! WE'D BETTER GET TO HIM AS SOON AS POSSIBLE!
17

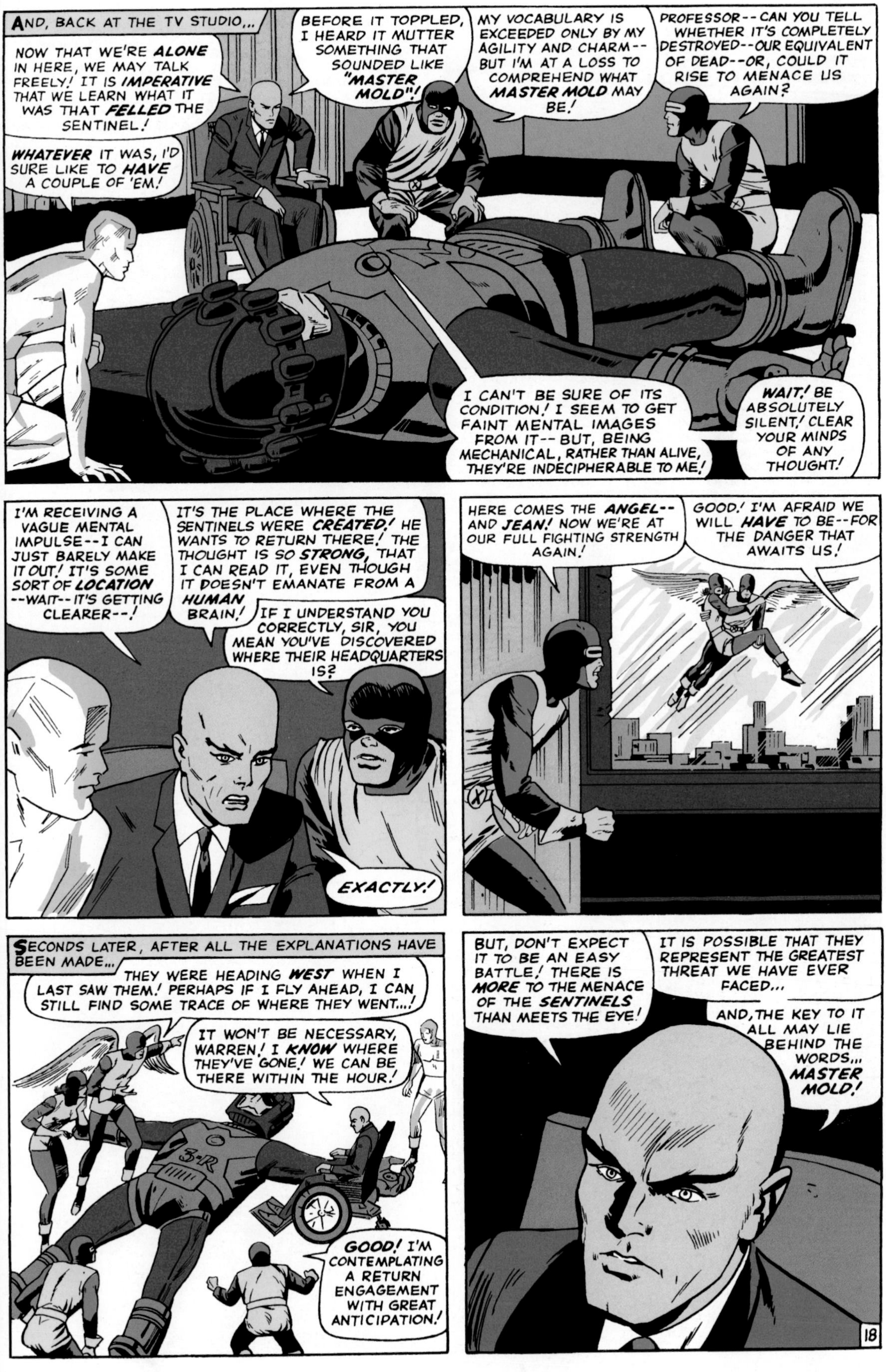
AND, BACK AT THE TV STUDIO...
NOW THAT WE'RE ALONE IN HERE, WE MAY TALK FREELY! IT IS IMPERATIVE THAT WE LEARN WHAT IT WAS THAT FELLED THE SENTINEL!
WHATEVER IT WAS, I'D SURE LIKE TO HAVE A COUPLE OF 'EM!
BEFORE IT TOPPLED, I HEARD IT MUTTER SOMETHING THAT SOUNDED LIKE "MASTER MOLD"!
MY VOCABULARY IS EXCEEDED ONLY BY MY AGILITY AND CHARM--BUT I'M AT A LOSS TO COMPREHEND WHAT MASTER MOLD MAY BE!
PROFESSOR--CAN YOU TELL WHETHER IT'S COMPLETELY DESTROYED--OUR EQUIVALENT OF DEAD--OR, COULD IT RISE TO MENACE US AGAIN?
I CAN'T BE SURE OF ITS CONDITION! I SEEM TO GET FAINT MENTAL IMAGES FROM IT--BUT, BEING MECHANICAL, RATHER THAN ALIVE, THEY'RE INDECIPHERABLE TO ME!
WAIT! BE ABSOLUTELY SILENT! CLEAR YOUR MINDS OF ANY THOUGHT!
I'M RECEIVING A VAGUE MENTAL IMPULSE--I CAN JUST BARELY MAKE IT OUT! IT'S SOME SORT OF LOCATION--WAIT--IT'S GETTING CLEARER--!
IT'S THE PLACE WHERE THE SENTINELS WERE CREATED! HE WANTS TO RETURN THERE! THE THOUGHT IS SO STRONG, THAT I CAN READ IT, EVEN THOUGH IT DOESN'T EMANATE FROM A HUMAN BRAIN!
IF I UNDERSTAND YOU CORRECTLY, SIR, YOU MEAN YOU'VE DISCOVERED WHERE THEIR HEADQUARTERS IS?
EXACTLY!
HERE COMES THE ANGEL--AND JEAN! NOW WE'RE AT OUR FULL FIGHTING STRENGTH AGAIN!
GOOD! I'M AFRAID WE WILL HAVE TO BE--FOR THE DANGER THAT AWAITS US!
SECONDS LATER, AFTER ALL THE EXPLANATIONS HAVE BEEN MADE...
THEY WERE HEADING WEST WHEN I LAST SAW THEM! PERHAPS IF I FLY AHEAD, I CAN STILL FIND SOME TRACE OF WHERE THEY WENT...!
IT WON'T BE NECESSARY, WARREN! I KNOW WHERE THEY'VE GONE! WE CAN BE THERE WITHIN THE HOUR!
GOOD! I'M CONTEMPLATING A RETURN ENGAGEMENT WITH GREAT ANTICIPATION!
BUT, DON'T EXPECT IT TO BE AN EASY BATTLE! THERE IS MORE TO THE MENACE OF THE SENTINELS THAN MEETS THE EYE!
IT IS POSSIBLE THAT THEY REPRESENT THE GREATEST THREAT WE HAVE EVER FACED...
AND, THE KEY TO IT ALL MAY LIE BEHIND THE WORDS... MASTER MOLD!
18

MEANWHILE, THE SENTINELS, AND THEIR NOW-CONSCIOUS HUMAN PRISONER, HAVE REACHED THEIR DESTINATION...

TURN ME LOOSE! LET ME GO!! I ORDER YOU TO RELEASE ME!

WE ARE SENTINELS! WE TAKE NO ORDERS! WE WERE CREATED TO PROTECT!

IT WAS HERE THAT WE WERE CREATED! IT IS HERE THAT MANY MANY MORE SENTINELS SHALL BE BORN!

NO! THERE MUST BE NO MORE OF YOU-- NOT UNTIL I LEARN WHAT I DID WRONG! NOT UNTIL I'VE BROUGHT YOU UNDER MY CONTROL AGAIN!

IT IS TOO LATE FOR THAT, HUMAN! THE ONLY WAY WE CAN PROTECT MANKIND IS BY CONQUERING IT! FOR, WE ARE SENTINELS!

INTO THE MASTER CHAMBER WITH HIM!

WITHOUT ANOTHER WORD, THE POWERFUL, ARTIFICIAL CREATURES BRING DR. TRASK INTO A HUGE, INCREDIBLY-CONSTRUCTED ROOM...

THIS IS MADNESS! YOU KNOW IT IS FORBIDDEN FOR ANY SENTINELS TO ENTER HERE,!! YOU MUST LISTEN TO ME-- I AM YOUR FRIEND--!

WE NEED NO FRIENDS! WE ARE SENTINELS! WE WERE BORN TO PROTECT!

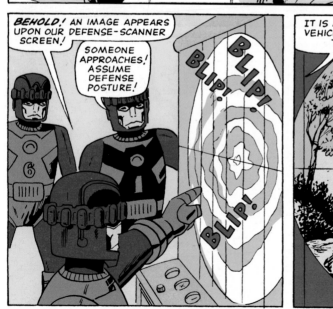

BEHOLD! AN IMAGE APPEARS UPON OUR DEFENSE-SCANNER SCREEN!

SOMEONE APPROACHES! ASSUME DEFENSE POSTURE!

BLIP! BLIP! BLIP! BLIP!

IT IS A HUMAN-OCCUPIED VEHICLE! IT ENTERS THE TARGET AREA!

THOSE INSIDE ARE THE ONES WE HAVE SEEN BEFORE! THEY ARE OUR ENEMIES!

19

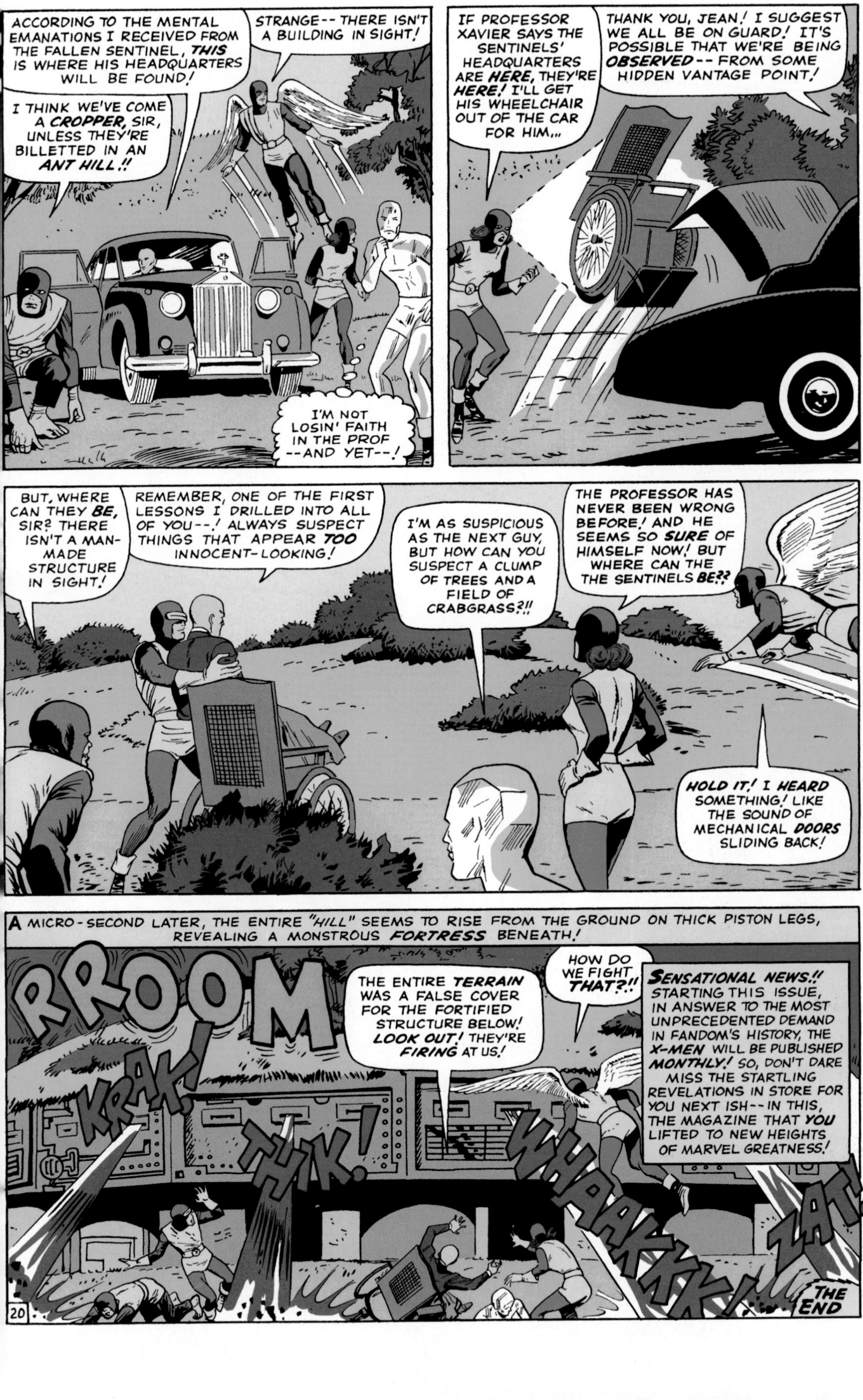

ACCORDING TO THE MENTAL EMANATIONS I RECEIVED FROM THE FALLEN SENTINEL, THIS IS WHERE HIS HEADQUARTERS WILL BE FOUND!
STRANGE-- THERE ISN'T A BUILDING IN SIGHT!
I THINK WE'VE COME A CROPPER, SIR, UNLESS THEY'RE BILLETTED IN AN ANT HILL!!
I'M NOT LOSIN' FAITH IN THE PROF --AND YET--!
IF PROFESSOR XAVIER SAYS THE SENTINELS' HEADQUARTERS ARE HERE, THEY'RE HERE! I'LL GET HIS WHEELCHAIR OUT OF THE CAR FOR HIM...
THANK YOU, JEAN! I SUGGEST WE ALL BE ON GUARD! IT'S POSSIBLE THAT WE'RE BEING OBSERVED-- FROM SOME HIDDEN VANTAGE POINT!
BUT, WHERE CAN THEY BE, SIR? THERE ISN'T A MAN-MADE STRUCTURE IN SIGHT!
REMEMBER, ONE OF THE FIRST LESSONS I DRILLED INTO ALL OF YOU--! ALWAYS SUSPECT THINGS THAT APPEAR TOO INNOCENT-LOOKING!
I'M AS SUSPICIOUS AS THE NEXT GUY, BUT HOW CAN YOU SUSPECT A CLUMP OF TREES AND A FIELD OF CRABGRASS?!!
THE PROFESSOR HAS NEVER BEEN WRONG BEFORE! AND HE SEEMS SO SURE OF HIMSELF NOW! BUT WHERE CAN THE SENTINELS BE??
HOLD IT! I HEARD SOMETHING! LIKE THE SOUND OF MECHANICAL DOORS SLIDING BACK!
A MICRO-SECOND LATER, THE ENTIRE "HILL" SEEMS TO RISE FROM THE GROUND ON THICK PISTON LEGS, REVEALING A MONSTROUS FORTRESS BENEATH!
RROOM
THE ENTIRE TERRAIN WAS A FALSE COVER FOR THE FORTIFIED STRUCTURE BELOW! LOOK OUT! THEY'RE FIRING AT US!
HOW DO WE FIGHT THAT?!!
SENSATIONAL NEWS!! STARTING THIS ISSUE, IN ANSWER TO THE MOST UNPRECEDENTED DEMAND IN FANDOM'S HISTORY, THE X-MEN WILL BE PUBLISHED MONTHLY! SO, DON'T DARE MISS THE STARTLING REVELATIONS IN STORE FOR YOU NEXT ISH-- IN THIS, THE MAGAZINE THAT YOU LIFTED TO NEW HEIGHTS OF MARVEL GREATNESS!
KRAK!
THK!
WHAAKKK!
ZAT!
THE END

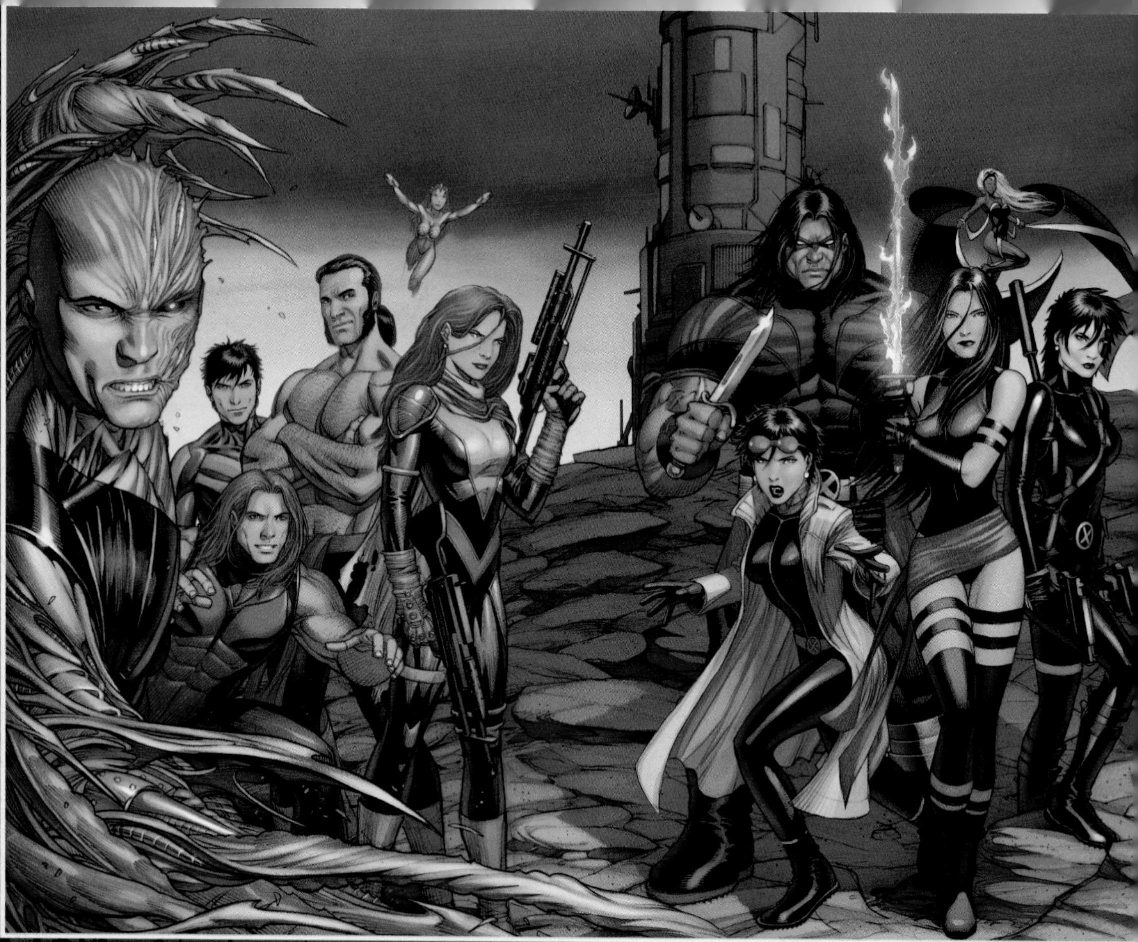

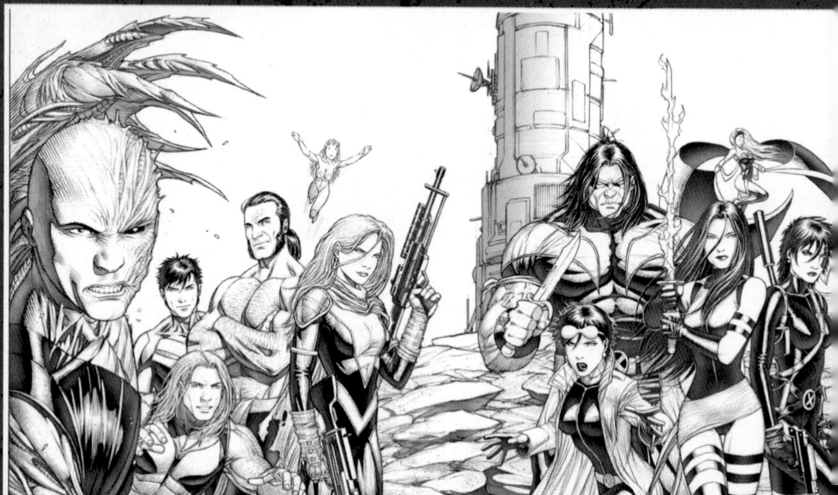

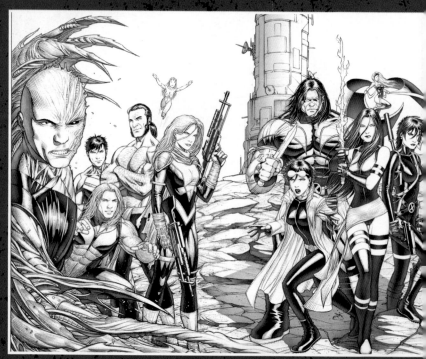

CYCLOPS & THE X-MEN
GENERATION HOPE #13, X-MEN #20, UNCANNY X-MEN #1

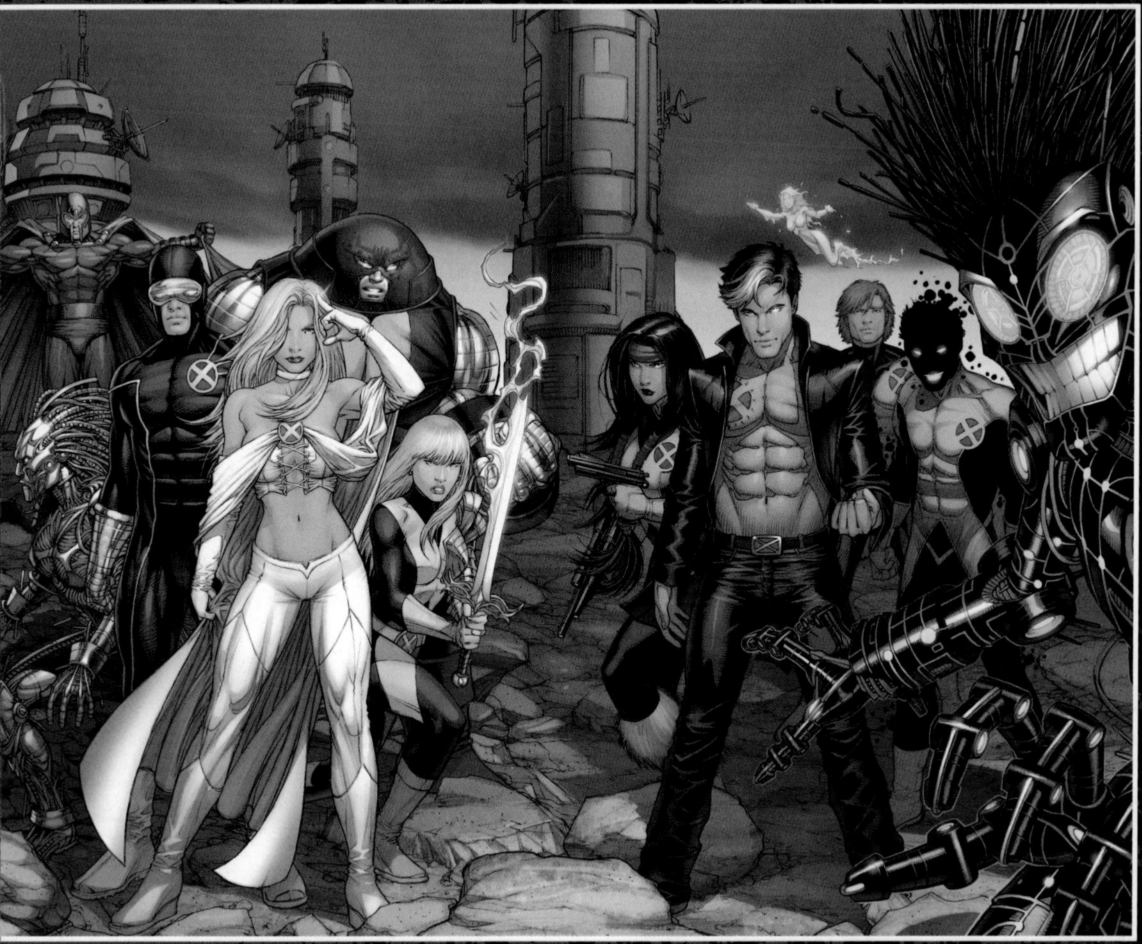

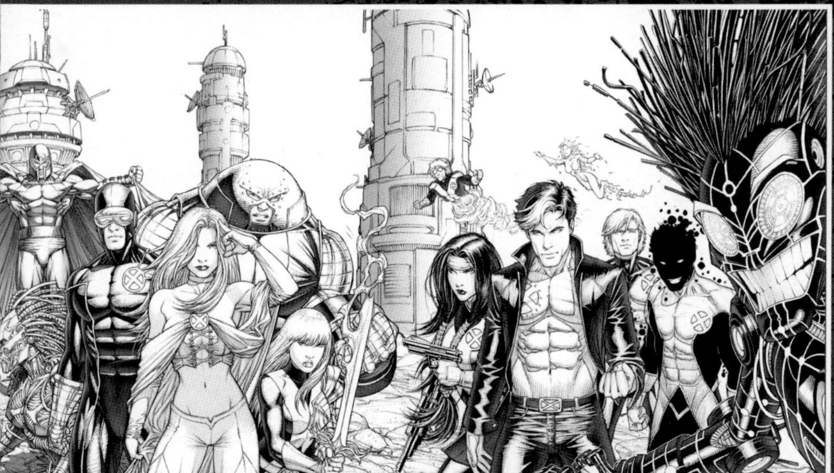

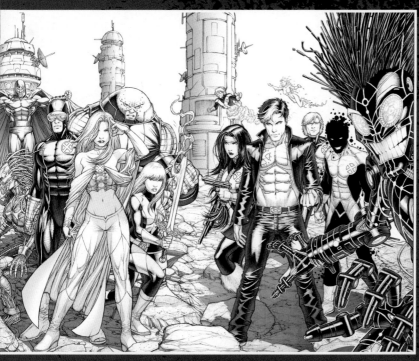

COMBINED VARIANTS
BY DALE KEOWN & JASON KEITH

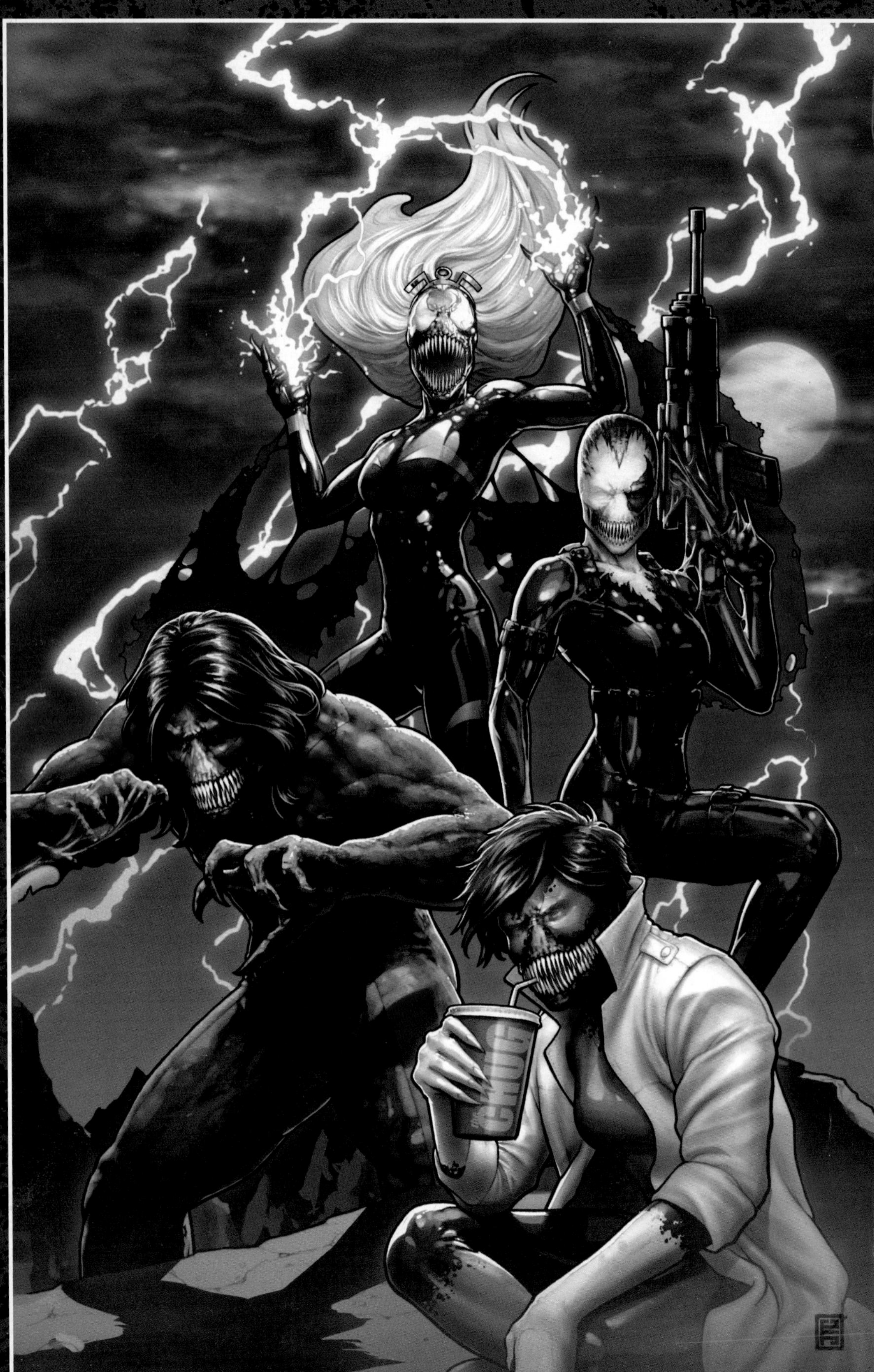

#23 VENOM VARIANT BY JOHN TYLER CHRISTOPHER

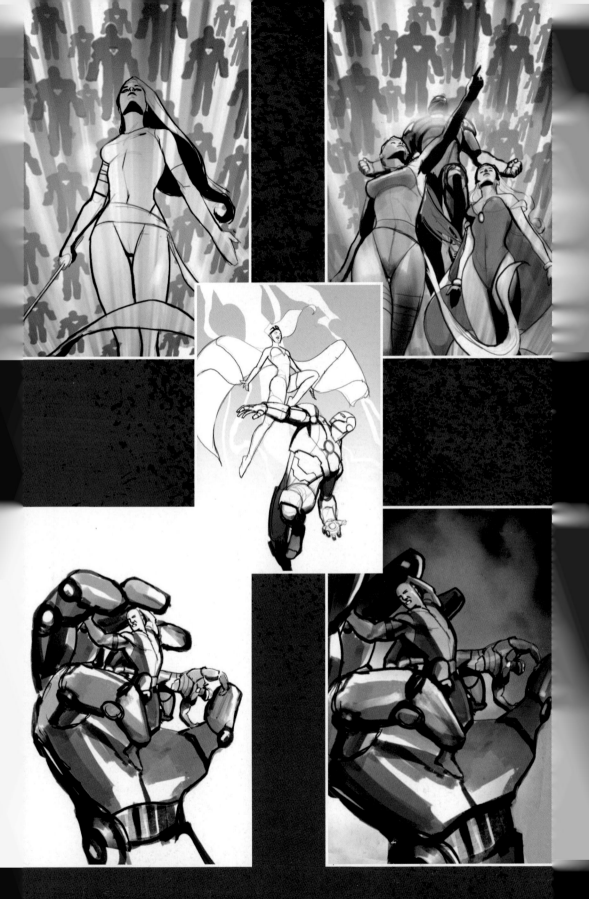

COVER SKETCHES BY ADI GRANOV

GET CAUGHT UP ON THESE GREAT X-MEN STORIES
"It's a solid, entertaining comic." - ComicBookResources.com
MARVEL PREMIERE EDITION
X-MEN
CURSE OF THE MUTANTS
GISCHLER · MEDINA
X-MEN: CURSE OF THE MUTANTS PREMIERE HC
978-0-7851-4846-3
MARVEL PREMIERE EDITION
GISCHLER BACHALO
X-MEN
WITH GREAT POWER
X-MEN: WITH GREAT POWER PREMIERE HC
978-0-7851-4848-7
MARVEL PREMIERE EDITION
YOST MEDINA TALAJIC
X-MEN
FIRST TO LAST
X-MEN: FIRST TO LAST PREMIERE HC
978-0-7851-5287-3
MARVEL
GISCHLER MOLINA PIERFEDERICI CONRAD
X-MEN
FF
X-MEN: FF PREMIERE HC
978-0-7851-6069-4
On Sale Now
MARVEL
www.marvel.com
TM & © 2012 MARVEL & SUBS

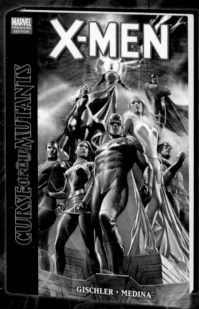

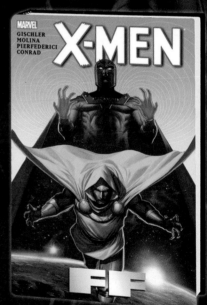